Volkswagen Station Wagon
and De Luxe Station Wagon

THE COMPLETE BOOK OF
CLASSIC VOLKSWAGENS

BEETLES, MICROBUSES, THINGS, KARMANN GHIAS, AND MORE

THE COMPLETE BOOK OF
CLASSIC VOLKSWAGENS

BEETLES, MICROBUSES, THINGS, KARMANN GHIAS, AND MORE

JOHN GUNNELL

Quarto is the authority on a wide range of topics.

Quarto educates, entertains and enriches the lives of
our readers—enthusiasts and lovers of hands-on living.

www.quartoknows.com

First published in 2017 by Motorbooks, an imprint of the The Quarto Group, 401 Second Avenue North,
Suite 310, Minneapolis, MN 55401 USA. Telephone: (612) 344-8100 Fax: (612) 344-8692.

quartoknows.com
Visit our blogs at quartoknows.com

Motorbooks titles are also available at discounts in bulk quantity for industrial or sales-promotional use. For
details contact the Special Sales Manager by email at specialsales@quarto.com or by mail at The Quarto
Group, Attn: Special Sales Manager, 401 Second Avenue North, Suite 310, Minneapolis, MN 55401 USA.

10 9 8 7 6 5 4 3 2 1

ISBN: 978-0-7603-4987-8

Library of Congress Cataloging-in-Publication Data

Names: Gunnell, John, 1947- author.
Title: The complete book of classic Volkswagens : Beetles, Microbuses,
    Things, Karmann Ghias, and more / John Gunnell.
Description: Minneapolis, MN, USA : Quarto Publishing Group USA Inc., 2017.
Identifiers: LCCN 2016054430 | ISBN 9780760349878 (hardbound)
Subjects: LCSH: Volkswagen automobiles–History. | Antique and classic cars.
Classification: LCC TL215.V6 G858 2017 | DDC 629.222–dc23
LC record available at https://lccn.loc.gov/2016054430

Acquiring Editor: Darwin Holmstrom
Project Manager: Alyssa Bluhm
Art Director: James Kegley
Layout: Kim Winscher
Front cover & title page illustration: Ed Jackson/artbyedo.com

Printed in China

CONTENTS

CHAPTER 1

WAR BABY

The purpose of this book is to tell you the complete story of air-cooled Volkswagen automobiles. The primary focus will be on the Type 1 Volkswagen, which most of us know as the Beetle or the "Bug." We'll cover every year of this model from 1946 through 1979 and will then take an overview look at the 1980–2003 Beetles manufactured and sold in other countries. We'll also study the three generations of air-cooled Volkswagen buses, several types of Karmann Ghias, and the Notchback, Fastback, and Squareback models that arrived in the early 1960s in an attempt to broaden the company's product offerings.

This prototype Beetle is a 1946 Volkswagen Type 11 Saloon from the Nethercutt Collection (San Sylmar Museum) in Sylmar, California. This is the very first Volkswagen imported into the United States. *Courtesy the Nethercutt Collection*

1930–1945 PEOPLE'S CAR PROJECT

It's no secret that the Volkswagen Beetle concept evolved as the one bright spot in a dark period of German history, when Adolf Hitler and his Nazi party were twisting nationalistic pride and militarism into ugly forces to drive a horrific political movement. What better way could there be to sway people in that era to your side than offering them a car for the masses? Henry Ford did this in the United States with his cheap and reliable Model T. It put Americans on wheels and made him wealthy. Hitler promised to put Germans on wheels with the "Volks-Wagen" (People's Car) and hoped it would make him very powerful.

The car itself didn't spring from Hitler's mind. It was the brainchild of Dr. Ferdinand Porsche, an engineering genius who devised the idea of a reliable, affordable car while working at Austro-Daimler. It was called the Type 130 WO1 and at least one prototype was made. It had a pusher-type layout with the engine in the rear, as well as a swing-axle rear suspension. Since Austro-Daimler wanted to build limousines for royalty, it wasn't very much interested in making an entry-level car. Porsche disagreed with that thinking and headed for the door.

In 1930, Porsche struck out on his own and formed an engineering consulting company. He called it Dr. Ing.

H.c. Ferdinand Porsche GmbH. This was the real start of the Volkswagen story. Porsche hired people that he had worked with before. Erwin Komenda was a car body designer. Joseph Kales was an expert in air-cooled engine technology. Dr. Porsche's son Ferry was the junior member of the group at twenty-one years old. Other members included Karl Fohlich (transmission), Josef Zadradnik (chassis), and Josef Mickl (aerodynamics). Porsche challenged his team to develop the small, cheap car he had envisioned.

Early in the new engineering firm's history came Project 12, which Porsche saw as a car perfectly suited for the Great Depression. Dr. Fritz Neumayer agreed with him. Neumayer wanted to take his Zündapp motorcycle company into the car-making business. However, the good doctor insisted on using a five-cylinder water-cooled radial engine. A job was a job and Porsche agreed.

The Type 12 was essentially a two-door sedan that from the cowl to the rear looked almost like a Citroën deux chevaux with a more rakish windshield. Up front it had a snob-hosed hood and long MG TF-style headlights protruding from the front fenders. It had valanced front fenders and rear fenders with large enclosures or "skirts." Three Type 12 prototypes with Reutter coachwork were built. These would ultimately evolve into the Beetle over the next fifteen years.

Underneath, the car had a backbone chassis, independent front and rear suspensions, and a rear-mounted engine. The front suspension used a

transverse leaf spring and swing axles were at the rear. The layout and overall design motif were very Beetle-like, even though there was still a lot of work to do.

Most of the car's basic elements were already in Porsche's thinking. The design team chose a rear-mounted engine because it eliminated the need for a long driveshaft. However, weight distribution concerns dictated that a lightweight engine be used. Aluminum and magnesium castings were the answer.

Porsche realized that an air-cooled engine also fit the project better. Having no radiator would save weight, and owners would not have to worry about coolant freeze-ups. If he used horizontally opposed cylinders, Porsche could go with a short crankshaft and mate it more easily to a transaxle. Instead of a ladder frame, the car could have a platform on a central backbone and an integral floorpan. A torsion bar front suspension and rear swing axles worked well too.

Zündapp nixed the Type 12 in 1932, but Porsche established a connection with NSU to develop yet another set of prototypes. These evolved from the basic Project 12 design parameters, but changed from the five-cylinder radial engine that Neumayer had requested to the horizontally opposed flat-four-cylinder type that Porsche and his team knew made more sense.

By 1933, Adolph Hitler had risen to power. The dictator was somewhat of a car enthusiast and many photos show him inspecting the latest models

A mechanical braking system was used on early Volkswagens. Drum brakes were fitted both front and rear. Standard equipment included 5.00 x 16-inch tires.

This 1949 Volkswagen cutaway chassis belongs to Mike Yager of Mid America Motorworks, a leading supplier of VW parts. This section of the rare auto show chassis lets you see how the transaxle works.

at new car shows. Hitler announced his desire to create not only the Autobahnen (high-speed highway network), but also his People's Car for the ordinary workingman's family. Hitler wanted a car that could do 100 kilometers per hour (62 miles per hour), get 33 miles per gallon, need minimal repair and maintenance, have space for four to five people, and have an air-cooled engine (since so few people in Germany had garages).

At the 1934 Berlin Auto Show, Hitler publicly endorsed many of the ideas that Dr. Porsche had developed for the Zündapp and NSU projects. Porsche was encouraged to continue his research and develop a new car that would be called the Volkswagen Series 3. Late in 1936, the final prototypes for this next concept were ready. They carried bodywork

crafted largely by Erwin Komenda. The German automaker's association undertook extensive testing of the car.

By 1937, it was determined that a separate government company would be set up to complete development of the car and bring it to production. A new factory was planned and built just to produce enough Volkswagens for all of the workers. With the assistance of Daimler-Benz, thirty prototype cars were prepared. This version of the Volkswagen was known as the Series 30 and was road tested by Nazi storm troopers. The cars had a removable engine lid and no rear window.

Plans were now being made to build a factory, to build Volkswagens. Dr. Porsche made two trips to the United States and met with American auto industry leaders, including Henry Ford. He also searched in

America for engineers of German extraction who wanted to come back there and help set up the factory.

Work began on the plant in mid-1938, with the first cars scheduled to emerge late the following year. Meanwhile, Porsche's design team kept refining the car until it finally was approved as the ready-for-production Series 38. This car was destined to become an automotive icon after the war in countries all over the globe. It was initially sold as the KdF-Wagen. *Kraft durch Freude* means "Strength through Joy." That was the name of a sponsoring Nazi group. The car quickly adopted the Volkswagen nickname that had been hung on it for several years. Both 704cc and 984cc air-cooled engines were installed in early versions.

The plan was to sell early Volkswagens using a stamp-purchase plan that would allow German workers to purchase stamps each week. When the worker's stamp "card" was filled up, he'd be the owner of a Volkswagen. World War II intervened and ended this scheme before civilian production ever really started. However, quite a few Germans would wind up bringing their filled-up stamp books in years later to try to redeem them for a car. In 1961, Volkswagen offered those people credit toward a new car purchase or a set amount of cash.

WAR MACHINES

Porsche never designed the Volkswagen to go to war, but war broke out before German workers could cash in their KdF-Wagen stamps. About 210 cars

On the left is a 1943 Volkswagen Type 82 (German Army designation Kfz.1) Kübelwagen or bucket car. On the right is the 1973 Type 181 that was marketed as "The Thing" with a base price of $2,700. *Archives/TEN: The Enthusiast Network Magazines, LLC*

were built before Volkswagen stopped production of civilian models in 1940. Instead of going to workers who had diligently saved their stamps, those cars were given to high-ranking Nazi officials. The factory stayed operational to make war goods and airplane parts. Dr. Porsche had already worked up some Beetle-based military vehicles. The first of these was the Type 62. If it looked crude, it might have been due to the fact that Porsche's team whipped it up in a month.

The Type 62 looked somewhat like a Volkswagen Thing with the doors and pillars removed and replaced by canvas. It rode on big 19-inch tires, but was basically a Beetle underneath.

When used during the Nazi invasion of Poland in 1939, with its gearing, the Type 62 could not be driven as slowly as foot soldiers marched. It was followed by a Type 2 version (AKA Type 82) on a sturdier platform with no-spin axles and reduction gears. The Type 82 had higher ground clearance and a stronger body by Ambi-Budd, a US firm.

The Type 82 is better known as the Kübelwagen (Bucket car) and this is the vehicle that the Volkswagen Thing is a replica of. The Kübelwagen was Germany's Jeep, although its 23-horsepower engine compared to 60 horsepower in a Jeep. On the other hand, the Kübelwagen had a longer wheelbase and wider track so it tipped

over far less. The Kübelwagen also had real doors and bodywork for better all-round protection and more seating room and luggage space inside the "bucket."

Most Kübelwagens had rear-wheel drive and got by fine with it due to their light weight and rear-mounted engine. For improved off-roading, the Nazis sometimes fitted their Kübelwagens with aircraft tires. Porsche easily developed four-wheel-drive versions of the vehicle, but they weren't much better in all-terrain use than the two-wheel-drive originals. However, the same type of four-wheel-drive system did improve a Beetle-type military vehicle, the Type 87

Kommandeurwagen. There was also a Type 83 van/ambulance Beetle variant.

Porsche's four-wheel-drive system was also used for the Type 166 Schwimmwagen—an amphibious version of the Kübelwagen with flotation tires and a special high-mounted exhaust system. Porsche chief designer Erwin Komenda created a new boat-style body structure for the Schwimmwagen. It used a 1,100cc engine with 25 horsepower that was made standard for Kübelwagens too.

ALL THE KING'S MEN: POSTWAR BRITISH CONTROL

In early April 1945, the American army entered the city where Hitler built the Volkswagen factory. Some eighteen thousand people lived there and many were housed in emergency quarters because the factory had been heavily bombed in Allied air raids. The town was placed under the command of Major Ivan Hirst. Efforts were made to get Ford interested in producing Volkswagens, but Ford Chairman Ernest Breech said, "I don't think what we're being offered here is worth a damn."

One official report stated the Volkswagen was "too ugly and noisy and quite unattractive to the average motorcar buyer." Due to such lack of interest, the Volkswagen plant was to be dismantled as part of war reparations. Hirst thought the factory deserved a better fate and persuaded the British Army to use Volkswagens for light transport. An order was placed for

twenty thousand units, the first of which went to occupying forces. Many of these were Type 21 Kübelwagens, the rarest type of Volkswagens to collect. A total of 1,785 units were made in 1945.

Late that May, the first town council meeting was held and hosted representatives appointed by the British military government. They chose Wolfsburg as the name of the town and the Volkswagen factory was temporarily named Wolfsburg Motor Works. Technically, the military government seized the company's assets. In addition to the cars used by the occupying forces, some Volkswagens were put to other uses, such as German postal vans. Repair work on British military vehicles was also carried out at the factory during this period.

Heinrich "Heinz" Nordhoff took over as general manager of the

Volkswagen factory on January 1, 1948. Formerly with Opel, Nordhoff directed the company in a brilliant fashion, steering it toward international distribution that began in 1949 with the exportation of Volkswagen sedans to the Netherlands. Nordhoff presided over the car's development into a 1950s phenomenon. By May 1949, the fifty thousandth Volkswagen made since the end of the war was built. On June 30, 1949, the Volkswagen Finance Company was formed. On July 1, 1949, a new export model (11A) was introduced at a price of 5,450 Deutsche Marks and a Karmann-bodied convertible was released.

On September 6, 1949, the British departed from the operation, returning the company to German control via military government directive No. 202.

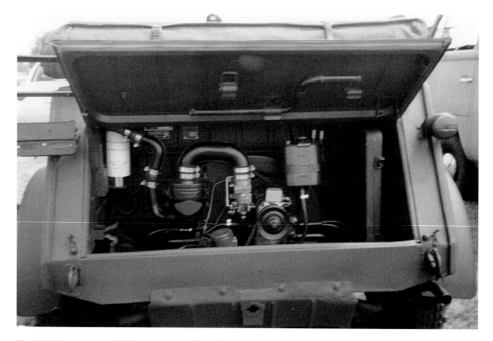

The Kübelwagen was VW's answer to the military jeep, but it was not a four-wheel-drive vehicle. Early Kübelwagens, like this 1942 version, used the original 985cc 30-horsepower Volkswagen flat four. Access to the engine was very simple.

1948: THE "VICTORY WAGON" COMES TO AMERICA

Ben Pon Sr., a businessman and former racing car driver from the Netherlands, called the Volkswagen his "Victory Wagon." It was the car that helped Ben Pon achieve his greatest success as an automobile dealer.

In 1898, Mijndert Pon opened a shop selling sewing machines, household items, and tobacco goods in Amersfoort. Later, he added Opel bikes and motorized bikes. Beginning in 1920, Pon sold Opel and Ford cars and Continental tires. Sons Ben

and Wijnand took over in 1931 and renamed it Pon's Automobielhandel. They became Volkswagen's first foreign distributors in 1947.

Export sales were very important to all European automakers in the early postwar years. World War II had devastated the economies of many nations and the exportation of automobiles was a way to help rebuild battered economies. The Pons were the first to sell Volkswagens outside of Germany.

On August 8, 1947, the brothers brought fifty-one Volkswagens into Holland. In 1949, new deluxe Export Sedans and Export Cabriolets went into production and two of the sedans were exported to Holland by the Pons and

then sent on to the United States. On January 8, 1949, in Rotterdam, the cars were loaded on Holland America Line's *Westerdam*. On January 17, the ship pulled into New York Harbor carrying the first Volkswagens to come to the United States. Max Hoffman's Hoffman Motor Car Company on Park Avenue in New York City was the first American dealership to officially take on Volkswagens.

However, the reaction to these new vehicles wasn't exactly warm in the United States. During a press conference on the *Westerdam*, automotive journalists slammed the Volkswagen for being "Hitler's homely-looking honey." That's when Pon came back at them with the term Victory Wagon. "We did win, after all!" he said.

Characteristics of early Volkswagens included single-acting rear shocks (1945–1951), a T-shaped luggage compartment handle (1945–1949), pullout door handles (1945–1959), and a license plate pressing on the rear engine cover (1945–1949). *Courtesy the Nethercutt Collection*

ABOVE: Note rear bumper design, black-out style lamps, and single passenger-side exhaust pipe on this 1948 Beetle. The license plate number on the rear was the same as the front, but the plate had a different shape. *Archives/TEN: The Enthusiast Network Magazines, LLC*

LEFT: This 1948 Beetle has less bright metal trim than later models would carry. There are no lamps on top of the front fenders. Note the B-GK-99 license plate on the front is of the wide, narrow British style. *Archives/TEN: The Enthusiast Network Magazines, LLC*

But he was wrong. Even though Pon had seen the Volkswagen's popularity in Holland grow and felt the same thing would happen in the United States, he couldn't interest dealers in the cars. He promoted the Volkswagens to East Coast car stores for three weeks, but none of them signed on. He sold one of the cars for $800 (reportedly to settle his bill at the Roosevelt Hotel). Another car was also sold that year, and then Hoffman took over and sold 157 Beetles in 1950.

Former Opel manager Heinz Nordhoff was the one to create Beetlemania in America. Starting in 1955, Volkswagen established a base of operations in Englewood Cliffs, New Jersey. That was the same year that the Wolfsburg plant first hit production of one million units. Volkswagen was smart enough never to underestimate the demand for cheap, affordable postwar transportation. In 1970, Volkswagen ran an ad showing six cars built in 1949: Tucker, Packard, De Soto, Studebaker, Hudson, and Beetle. "Where are they now?" the ad asked. The copywriters noted the Volkswagen, "2,200 improvements later," was still around!

CHAPTER 2

SPLIT WINDOW

The January 1950 issue of *Motor Trend* carried a reader's letter from Hans B. Kirchner of Long Beach, California, an early Volkswagen Beetle fan. It was entitled "60,000 miles in a Volkswagen."

Kirchner told of how he had purchased a Volkswagen in 1947 and used it to travel the Southern Alps to Italy. He had crossed the Großglocknerstraße (highest highway in Austria) and Germany in his car, then brought it to the United States. He drove it from coast to coast, including Southern and Northern California, and brought it to Long Beach in 1949.

Kirchner's car must have been one of very few Volkswagens in the country at that time, but this situation was going to change. The 1950s would see the "People's Car" soar to sales and production records, not only in the United States, but throughout the world. When the company swung into its twentieth year of production, in 1959, it claimed that it had built 2.5 million cars since 1939. Of those, all but 96,182 were manufactured during the 1950s.

Black-and-white Volkswagen catalog art of 1950–1951 subtly emphasizes the small size of the car compared to the world around it. At the same time, it leaves the impression that the Beetle could "climb every mountain."

The changes began on January 1, 1950, when Heinz Nordhoff was appointed general director and took charge of the Volkswagen factory and made the bold decision to increase production. As things turned out, the company produced 81,979 cars by the end of the year, compared to 46,146 in 1949. The 1950 total was nearly double that of a year earlier and included the 100,000th Beetle, which was built on March 4.

It is also interesting to note that only 270 Volkswagens were sold in the United States in 1950. However, Nordhoff knew that he had 15,000 German buyers on a waiting list, along with 7,000 customers in other countries. So, nearly half the cars that left the factory in 1950 already had customers waiting for them.

Motor Trend tested a Volkswagen Beetle in late 1950. "Roadability is said to be phenomenal for a light sedan," advised the magazine. The German car was said to be rapidly becoming an "outstanding success." The magazine noted that "several hundred" had been sold in the New York area.

Several hundred sales in any country were not going to turn the Volkswagen into a success, and Nordhoff knew that he needed to tap into the large United States automobile market, but it wasn't going to be easy. In 1950, Volkswagen needed America, but Americans had no burning desire to trade their Buicks and Packards in on a small, noisy car with a tiny engine.

Nordhoff also had problems on the home front because postwar currency reforms in Germany had replaced Reichsmarks with Deutsche Marks and all of Volkswagen's business had been conducted with the older currency. In other words, the company literally had no spending cash. To solve this problem, Nordhoff turned to the German Volkswagen dealers and asked them to bring Deutsche Marks to the factory to keep production going. The dealers held him in such high esteem that they helped bail the company out—a move that ultimately paid off for them.

Ben and Wijnand Pon failed to ignite American interest in the Volkswagen Beetle in 1949, and Ben Pon told Nordhoff that it was premature to expect the cars to sell in the United States because dealers there did not know how to service them. Americans had become convinced that all foreign cars were prone to breakdowns and pricey to repair.

Of course, the relatively new car magazines in America were open-minded about imports for several reasons. They were not yet getting a lot of manufacturer support from the "Big Three" in the States and being new, they needed advertising. Imported cars made interesting reading and the magazines knew that European companies exporting cars to the United States needed American dollars to rebuild their war-torn economies. The US magazines were anxious to trade ink for ads in 1950.

Motor Trend even started a Transatlantic Newsletter section of the magazine to report on imported cars. The July 1950 *Motor Trend* featured a photo of a Volkswagen and a Porsche with a caption reading, "The cars in this pleasant Alpine setting are both engineered by Dr. Ferdinand Porsche." In the September 1950 Transatlantic Newsletter, the imported car columnist noted, "Volkswagen's latest models have been reduced in price and improved in quality. Lockheed hydraulic brakes are now standard (on cars produced after March 1950). Cooling air to the engine is at last thermostatically regulated."

Shortly after being appointed Volkswagen boss, Heinz Nordhoff made Max Hoffman of New York City the exclusive US agent for Volkswagen sales east of the Mississippi River. As the *New York Times* noted in a headline, "Max Hoffman Made Imports Less Foreign to Americans."

Hoffman handled car sales the way art dealers sold paintings. He specialized in the importation of European luxury cars, and some of them, such as the British Jaguar, were hard to get. He would make deals to secure a Jaguar for a wealthy client if he or she agreed to buy a Volkswagen too. In 1950, Hoffman sold around 330 Volkswagens.

Hoffman was more of a wholesaler than a customer-friendly dealer. He preferred being a supplier to other dealers, because then he could sell them several cars and not have to worry about advertising, dealer preparation and after-the-sale servicing. Hoffman got the Volkswagen ball rolling in the United States, but he was not exactly what Nordhoff had in mind for long-term US operations.

Nordhoff had listened to what Pon told him in 1949 and his vision was focused on establishing a coast-to-coast dealer network with modern sales and service facilities in many markets. However, from 1950 until 1953, US sales were handled through Max Hoffman's place on Park Avenue.

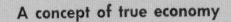
A concept of true economy

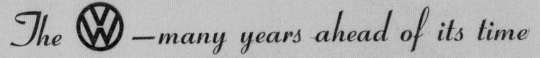
The VW—many years ahead of its time

THE STANDARD SEDAN

for highest value at lowest cost

The Standard Sedan could be identified by looking for the horn attached to the outside of the front bumper bracket, which eliminated the use of a protective grille. It had painted hubcaps and bumpers.

1950

Early sales brochures described the Beetle as "The Amazing Volkswagen." They said the car was fun to drive, easy to park, and had a low initial cost. Other features and benefits included its low fuel consumption, its extremely low maintenance costs, and its ample legroom. The copywriters claimed that its "upkeep averages less than bus fare." The air-cool engine was hyped as another Volkswagen advantage.

The Beetle's 69-ci engine used finned cylinders with cast-iron cylinder liners. It developed 24.5 horsepower at 3,300 rpm and delivered 51 pound-feet of torque at 2,000 rpm. A Solex carburetor was fitted and a six-volt electrical system was all that was required in 1950. The Beetle had a 37-foot turning radius and required 2.4 turns of the steering wheel. The car's rear engine and rear-drive setup was novel to Americans, though not to many Europeans. Early cars made before March 1950 had mechanical brakes.

The Beetle's body construction was that of a steel single-unit body

The answer to discriminating demands.

The VW —proven everywhere, desired everywhere

THE SUNSHINE ROOF SEDAN
— suitable for any weather.

A full-length canvas sunroof became available in April 1950. The sunroofs were manufactured by the Golde Company in Germany and installed by Volkswagen on the assembly line. Early "sunshine roofs" had square corners.

mounted on a stamped-steel floorpan. Throughout its history, the Beetle avoided major changes, but a few visual clues told you about the specific car you were looking at. In August 1949, many changes associated with 1950 Volkswagen models were seen. They included a redesigned fuel tank, the addition of a fuel filler cap with a VW emblem, and a heavier duty front axle.

On some 1950 Volkswagens, the old, single-acting lever-type shock absorbers were replaced with a new double-acting type. The left-hand door lost its armrest and running-in stickers were no longer placed on the windshield. On August 28,

a new seven-digit chassis numbering system was adopted. September brought changes to the clutch disc and piston clearance specs. In the suspension, a track rod with left- and right-hand threading was made standard.

In October 1949, Volkswagen stopped providing an engine crank-starting handle. A beefier clutch lever was put into production. Inside, the use of a brown molded-type rubber front floor mat and rubber footwell trim began. Rubber rear floor mats were no longer used. An accelerator pedal with a larger roller was adopted in October and the runner for the driver's seat was raised a bit. In

December 1949, the push rod tubes were changed to have corrugated ends only.

The 1950 Volkswagen models included the Standard Saloon (sedan) and the Deluxe Export Saloon, along with a rare Cabriolet (convertible). About two months into the year, a sunroof was made available for the sedan and buyers who liked this option could order it at additional cost.

"Export" models were designed for the taste of export (mainly American) buyers and came with fancier equipment than that used on the Standard model in Germany. The Export Sedan was identifiable by its chrome bumpers, bright

CHAPTER 2

hubcaps, chrome headlight rims, and shiny door handles. The Export interior appointments were also of a better quality.

The new Cabriolet was based on the two-door sedan. It had a convertible top that was unusually bulky when folded. Four-wheel independent suspension was featured. The Standard Sedan could be identified by looking for the horn attached to the outside of the front bumper bracket, which eliminated the use of a protective grille. On the Export Sedan, the horn was attached under the left fender, behind a small grille.

Running changes were made to the Volkswagen sedan throughout 1950. In January, the crankcase was modified to alter the oil level and to allow complete draining of the oil. The use of an oil splash guard was discontinued and the number 4 main bearing was grooved. Another change was the gasket between the cylinder and cylinder head.

Up front, the upper torsion bar now had the same five leafs as the lower one (instead of four). A larger knob was used on the lock cable for the up-front trunk. The main beam and turn-signal indicator lights were on the left side of the dashboard, with the generator and oil warning lights on the right. The oil dipstick was given a black phosphate coating. A sealing ring was used between the headlights and front fenders.

In February 1950, Volkswagen began using a 19mm hexagonal oil drain plug on some cars. The accelerator cable elbow was replaced by a pin-and-clip arrangement. The cord carpets, previously used in the rear, were replaced with Honey Brown molded-rubber mats. Starting in March, some Export Sedans and Karmann-bodied

Cabriolets received the hydraulic brakes that *Motor Trend* mentioned. They were made standard on all Type 11A and Type 15 cars a month later.

Volkswagen began stamping its chassis number on the vertical side panel of the left-hand rear crossmember, instead of on the smooth surface of the chassis tunnel. The exhaust pipe diameter was also enlarged. In April 1950, the door windows got a curved cutout at the front upper "corner" for improved draft-free fresh-air ventilation and a locking right-hand door handle went into production. On April 28, Volkswagen put the Sunroof Sedan into production. The next day, a new turn handle was used with the heater flap cable.

In May 1950, a heating pipe with noise suppressors was adopted. Volkswagen changed to automatic cooling-air regulation, which eliminated use of the swivel-handled control valve. A thermostat that reacted to engine temperature instead regulated the air-control valve. A connecting pipe was added to the exhaust box to help preheat the gas/fuel mixture.

Mahle Autothermic pistons went into some engines and a brake fluid reservoir with a float replaced the old filter type. The diameters of the master cylinder and rear-wheel cylinders were reduced. In June, ashtrays were added to the dashboard and the rear right interior side panel. A single-spring clutch also became standard equipment.

Volkswagens were identified by a serial number stamped into a plate on the front center underhood area. It was repeated at the back of spare tire and also stamped on the chassis tunnel (backbone) below the rear seat. The car's

engine number was stamped on the generator support and on the crankcase. The serial number range was 138555–220471. The model year ended on December 31, 1950, with chassis number 220133 and engine number 265999.

SPLIT WINDOW FACTS

▐▌ A used 1948 Volkswagen was advertised in the August 1954 issue of *Motor Trend*. The car was in nice condition with a radio and paint. Mr. B. Dierke of Chicago was asking $25 but offered to "trade up on an MG."

▐▌ According to *Ward's 1952 Automotive Yearbook*, 157 Volkswagens were registered in the United States in calendar-year 1950.

▐▌ In 1950, *Motor Trend* magazine seemed more interested in the German DKW than it was in the Volkswagen.

▐▌ Even before World War II, Dr. Ferdinand Porsche was heard to compare the shape of his People's Car to that of a "May Beetle."

▐▌ In 1950, *Motor Trend* observed that a Volkswagen was capable of 34-miles-per-gallon fuel economy. In addition, the car could easily hit 60 miles per hour.

▐▌ In 1952, the Volkswagen was so little known that *Ward's Automotive Yearbook*, which rarely makes mistakes, misspelled the company's name as "Volkswagon."

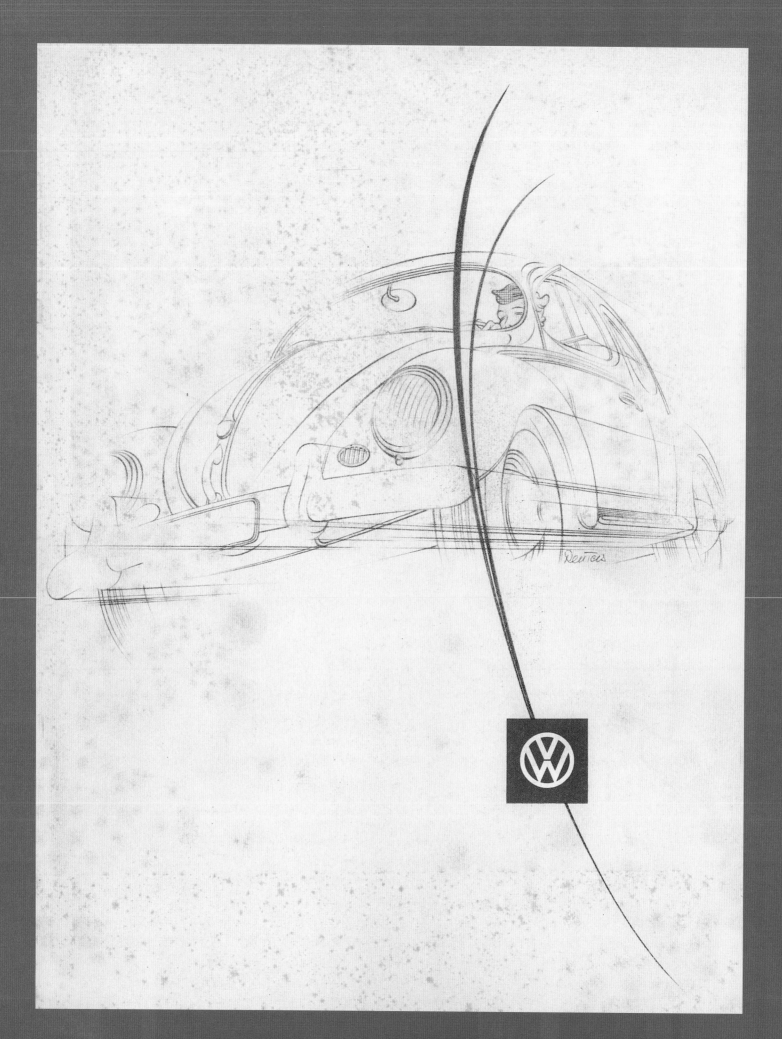

On January 30, 1951, Dr. Ferdinand Porsche, the father of Volkswagen, passed away at age seventy-five. With international communications being much slower in 1951, it wasn't until June that *Motor Trend* noted his passing. "He was best known for his revolutionary Volkswagen and recent Porsche automobile and for his famous rear-engined racing machines, which were operated by Auto Union between '34 and '37," said the magazine.

Volkswagenwerk GmbH produced 93,709 vehicles at its Wolfsburg, West Germany, factory in model-year 1951. Hoffman Motor Car Company sold 550 of those cars in the United States and *Ward's* reported that 390 Volkswagens were registered in the United States in calendar-year 1951. On October 5, 1951, the 250,000th Volkswagen made since the end of the war was built.

The 1951 Volkswagen Beetle continued with split-rear window styling. When viewing the car from that angle, the windows truly looked like the eyes of a Beetle. One obvious change to the cars was the addition of pullout ventilation flaps on the body panel between the front fenders and door. These had a boomerang shape on one side and other side was straight. The front quarter air vents were unique to cars built between January 6, 1951, and October 1952.

At least twenty-four other noticeable changes were phased in during the 1951 assembly run. The generator pulley was also redesigned in January 1951, a sleeve for guiding the accelerator cable return spring was

BLICK INS INNERE

DER GENUSS DES FAHRENS beginnt schon, wenn man den Wagen betritt, denn formschön und zweckmäßig ist auch die innere Architektur des VW. Die Cord- (beim Standard-Modell Tuch-) Polsterstoffe wie auch die Tür- und Wandverkleidungen harmonieren in modischen Farben und Mustern mit dem neuen Farbsortiment der Lackierung und den elfenbein (beim Standard-Modell dunkel) gehaltenen Griffknöpfen und Rosetten. Sitze und Lehnen sind hinsichtlich weicher Federung und haltbietender Plastik (Randwülste aus Schaumgummi) geradezu ideal konstruiert. Die Vordersessel sind auch während der Fahrt einzeln verstellbar und haben stärker geneigte Lehnen; die breite Sitzbank im Fond bietet erforderlichenfalls drei Personen Platz, denen durch großen Abstand zwischen Vorder- und Hintersitzen und durch Erweiterung des Fußraumes ausreichende Bewegungsfreiheit geschaffen wurde. Bei Dunkelheit spendet eine im Dachholm links überm Fahrersitz eingebaute Innenleuchte gute Helligkeit, während das angenehme, beliebig regulierbare Flutlicht des Zentralinstruments das Gefühl einer sicheren Geborgenheit noch erhöht. In der ebenso modern-geschmackvollen wie technisch durchdachten Armaturentafel vereinigt sich in handlicher Anordnung lückenlos alles, was zum Fahren notwendig oder nützlich ist:

1. WINKERHEBEL an der Lenksäule, von der linken Hand mit *einem* Finger zu betätigen

2. Großes ZENTRALINSTRUMENT mit Tachometer, Kilometerzähler und den im Zifferblatt harmonisch eingefügten Kontroll-Leuchten für Lichtmaschine und Kühlung (rot), Öldruck (grün), Fernlicht (blau) und Winker (Doppelpfeil)

3. Sehr ansprechendes, überraschend griffiges ZWEISPEICHEN-LENKRAD, hellfarben getönt, mit schwarz-goldenem, wappengeschmücktem Signalknopf (Export-Modell)

4. Flinke SCHEIBENWISCHER mit weitem Ausschlag und festem Aufdruck, beim Export-Modell mit automatischer Rückkehr in Tiefstellung beim Abschalten

5. Platz für RUNDFUNKSKALA und Bedienungsknöpfe, links daneben ein Zugschalter für Scheibenwischer, ferner ein Dreh-Zugschalter für Scheinwerfer und die feinregulierbare Beleuchtung des Zentralinstruments

6. Hinter geschmackvollem Ziergitter der große Raum für den Einbau eines RADIOGERÄTES

7. Handlich rechts vor dem Fahrer der Zugknopf für die LUFTKLAPPE ALS STARTERHILFE

8. Kombiniertes ZÜND-ANLASS-SCHLOSS; Zündschlüssel ist gleichzeitig auch Türschlüssel

9. Versenkbarer, großer KIPP-ASCHER

10. Schließbarer, geräumiger HANDSCHUHKASTEN

UNMITTELBAR IM BLICKFELD DES FAHRERS liegt das geschmackvoll und übersichtlich eingeteilte Zentralinstrument, das bei Dunkelheit beleuchtet werden kann und in dem alle während der Fahrt zu überwachenden Kontrollorgane zusammengefaßt sind.

OPPOSITE: The Volkswagen Beetle was, at its core, a simple answer to affordable transportation and the artwork used to promote the car was also simple. This elegant example from 1951 has a sketch pad feel to it.

LEFT: The Volkswagen dashboard included a directional signal stalk, a circular gauge with a kilometer speedometer and tachometer, a horn button with the Wolfsburg crest, a bright metal grille, an ashtray, a glove box, and other features.

SPLIT WINDOW

added, and engineers replaced the original magnesium-aluminum alloy crankcase with an electron type that had been experimented with earlier.

On February 5, Volkswagen decided to bench test the Standard Saloon rather than run it in on a test track. In March, a synthetic cam gear was put into production and the exhaust silencer pipe was modified. "Windows" appeared in both halves of the crankcase starting in April. A Wolfsburg crest was added to the front hood of Export models, which could also be identified by their polished

aluminum side trim, chrome-plated door handles, and bright metal hubcaps. Bright metal trim was also added around the windshield of Export models.

Volkswagen moved its front heater flaps inside the heat exchangers. A locking glove compartment was added to the Cabriolet so owners could keep their belongings stored there more secure. Cabriolets were also converted to concealed door hinges, a single interior door pocket on each side, and an additional interior-light switch.

In April 1951, Volkswagen's six-volt generator was uprated and, in July, a rubber boot was added to cover the hand-brake lever. In August, the front quarter panel ventilation flaps were improved through the use of a new mesh screen and an operating lever. Volkswagen serial numbers were in the same locations and the serial number range was 220472–313829. The model year ended on December 31, 1951, with chassis number 313829 and engine number 379470.

1952

Little by little, Volkswagen was expanding production, although the output for model-year 1952 wasn't likely to shake up the auto world or the fat cats in Detroit. In the United States, for instance, *Ward's* reported just 601 registrations of new Volkswagens. However, total annual production was now into six figures with 114,348 vehicles leaving Wolfsburg. During the fourth quarter of the year, Volkswagen workers were building 734 cars per day. The great majority of those were Beetle sedans, although a small number of Cabriolets and Microbuses were made. On September 11, 1952, Volkswagen of Canada was formed to market Volkswagens in Canada. For the year, 41.4 percent of all Volkswagens made were exported, but it's pretty apparent that most did not come to America.

Late 1951 changes carried over for 1952 models included strengthened jacking points on Beetles. The front quarter vents with handles continued to cool Volkswagen drivers

and passengers. For cost savings, Volkswagen stopped putting wheel bolts in the factory tool kit. In November 1951, the rear seat bolsters that had been used in the Export Sedan since 1949 were discontinued and the exhaust valves were improved. Starting in December 1951, new six-volt 0.6-watt dashboard indicator lamps were used.

As usual, Volkswagen's new model year started on January 1, 1952, and the Beetle would see numerous changes over the next twelve months, although they were phased in, rather than all done at the same time. Take the addition of vent windows in the doors. This change is often thought of as a way to spot a 1952 Beetle, although it wasn't made until October 1, 1952. So, it is possible to have a 1952 Volkswagen with the split-rear windows and side vent windows. In fact, as noted later in this chapter, it is possible to have an early 1953 Beetle with this configuration.

In January 1952, using a hollow bolt with a felt ring was a change

made to prevent grease leaks, and the handbrake lever boot on the chassis tunnel of Export models was modified. Starting in February, the hydraulic brake reservoir no longer had a float and Volkswagen made some electrical changes involving parking lights, which were in the headlight and attached to a different system terminal. In March, a Klettermaxe jack was added to the tool kit. Also in March, the use of a connecting pipe between the tailpipe and the exhaust silencer was dropped. In May, the use of double-valve springs stopped and a single-valve spring was used. In June, the diameter of the clutch cable adjusting nut was reduced. A new clutch cable operating lever with a conical eye was also adopted.

No serial number locations changed in 1952. The starting number was 313830 and the ending number was 428156. The model year officially ended on December 31, 1952, with chassis number 397023 and engine number 481713.

ABOVE: From the side view, this 1949 Volkswagen Beetle can be identified as a 1948–1949 model by the lack of vent windows (introduced in 1952) and lack of bright metal body side moldings. The chrome bumpers indicate it is a 1949.

RIGHT: The design of the 1946–1949 dashboard changed little from that of the 1938 Volkswagen prototype with open glove boxes on either side and a VW emblem on the right-hand blanking plate. The speedometer had very few changes too.

Early 1953

When the year began, Volkswagen was planning to produce one hundred sixty thousand passenger cars in 1953, but strangely enough it was hard to determine who actually owned the company. Since 1945 a certain amount of the company's profits had been put into escrow, awaiting a decision by the West German courts as to ownership. There was $50 million in the kitty.

Regardless of how that situation shook out, more than two hundred thousand Volkswagens had been exported from Germany by that point. And they had been sold in eighty-three different countries. The German automaker was definitely starting down the road to success and was about to modernize the looks of the Beetle with what, for Volkswagen, was a big change—a one-piece rear window. However, this change did not occur until March, so the early 1953 cars were carryover 1952 models, although they featured some late 1952 improvements.

The changes introduced on early 1953 Volkswagens (and continued on for late 1953 models) included a new rotary knob for adjusting the heater output. The front torsion bar suspension got a sixth leaf and the travel length of the front telescopic shock absorbers was increased.

A new 28 PCI carburetor was used. The transmission used in the Export sedan had synchronizers on all gears except first gear. New rubber-and-steel gearbox mountings were also used.

In the rear suspension, torsion bar diameters were reduced a bit. Volkswagen also switched to smaller-but-wider 5.60-15 wheels and the brake system rear-wheel cylinders had a smaller diameter. As mentioned in the 1952 information, vent windows were added to the doors on October 1, 1952, and they continued to be used in all 1953 models. Other improvements were made to the heating system demisters and noise suppression was better. The door window regulators required just over three turns of the crank handle to fully lower the windows, rather than 10½ turns.

The engine lid at the rear of the Beetle had a T-handle instead of a vertical one. The bumpers had a broader section (profile) and beefier guards. Polished anodized metal moldings replaced the old aluminum body trim. The rear light lenses had heart-shaped brake lamp lenses on top of each taillight.

For better security the glove compartment received a lid and a push-button latching mechanism. The

dashboard was completely redesigned and rubber floor mats with press studs were also new. A new ashtray was on the passenger side of the dash and the car had different cloth upholstery.

The fuse box for the brake/taillights was on the reverse side of the dashboard. The starter button was now on the left side of the steering wheel. The turn-signal indicator switch was to the left of the column. A new larger-diameter speedometer was fitted. The horn was now concealed behind a decorative oval grille. The horn button on the center of the steering wheel had a Wolfsburg crest.

Wider-sweeping windshield wipers were fitted as well as new battery hold-down springs. Single-pull switches were used for the lights and the wipers. Volkswagen continued making running changes to its "People's Car" in 1953, but made fewer modifications than in the past few years. An oil-bath air cleaner with a clamping strap was introduced. The carburetor air-correction jet was revised and bronze check valves replaced the steel ones. Engine valve clearances were reduced. New adjustable door striker plates appeared on production cars beginning on Valentine's Day.

ABOVE: Joseph Cecil spent nine years in Germany and picked up the language, a German wife, and a rare Model 11E Beetle. His 1952 Volkswagen Model 11E—immediately identifiable to collectors by its split rear window—is one of few that survive outside the VW museum in Wolfsburg. Note the painted hubcaps, rollback sunroof, and split rear window treatment.

RIGHT: This photo shows the white interior of Joseph Cecil's 1952 Volkswagen Model 11E Sunshine Sedan. The dashboard now has twin gauge clusters.

1950

VOLKSWAGEN SEDAN

PAINT COLORS

L11 Pastel Green	**L50** Coral Red
L13 Medium Green	**L51** Bordeaux Red
L14 Reseda Green	**L70** Medium Brown
L21 Pearl Gray	**L71** Beige
L23 Silver Gray	**L76** Brown Beige
L32 Dark Blue	**L87** Pearl White
L41 Black	

INTERIORS

STANDARD Beige cloth
OPTIONAL (ALL MODELS)
Beige leatherette
(*determined by body color)
Red leatherette
(*determined by body color)

HEADLINER Beige or Gray, depending on body color
CARPETS Gray Beige or Honey Brown, depending on body color
FLOOR MATS (STANDARD) Black rubber (**DELUXE EXPORT MODEL**) Black or Beige mat, depending on choice and body color

MODEL AVAILABILITY	Standard 2-door Sedan ($1,280)
	Deluxe 2-door Sedan ($1,480)
	Deluxe 2-door Sunroof Sedan ($1,560)
	2-door Cabriolet Convertible ($1,997)
WHEELBASE	94.5 inches
LENGTH	160.2 inches
WIDTH	60.5 inches
HEIGHT	(sedan) 61.0 inches
WEIGHT	(sedan) 1,600 lbs.
TREAD	(front/rear) 51.0/49.2 inches
TIRES	(sedan) 5.00 x 16
BRAKES	front/rear drum (hydraulic after March/April 1950)
WHEELS	steel disc
FUEL TANK	8.8 gallons
FRONT SUSPENSION	king pins with transverse torsion bars and upper/lower trailing arms
REAR SUSPENSION	swing axles with trailing arms and torsion bars
STEERING	worm and cap nut
ENGINE	1,131cc 24.5-horsepower horizontally opposed four-cylinder, overhead valve, air cooled, light alloy block and head
TRANSMISSION	four-speed manual
FINAL DRIVE RATIO	4.43:1

1951

VOLKSWAGEN SEDAN

PAINT COLORS

L11 Pastel Green	**L37** Medium Blue
L13 Medium Green	**L41** Black
L14 Reseda Green	**L55** Maroon Red
L21 Pearl Gray	**L70** Medium Brown
L23 Silver Gray	**L73** Chestnut Brown
L31 Dove Blue	**L87** Pearl White
L32 Dark Blue	**L90** Sand Beige
L36 Azure Blue	

INTERIORS

STANDARD (ALL MODELS) Beige cloth
OPTIONAL (ALL MODELS)
Beige leatherette
(*determined by body color)
Red leatherette
(*determined by body color)

HEADLINER Beige or Gray, depending on body color
CARPETS Gray Beige or Honey Brown, depending on body color
FLOOR MATS (STANDARD) Black rubber (**DELUXE EXPORT MODEL**) Black or Beige mat, depending on choice and body color

MODEL AVAILABILITY	Standard 2-door Sedan ($1,295)
	Deluxe 2-door Sedan ($1,480)
	Deluxe 2-door Sunroof Sedan ($1,550)
	2-door Cabriolet Convertible ($2,296)
WHEELBASE	94.5 inches
LENGTH	159.3 inches
WIDTH	60.6 inches
HEIGHT	(sedan) 59.1 inches
WEIGHT	(sedan) 1,600 lbs.
TREAD	(front/rear) 50.8/49.2 inches
TIRES	(sedan) 5.00 x 16
BRAKES	hydraulic, front/rear drum
WHEELS	steel disc
FUEL TANK	8.8 gallons
FRONT SUSPENSION	king pins with transverse torsion bars and upper/lower trailing arms
REAR SUSPENSION	swing axles with trailing arms and torsion bars
STEERING	worm and cap nut
ENGINE	1,131cc 24.5-hp horizontally opposed four-cylinder, overhead valve, air cooled, light alloy block and head, finned cylinders with cast-iron liners
TRANSMISSION	four-speed manual
FINAL DRIVE RATIO	4.43:1

1952

VOLKSWAGEN SEDAN

PAINT COLORS

L11 Pastel Green	**L37** Medium Blue
L13 Medium Green	**L41** Black
L14 Reseda Green	**L55** Maroon Red
L21 Pearl Gray	**L70** Medium Brown
L23 Silver Gray	**L73** Chestnut Brown
L31 Dove Blue	**L87** Pearl White
L32 Dark Blue	**L90** Sand Beige
L36 Azure Blue	

INTERIORS

STANDARD (ALL MODELS)
Beige cloth

OPTIONAL (ALL MODELS)
Beige leatherette
(*determined by body color)
Red leatherette
(*determined by body color)

HEADLINER Beige or Gray, depending on body color

CARPETS Gray Beige or Honey Brown, depending on body color

FLOOR MATS (STANDARD) Black rubber **(DELUXE EXPORT MODEL)** Black or Beige mat, depending on choice and body color

MODEL AVAILABILITY	Standard 2-door Sedan ($1,395)
	Deluxe 2-door Sedan ($1,595)
	Deluxe 2-door Sunroof Sedan ($1,667)
	2-door Cabriolet Convertible ($2,395)
WHEELBASE	94.5 inches
LENGTH	159.4 inches
WIDTH	60.6 inches
HEIGHT	(sedan) 59.1 inches
WEIGHT	(sedan) 1,600 lbs.
TREAD	(front/rear) 50.8/49.2 inches
TIRES	(sedan) 5.00 x 16
BRAKES	hydraulic, front/rear drum
WHEELS	steel disc
FUEL TANK	8.8 gallons
FRONT SUSPENSION	king pins with transverse torsion bars and upper/lower trailing arms
REAR SUSPENSION	swing axles with trailing arms and torsion bars
STEERING	worm and cap nut
ENGINE	1,131cc 24.5-hp horizontally opposed four-cylinder, overhead valve, air cooled, light alloy block and head, finned cylinders with cast-iron liners
TRANSMISSION	four-speed manual
FINAL DRIVE RATIO	4.43:1

EARLY 1953

VOLKSWAGEN SEDAN

PAINT COLORS

L11 Pastel Green	**L55** Maroon Red
L21 Pearl Gray	**L70** Medium Brown
L36 Azure Blue	**L73** Chestnut Brown
L37 Medium Blue	**L90** Sand Beige
L41 Black	

INTERIORS

STANDARD (ALL MODELS)
Beige cloth

OPTIONAL (ALL MODELS)
Beige leatherette
(*determined by body color)
Red leatherette
(*determined by body color)

HEADLINER Beige or Gray, depending on body color

CARPETS Gray Beige or Honey Brown, depending on body color

FLOOR MATS (STANDARD) Black rubber **(DELUXE EXPORT MODEL)** Black or Beige mat, depending on choice and body color

MODEL AVAILABILITY	Standard 2-door Sedan ($1,056)
	Deluxe 2-door Sedan ($1,675)
	Deluxe 2-door Sunroof Sedan ($1,790)
	2-door Cabriolet Convertible ($2,350)
WHEELBASE	94.5 inches
LENGTH	159.4 inches
WIDTH	60.6 inches
HEIGHT	(sedan) 59.1 inches
WEIGHT	(sedan) 1,600 lbs.
TREAD	(front/rear) 50.8/49.2 inches
TIRES	(sedan) 5.00 x 16
BRAKES	hydraulic, front/rear drum
WHEELS	steel disc
FUEL TANK	8.8 gallons
FRONT SUSPENSION	king pins with transverse torsion bars and upper/lower trailing arms
REAR SUSPENSION	swing axles with trailing arms and torsion bars
STEERING	worm and cap nut
ENGINE	1,131cc 24.5-hp horizontally opposed four-cylinder, overhead valve, air cooled, light alloy block and head, finned cylinders with cast-iron liners
TRANSMISSION	four-speed manual
FINAL DRIVE RATIO	4.43:1

CHAPTER 3

SMALL OVAL WINDOW

By mid-1953, the Volkswagen phenomenon was really beginning to take hold in America. Production for 1953 would be 151,323 units. According to *Ward's Automotive Yearbook*, 1,237 new Volkswagens—nearly 10 percent of the entire model-year production total—were registered to owners in the United States in calendar-year 1953. And to top off this new awareness of the brand, *Ward's* even spelled Volkswagen correctly for the first time!

The oval rear window was introduced in 1953 and used through 1957. Vent windows were added to the Deluxe Export Sedan in October of 1952. This illustration of the Deluxe Beetle sedan is used in many sales catalogs.

Volkswagens were also getting good reviews in car magazines. "Handling qualities are exceptional," declared *Motor Trend* of the Beetle in 1953. "You can break the rear end loose, but only if you work at it." The reviewer noted that the Beetle's interior trim was "as good as in some cars costing an additional $1,000."

One of the reasons that the Volkswagen was more in the spotlight in America in 1953 was the fact that the company's first dealerships opened that year. Heinz Nordhoff's agreement with Max Hoffman had expired and this left the US marketplace open to new distributors and dealers. Volkswagen management divided the country into two territories, east and west of the Mississippi River. Volkswagen then sent the mechanics and their families over from Germany. Each dealer was assigned one or more factory mechanics to assure that parts and service departments would meet stringent requirements.

These operational changes were in line with the ideas that Nordhoff envisioned after Ben Pon explained to him the problems involved in bringing the Beetle to America. The general director had never forgotten the advice he received, and in 1953, he was able to start franchising dealerships across the United States that would not only sell cars, but also provide service for them. It was a perfect storm and the roots of the Volkswagen tidal wave were in place.

Magazines such as *Motor Trend* not only began to feature Volkswagen photos and articles, but they did so repeatedly. Volkswagen got ink in that particular

The late 1953 Volkswagen Beetle Cabriolet Convertible retailed for $2,350 and offered buyers a chance to get a tan as deep as the cloth top on this beauty. At $1,677, the Deluxe Sunroof model was a cheaper way to suntan.

publication no less than three times during 1953. In the September issue, Dr. Ferdinand Porsche was mentioned as the creator of the Volkswagen and Porsche automobiles. In October, an article entitled "Seven Economy Cars" covered the Volkswagen sedan in minute detail. "The whole car is crammed with features as unusual as the engine," the magazine said. "Do you want a car that breaks sharply with tradition and does so with undeniable competence? If so, the Volkswagen deserves your attention," the magazine said.

An article entitled "German Auto Industry" appeared in the December 1953 *Motor Trend*. "Best known German export car is the Volkswagen, rear-powered by an air-cooled flat four and finished like an expensive car," said the caption under the picture of a Beetle sedan. The article also stated, "For 1953, the Volkswagen plant alone expects a production of 160,000 passenger cars."

All the Worlds' 1954 Cars (put together in 1953) said, "To date, over 2,000 Americans and 500,000 Europeans have bought these durable, economical, well-finished and sprightly Volkswagens."

The *Motor Trend Worldwide Yearbook 1954* gushed over the latest Volkswagen: "The Deluxe Export Sedan and Cabriolet offer between 30 and 32 miles to the US gallon. The 24.5-horsepower engine does not sound overly exciting; however, the Volkswagen combines simplicity, ease of repair and cheapness of replacement parts, which led to the Model T's fabulous popularity. Although the normal maximum speed does not exceed 65 mph, that speed is accomplished at just over 3,000 rpm, a noteworthy factor in reducing engine wear. Its pound- per-horsepower ratio is a relatively unimpressive 63.43, but despite this, the Volkswagen can hold its own under normal traffic conditions. The ride offered by this surprisingly roomy car is fairly comfortable. Its handling qualities are superior, aside from a tendency toward overly quick steering in the turns."

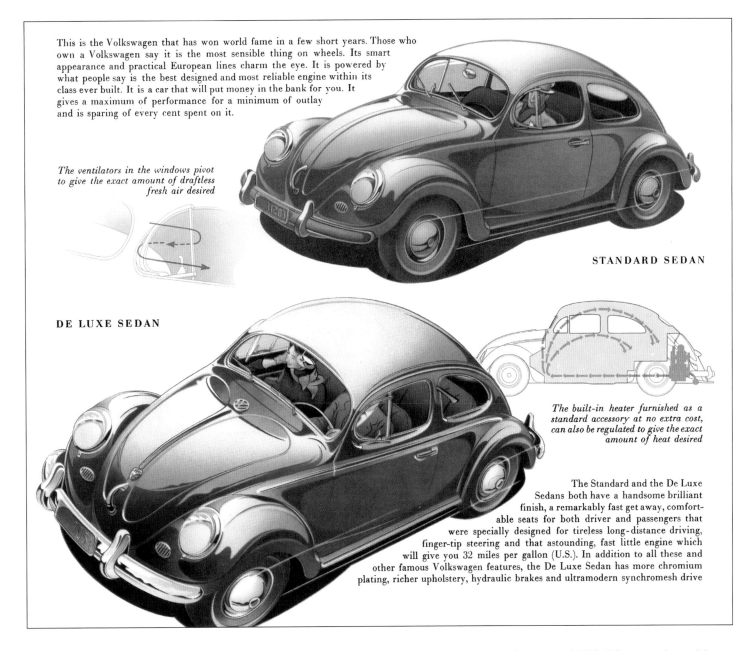

This is the Volkswagen that has won world fame in a few short years. Those who own a Volkswagen say it is the most sensible thing on wheels. Its smart appearance and practical European lines charm the eye. It is powered by what people say is the best designed and most reliable engine within its class ever built. It is a car that will put money in the bank for you. It gives a maximum of performance for a minimum of outlay and is sparing of every cent spent on it.

The ventilators in the windows pivot to give the exact amount of draftless fresh air desired

STANDARD SEDAN

DE LUXE SEDAN

The built-in heater furnished as a standard accessory at no extra cost, can also be regulated to give the exact amount of heat desired

The Standard and the De Luxe Sedans both have a handsome brilliant finish, a remarkably fast get away, comfortable seats for both driver and passengers that were specially designed for tireless long-distance driving, finger-tip steering and that astounding, fast little engine which will give you 32 miles per gallon (U.S.). In addition to all these and other famous Volkswagen features, the De Luxe Sedan has more chromium plating, richer upholstery, hydraulic brakes and ultramodern synchromesh drive

By mid-1953, the era of Volkswagens that looked almost identical to the prewar KdF-Wagen was over. In the first quarter of 1953, Volkswagen changed the rear split window of the Beetles to a slightly larger oval window.

This right-hand-drive 1953 Volkswagen Beetle was in the famous Auto Collections on the fifth floor of the Linq Hotel and Casino in Las Vegas, Nevada. It was for sale with an asking price of $49,500. Rob Williams, manager of the Auto Collections, is a Volkswagen aficionado.

Late 1953

By mid-1953, the era of Volkswagens that looked almost identical to the prewar KdF-Wagen was over. In the first quarter of 1953, Volkswagen changed the split rear window of the Beetles to a slightly larger oval window. This oval window was said to increase visibility out of the rear of the car up to 33 percent. The new design would last until 1958, when the larger rear window that most people see in Beetles today was adopted. Today, the split-window and small-oval-window cars are much rarer than the later Beetles with larger rear windows.

Also in March, the Volkswagen's electric fuses were changed to a brass-wire type. The fuel tank filler neck doubled in size to 80mm and new reflecting trim moldings were adopted. The ashtray lid in the dashboard sported a new, short-horizontal handle. A new interior light came with an on-off switch and a 10-watt bulb instead of a 5-watt bulb. A wider, new combined indicator arrow appeared in the speedometer. In July, a new rearview mirror that was integral with the sun visor was introduced and the quarter windows had new locking catches. The serial numbers for both early and late 1953 sedans were 428157–575414.

It's hard to say whether the growing competition among car magazines was pushing the envelope, or whether their testing methods were improving, or whether they were just after more advertising dollars, but by 1953 the Beetle's top speed was being reported as 66 miles per hour instead of the earlier figure of 60 miles per hour seen in many articles. The 0–60 miles-per-hour time published for the Beetle was 42.1 seconds. Average fuel miles was reported as 22–28 miles per gallon in one 1953 article. That compared to a figure of 34 miles per gallon published in earlier coverage.

1954

By the start of 1954, Nordhoff was "ready to roll" in the US auto market. His deal with Max Hoffman was over, new dealers were signing up, new facilities were going up, and factory-trained mechanics were in place to support the new dealer network. In January 1954, Will Van de Kamp was sent from Germany to take charge of Volkswagen sales in the eastern United States and Geoffrey Lange also arrived from Germany to oversee Western sales.

Van de Kamp had previously worked as a Volkswagen field representative in Germany. Lange was a salesman and had formed a close relationship with West Coast sports car guru John von Neumann, who had bought many cars from

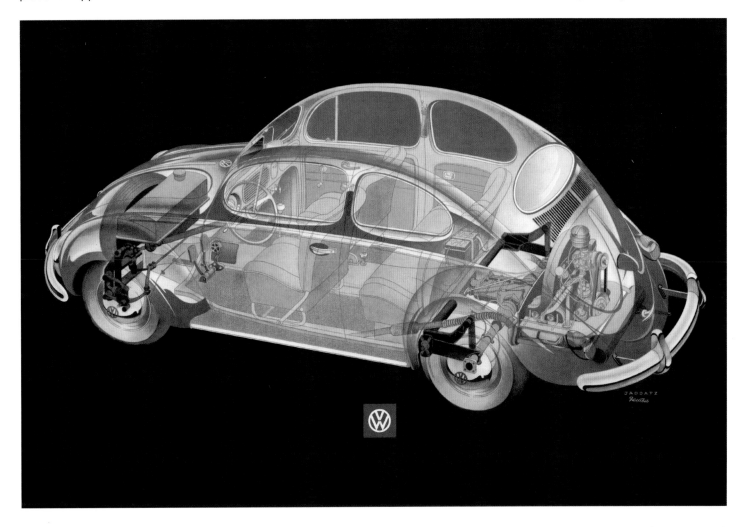

This ghost view of an early oval window sedan reveals all the innovations and advanced early-1950 technology built into the Beetle, including the rear-mounted, air-cooled engine and the novel front and rear suspension setups.

Hoffman and had developed a respect for the Porsche-designed Beetle.

Volkswagen's total sales took a big leap to 202,174 cars in 1954. That was about 50,000 more than the previous year. *Ward's* reported that 6,344 new Volkswagens were registered in the United States. On September 10, 1954, the 100,000th Volkswagen left the Wolfsburg factory. For the first time, Volkswagen generated one billion Deutsche Marks for the year. The company also focused on keeping the momentum going by starting an annual success bonus for its workers.

Late 1953 changes used on 1954 Volkswagen models included eight-leaf torsion bars and greaseless front wheel bearing caps. In October 1953, an uprated generator was used on some cars. The following month, Volkswagen went to a heater control knob with no inscription on it. A new steering wheel with two downward-pointing spokes was introduced. It provided a clearer view of the speedometer.

In December 1953, Volkswagen received its first new engine in a decade. The larger 1,192cc engine with a bore and stroke of 77 x 64mm was introduced early in the year. It had a 6.1:1 compression ratio, compared to the previous 5.8:1 and went from 24.5 to 30 brake horsepower at 3,400 rpm. Volkswagen continued with a six-volt electrical system, four main bearings, solid valve lifters, and a Solex downdraft carburetor.

The 1954 Volkswagen also received an oil-bath air cleaner. Larger heating outlets up front (instead of at the rear) featured a protective grille. The new 160-watt generator

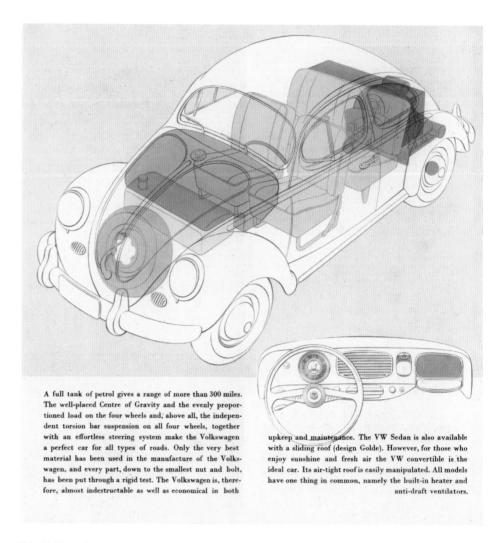

A full tank of petrol gives a range of more than 300 miles. The well-placed Centre of Gravity and the evenly proportioned load on the four wheels and, above all, the independent torsion bar suspension on all four wheels, together with an effortless steering system make the Volkswagen a perfect car for all types of roads. Only the very best material has been used in the manufacture of the Volkswagen, and every part, down to the smallest nut and bolt, has been put through a rigid test. The Volkswagen is, therefore, almost indestructable as well as economical in both upkeep and maintenance. The VW Sedan is also available with a sliding roof (design Golde). However, for those who enjoy sunshine and fresh air the VW convertible is the ideal car. Its air-tight roof is easily manipulated. All models have one thing in common, namely the built-in heater and anti-draft ventilators.

This 1954 catalog art aimed at the United States depicted a ghost view of the Deluxe Sedan. This piece does a good job of promoting the cars' technical features.

replaced the previous 130-watt model. Inside the cars, adjustable automatic instrument illumination was provided. The windshield wipers were improved and finished with metallic paint (instead of chrome plating).

Volkswagen tool kit ingredients were shuffled around again and the use of a push-button starter was discontinued. The engine distributor was built with a new type of vacuum control (cars only) and a new over-center battery clamp was used. By

late December 1953, the door and ignition locks were made identical.

The new model year officially started in January 1954, the same month that Volkswagen adopted a dipstick with an integral loop handle and cap. In February, Volkswagen began marking the month and year of production on the underside of the oil cooler. In March, a new style starting crank was supplied. It was made of 3mm gauge seamless tubing.

In April 1954, the Volkswagen distributor was upgraded with improved springs for the bob weights. In May, the carburetor was improved with a nylon float. Body paint on the Cabriolet was changed from cellulose to synthetic resin. Volkswagen added a driving mirror with two sun visors, a passenger grab handle, a tailpipe extension, and several interior changes. In July 1954, the filter mesh was removed from the oil filter cap.

— 1955 —

What a big difference in only six years! By the end of 1955, Volkswagen would stand tall as the third largest seller of imported cars in the United States. And since the US market was the 500-pound gorilla, that meant that Wolfsburg was hopping. How true. The plant produced 279,986 cars. Car magazines were filled with pictures of assembly lines cranking out Volkswagen products. And to top things off, 28,907 Volkswagens were registered in the United States.

"Having shot in a short time to the top of imported car sales lists, the familiar VW is worth a close look," *Motor Trend* said. "For a lot of people, [Volkswagen] gives near-sports feel, comfort, high quality, economy, practical innovations."

On August 5, 1955, the one millionth Volkswagen came off the assembly line in Germany. Volkswagen of America was also founded on October 27, 1955. This trading company, formed in Englewood Cliffs, New Jersey, was responsible for US sales of Volkswagen

The 1954 Beetle dashboard featured a cool-looking horizontal bars grille in its center. Circular instruments were on the left and the ashtray was on the right. The white two-spoke steering wheel was nice looking, but obscured the driver's view of instruments.

products. In Germany, the production of the Volkswagen Beetle actually passed the one thousand-units-per-day mark.

In 1955, Volkswagen switched to making product changes on a model-year basis, with the model year running from August of one year to August of the next. Very few changes were made this year though. Starting on April 1, 1954, cars sold in the United States, Canada, and Guam had been changed to fender-mounted turn signals instead of semaphores. All Volkswagens after this had turn signals.

On August 31, 1954, some engine improvements went into effect and the distributor rotor arm was redesigned to stay dust free. Volkswagen said that its engines no longer required a break-in period. Other changes made to the Beetle included the spare V-belt being dropped from the tool kit contents.

In October, the "window" lens on the brake light housing was discontinued and new double-filament bulbs were used in cars destined for the United States and Canada. Volkswagen also began using shatterproof windshield glass. A new taillight housing with a drain hole in it also went into production. In December, the door hinge was modified to use an oil slot, instead of a hole, for hinge pin lubrication. A key-type starter replaced the earlier push-button starter and a three-way dome light was installed. Car numbers for 1955 were 722935–929745.

About the Volkswagen interior, *Motor Trend* (June 1955) said, "Interiors are odd-smelling, durable plastic with most screws concealed, workmanship expected of much more expensive car."

1956

Volkswagen had 50.9 percent of market for imported cars in the United States this year. In all, 333,190 Beetles, Transporters, and Karmann Ghias left the factory in Germany. The other models are covered in a different chapter of this book. According to *Ward's Automotive Yearbook*, 50,011 new Volkswagens were registered in the United States in calendar-year 1956.

The May 1956 issue of *Motor Trend* showed the new Karmann Ghias coupe, a Volkswagen microbus, and thirteen Beetle sedans on the cover. Inside was a comparison road test of the '56 Volkswagen and Renault. Magazine test driver Pete Molson wrote, "There is a combination of civilized US-type comfort and fun in the VW that the Renault does not approach."

Carrosserie Zund of Switzerland made a large, wraparound rear window treatment. In Germany, a Volkswagen-base car called the Rometsch Sportwagen was available on a built-to-order basis. One brought into the United States by Beverly Hills, California, dealer Jack Berman was showcased in the September 1956 edition of *Motor Trend*. It was the first (and possibly only) such car to reach America. Available as a package priced at $2,995 for a coupe and $3,195 for a convertible, it included a completely custom body with a full wraparound rear window that had a touch of Studebaker Starlight Coupe to it.

Most of Volkswagen's changes for 1956 went into effect on August 4, 1955, when the taillights were redesigned and mounted higher on the fenders. Twin tailpipes jutted out the rear of the car (bright tailpipes on Export models). A new easy-grip steering wheel had deeper-set spokes and a smaller hub.

Door panels on Export models received leatherette trim. The interior door handles now operated toward the rear of the car. The jack attached with a snap-on clip and was nearer the spare tire than before. The front seats were made wider. Seats in the Export Sedan were on a higher-at-the-front rail and adjusted three ways. The gearshift lever was now bent backward.

In February 1956, Volkswagens received a distributor with a new power curve. Beginning in March, the Export Saloon had reduced ground clearance. April brought 15mm longer front seats with rubber-based hair padding. In June, the engine vacuum pipe was moved from above the choke cable to under the accelerator cable.

During 1956, tubeless tires were tested on eight hundred cars. The test must have been successful, as these tires were installed on all VWs a short time afterward. Other new-for-1956 features included self-cancelling directional lights and adjustable seat backs. Chassis numbers for the 1956 Beetles started at 929746 and ended with 1246618.

ABOVE: Whitewall tires were a Volkswagen factory option and gave the German economy car more of an upscale appearance. The split "towel rack" rear bumper guard was standard equipment. *Archives/ TEN: The Enthusiast Network Magazines, LLC*

RIGHT: Volkswagen's 1956 engine was a 72.7-cid overhead-valve flat four that generated 36 horsepower at 5700 rpm and 56 pound-feet of torque at 2000 rpm. The inherently vibration-free power plant had a top speed of 68 miles per hour *Archives/TEN: The Enthusiast Network Magazines, LLC*.

OPPOSITE: A comparison test in *Motor Trend* in 1956 pitted the Beetle against the Renault 4-CV. The editors said they would no longer laugh at the French car, but that the Volkswagen had a civilized US-type comfort the 4-CV couldn't match. *Archives/ TEN: The Enthusiast Network Magazines, LLC*

A gorgeous piece of catalog art showing a 1956 Volkswagen Type 15 Cabriolet. The coachbuilding firm of Wilhelm Karmann in Osnabrück, Germany, carried out the ragtop conversions for Volkswagen.

1957

The Volkswagen Beetle was the most popular, foreign-made transportation sedan in the United States in 1957 according to Trend Books' *Cars of the World* annual. The German car's highlight was its rear-mounted, air-cooled engine. The 72.74-cubic-inch powerplant developed 36 horsepower (US version) at 3,700 rpm.

The Volkswagen's downdraft carburetor was installed immediately above a hot spot that preheated the air-fuel mixture before combustion. The four-speed synchromesh transmission had helically cut gears for silent operation. A 68-mile-per-hour top speed was claimed and fuel economy was reputed to be 30 miles per gallon.

As in the past, the Volkswagen body featured welded, pressed steel construction. The body was bolted to the platform-type chassis. All four wheels were independently sprung through adjustable torsion bars. Rebound, front and rear, was checked by four double-acting telescopic shock absorbers.

Volkswagen's popularity continued to march upward with the manufacture of 380,561 cars for worldwide distribution in 1957. According to *Ward's*, 64,242 Volkswagens were registered in the United States. As production increased, so did a need for additional manufacturing space. Volkswagen took over the Henschel factory in Germany and also started a subsidiary in Australia. Despite the increase in registrations, Volkswagen's share of the import car market fell from almost 51 percent in 1956 to 31.1 percent in 1957. However, the "Big 3" in this market segment were Volkswagen first, Renault second, and British Ford third.

Volkswagen's changes for 1957 started appearing on cars leaving the factory in August 1956. They included an adjustable door lock plate, new ignition coil specs, and a light alloy cam timing gear. Starting in September, the VW emblems on the hubcaps were finished in black. A new

Cabriolet top was fastened with brass pins and studs instead of steel ones.

Starting in October, a new starter with four commutator brushes was used. All home-market cars now had an outside rearview mirror. The door hinges no longer had lubrication nipples. December brought new Pearl Blue and Bamboo colors for the Cabriolet, but Iris Blue and Sepia Silver were dropped.

There was slightly more room throughout the Beetle, including in the front luggage compartment. Numerous changes were made to Volkswagens throughout 1957. In January, the front heater outlets were moved rearward, to within a foot of the doors, to improve heat distribution. This required some modifications to the body side panels. In February, a new windshield wiper motor was installed and license plate lighting was improved. After the first week of June, a steering wheel with twice as many (48) splines was used.

The serial number range (for Beetle sedans and Karmann Ghias) ran from 1246619 to 1600439.

LATE 1953

VOLKSWAGEN SEDAN

PAINT COLORS

L11 Pastel Green
L19 Atlantic Green
L35 Metallic Blue
L37 Medium Blue
L41 Black

L73 Chestnut Brown
L225 Jupiter Brown
L271 Texas Brown
L272 Sahara Tan

INTERIORS

STANDARD (ALL MODELS)
Gray Beige cloth
OPTIONAL (ALL MODELS)
Beige leatherette
(*determined by body color)
Black leatherette
(*determined by body color)
Red Beige leatherette
(*determined by body color)

HEADLINER
Beige or Gray, depending on body color
CARPETS
Gray Beige or Honey Brown, depending on body color
FLOOR MATS
(STANDARD) Black rubber

MODEL AVAILABILITY	Standard 2-door Sedan ($1,056)
	Deluxe 2-door Sedan ($1,655)
	Deluxe 2-door Sunroof Sedan ($1,675)
	2-door Cabriolet Convertible ($2,350)
WHEELBASE	94.5 inches
LENGTH	160.2 inches
WIDTH	60.6 inches
HEIGHT	(sedan) 59.1 inches
WEIGHT	(sedan) 1,600 lbs.
TREAD	(front/rear) 50.6/49.08 inches
TIRES	(sedan) 5.50 x 15
BRAKES	hydraulic, front/rear drum
WHEELS	steel disc
FUEL TANK	8.8 gallons
FRONT SUSPENSION	king pins with transverse torsion bars and upper/lower trailing arms
REAR SUSPENSION	swing axles with trailing arms and torsion bars
STEERING	worm and cap nut
ENGINE	1,131cc 24.5-hp horizontally opposed four-cylinder, overhead valve, air cooled, light alloy block and head, finned cylinders with cast-iron liners
TRANSMISSION	four-speed manual
FINAL DRIVE RATIO	4.40:1

1954

VOLKSWAGEN SEDAN

PAINT COLORS

L41 Black
L213 Iceland Green
L225 Jupiter Gray
(Standard Sedan only)

L227 Strato Silver
L271 Texas Brown
L275 Light Beige
L276 Ultramaroon

INTERIORS

CLOTH INTERIOR
Beige/Green/Gray/Slate Blue, depending on body color
HEADLINER
Beige/Gray, depending on body color

CARPETS
Gray Beige/Gray Blue/Honey Brown, depending on body color
FLOOR MATS
(Provided) Black rubber

MODEL AVAILABILITY	Standard 2-door Sedan ($1,395)
	Deluxe 2-door Sedan ($1,495)
	Deluxe 2-door Sunroof Sedan ($1,575)
	2-door Cabriolet Convertible ($1,995)
WHEELBASE	94.5 inches
LENGTH	160.2 inches
WIDTH	60.6 inches
HEIGHT	(sedan) 59.1 inches
WEIGHT	(sedan) 1,565 lbs.
TREAD	(front/rear) 50.8/49.2 inches
TIRES	(sedan) 5.60 x 15
BRAKES	hydraulic, front/rear drum
WHEELS	steel disc
FUEL TANK	8.8 gallons
FRONT SUSPENSION	king pins with transverse torsion bars and upper/lower trailing arms
REAR SUSPENSION	swing axles with trailing arms and torsion bars
STEERING	worm and cap nut
ENGINE	1,192cc 30-hp horizontally opposed four-cylinder, overhead valve, air cooled, light alloy block and head, finned cylinders with cast-iron liners
TRANSMISSION	four-speed manual
FINAL DRIVE RATIO	4.40:1

1955

VOLKSWAGEN SEDAN

PAINT COLORS

L41 Black
L225 Jupiter Gray (Standard Sedan only)
L227 Strato Silver

L313 Reed Green
L315 Jungle Green
L324 Polar Silver
L370 Nile Beige

INTERIORS

CLOTH INTERIOR Beige/Green/Gray/Rusty Red, depending on body color

HEADLINER Beige/Gray/Brown Beige, depending on body color

FLOOR MATS (Provided) Black rubber

MODEL AVAILABILITY	Deluxe 2-door Sedan ($1,595)
	Deluxe 2-door Sunroof Sedan ($1,675)
	2-door Cabriolet Convertible ($2,195)
WHEELBASE	94.5 inches
LENGTH	160.2 inches
WIDTH	60.6 inches
HEIGHT	(sedan) 59.1 inches
WEIGHT	(sedan) 1,609 lbs.
TREAD	(front/rear) 50.8/49.2 inches
TIRES	(sedan) 5.60 x 15
BRAKES	hydraulic, front/rear drum
WHEELS	steel disc
FUEL TANK	8.8 gallons
FRONT SUSPENSION	king pins with transverse torsion bars and upper/lower trailing arms
REAR SUSPENSION	swing axles with trailing arms and torsion bars
STEERING	worm and cap nut
ENGINE	1,192cc 30-hp horizontally opposed four-cylinder, Soverhead valve, air cooled, light alloy block and head, finned cylinders with cast-iron liners
TRANSMISSION	four-speed manual
FINAL DRIVE RATIO	4.40:1

1956

VOLKSWAGEN SEDAN

PAINT COLORS (EARLY AUGUST 1955–MARCH 1956)

L41 Black
L225 Jupiter Gray (Standard Sedan only)
L227 Strato Silver

L313 Reed Green
L315 Jungle Green
L324 Polar Silver
L370 Nile Beige

PAINT COLORS (LATE APRIL–JULY 1956 & 1957)

L41 Black
L225 Jupiter Gray (Standard Sedan only)
L240 Agave Green
L324 Polar Silver

L331 Horizon Blue
L351 Coral Red
L378 Prairie Beige
L412 Diamond Green

INTERIORS

CLOTH INTERIOR Green/Gray/Blue/Rusty Red, depending on body color

HEADLINER Beige/Gray/Brown Beige, depending on body color

FLOOR MATS (Provided) Black rubber

MODEL AVAILABILITY	Deluxe 2-door Sedan ($1,495)
	Deluxe 2-door Sunroof Sedan ($1,575)
	2-door Cabriolet Convertible ($1,995)
WHEELBASE	94.5 inches
LENGTH	160.2 inches
WIDTH	60.6 inches
HEIGHT	(sedan) 59.1 inches
WEIGHT	(sedan) 1,609 lbs.
TREAD	(front/rear) 50.8/49.2 inches
TIRES	(sedan) 5.60 x 15
BRAKES	hydraulic, front/rear drum
WHEELS	steel disc
FUEL TANK	8.8 gallons
FRONT SUSPENSION	king pins with transverse torsion bars and upper/lower trailing arms
REAR SUSPENSION	swing axles with trailing arms and torsion bars
STEERING	worm and cap nut
ENGINE	1,192cc 36-hp horizontally opposed four-cylinder, overhead valve, air cooled, light alloy block and head, finned cylinders with cast-iron liners
TRANSMISSION	four-speed manual
FINAL DRIVE RATIO	4.40:1

1957

VOLKSWAGEN SEDAN

PAINT COLORS (LATE APRIL–JULY 1956 & 1957)

L41 Black
L225 Jupiter Gray (Standard Sedan only)
L240 Agave Green
L324 Polar Silver

L331 Horizon Blue
L351 Coral Red
L378 Prairie Beige
L412 Diamond Green

INTERIORS

CLOTH INTERIOR Green/Gray/Blue/Rusty Red, depending on body color

HEADLINER Beige/Gray/Brown Beige, depending on body color

FLOOR MATS (Provided) Black rubber

MODEL AVAILABILITY	Deluxe 2-door Sedan ($1,495)
	Deluxe 2-door Sunroof Sedan ($1,575)
	2-door Cabriolet Convertible ($1,995)
WHEELBASE	94.5 inches
LENGTH	160.2 inches
WIDTH	60.6 inches
HEIGHT	(sedan) 59.1 inches

WEIGHT	(sedan) 1,609 lbs.
TREAD	(front/rear) 50.8/49.2 inches
TIRES	(sedan) 5.60 x 15
BRAKES	hydraulic, front/rear drum
WHEELS	steel disc
FUEL TANK	8.8 gallons
FRONT SUSPENSION	king pins with transverse torsion bars and upper/lower trailing arms
REAR SUSPENSION	swing axles with trailing arms and torsion bars
STEERING	worm and cap nut
ENGINE	1,192cc 36-hp horizontally opposed four-cylinder, overhead valve, air cooled, light alloy block and head, finned cylinders with cast-iron liners
TRANSMISSION	four-speed manual
FINAL DRIVE RATIO	4.40:1

The oval window adopted in 1953 remained in use until August 1957. This 1957 Beetle owned by John Ammond has the American-style bumper guards that were of split design to allow the trunk lid to be raised.

CHAPTER 4

1	Luggage compartment under front hood	8	Heater outlet
2	Steering column lever operating direction indicators	9	Sliding seat mounted on guide rails
3	Pedal assembly	10	Lever for adjusting backrest
4	Adjustable sun visor	11	Coat hook and assist strap
5	Defroster vent	12	Hinged ash-tray
6	Ventilation wings with inside catch	13	Luggage compartment behind rear seat
7	Arm-rest	14	License-plate lamp
		15	Stop-lights combined with tail-lights and reflectors

BIG WINDOW

In April 1958, *Motor Trend*'s Walt Woron wrote an article about the German auto industry and a visit he paid to the Volkswagen plant: "When you stand at one end of a corridor on the *office* side of the factory, you cannot see the other end," he marveled. "You see cars rolling off the ends of four assembly lines at the rate of one every thirty seconds. Then, and only then, do you get the true impression of Volkswagenwerk GmbH, located in the small town of Wolfsburg, near Hanover, in Western Germany, just seven short miles from the Iron Curtain."

This Volkswagen catalog art from 1959 illustrates fifteen of the Beetle's selling features, including room for two large suitcases and a bag in the behind-the-seat luggage compartment.

Woron should not have been surprised at the speedy pace of production. During 1958, Volkswagen manufactured 451,526 cars with serial numbers 1600440 through 2007615. By that year, about 818,000 Volkswagens had been registered in Germany since the start of production. In the United States, 78,261 of the new-for-1958 "big window" models were registered. The German automaker's share of the US imported car market had grown tremendously. It was zero in 1948 and 20.7 percent ten years later. And it was only the beginning!

With the assembly lines humming and Wolfsburg's lines running steadily to build more cars, Volkswagen engine production was transferred from there to a new addition at another factory the company operated in Hanover, Germany.

1958

As usual, Volkswagen's main 1958 product changes came after the company's holiday break, late in the summer of 1957. A number of changes took place on August 1. Major appearance changes included a larger windshield and the "big window" treatment at the rear that would last through the mid-1960s.

The new windshield narrowed the front corner posts. This was deemed a safety feature because it improved forward vision. It also changed the Beetle's 1930s look quite a bit. Changes were also made to the windshield, which was slightly deeper. Both of these were considered major changes for a company that prided itself on making only small changes over many years. The Volkswagen Beetle was definitely a "why change a good thing?" type of car.

RIGHT: Variations of this illustration were used on several Volkswagen literature pieces, including the catalog produced for the eastern United States. This version showing the Wolfsburg factory dates from 1958.

OPPOSITE PAGE: Volkswagen copywriters went back and forth on whether the open car was a Convertible or a Cabriolet. In different brochures, the model on top is called a "Sun Roof" or a "Sunroof" and it was originally called the Sunshine Sedan.

SUN ROOF

Volkswagen Sedans offer a pleasant surprise when they are equipped with a Golde Sun Roof. With a sweep of the hand you can fold the top back and enjoy the fresh air and sunshine. With the Sun Roof closed, the car is just as weatherproof in bad weather as if it had a steel top. All Volkswagen models have ventilator wings in the windows for draftless ventilation.

CONVERTIBLE

If you like to drive a sporty car and enjoy sunshine to the full, the Volkswagen Convertible is the car for you. Wherever you drive or park a Volkswagen Convertible, it attracts the admiring attention of all eyes. Volkswagen has built in the Convertible the car of your dreams. Like all other Volkswagen models, the Convertible has no waste space or superfluous weight. Not an inch of space is unexploited and every ounce of weight is put to good use. The Convertible is the fastest and easiest handling car in turbulent city traffic. Put the top up on a Convertible and you can drive through a cloud-burst in comfort. It is absolutely impervious to rain, wind, dust and cold. — It is hard to talk a woman into a Sedan when she has once seen the graceful lines of the Convertible (body by Karmann).

The car also had a completely new dashboard with the radio loudspeaker to the left of the steering wheel, all-new control knobs, and a glove box lid that dropped automatically when a button was pushed. Export and Cabriolet models had a bright metal molding running across the center of the dash from side to side. The old-fashioned roller-type gas pedal was replaced by pad type.

A higher, but smaller, air cleaner was fitted to the Volkswagen engine and fuel economy went up to 35–40 miles per gallon. The windshield wipers were moved closer together for a wider sweep. Several modifications were made to the car bodies. The cool-air inlets were redesigned to improve drainage. The engine cover was sealed better from moisture. Modifications were made to the license plate light.

A second group of changes came on September 16, 1957. The steering column was shortened, a new steering wheel was used, more new colors were introduced, and Volkswagen improved its seats. In addition, soundproofing was improved and outlets with short vertical louvers were added below the rear window of sedans. Cabriolets did not have louvers on their thinner panel below the window. Instead, they had louvers on either side of the engine cover.

In October, Volkswagen started using a different type of bulb in the license plate and brake indicator lamps. On December 20, Volkswagen offered maintenance-free tie rods as an option in twenty thousand cars.

A small number of additional changes were made during calendar-year 1958. In January, many Cabriolets (depending on body color) received Pearl White wheels and the factory began using magnetic oil drain plugs on export sedans. A control flap was also added to the rear window demister system.

In February, coat hooks were an addition to the interior. In March, the spark plug wrench that came with the car was changed to a rubber-sleeve type instead of the retaining-spring type. In April, Volkswagen began using 13mm bolts to attach mudguards, running boards, and horns. On April 29, Wolfsburg initiated use of a rolled bronze swivel-pin bushing, with a lengthwise slit, in the steering system. A plastic carburetor venturi tube replaced the aluminum type in June. Starting in July, the distributor rotor and spark plug caps were different.

In April 1958, *Motor Trend* selected the Volkswagen Beetle as The Best Foreign Car Buy in the $1,500–$2,000 range. "You have to go a long way to beat the Volkswagen as the best dollar-for-dollar buy in the economy class," said the write-up. The magazine found Volkswagen's paint, trim, and upholstery of incredibly high quality and credited its full torsion bar suspension for "top-of-the-list" ride quality. Real-life top speed was said to be in the 70–72-miles-per-hour bracket, although the speedometer read 80 miles per hour.

"The air-cooled, flat-opposed, four-cylinder engine, nestling aft, never overworks itself," said *Motor Trend*. "Piston speed at full throttle is ridiculously low." The write-up noted that the seats did not offer much support and mentioned the fact that there were no instruments, except for a speedometer and monitor lights for the oil and generator. Visibility was highly praised, however.

The magazine also warned: "Don't overfill the front-mounted gas tank or you'll ride with fumes." On the plus side, it pointed out that Volkswagen's service and parts situation was "likely the best in America." We personally remember the brand new Volkswagen dealership in our hometown of Staten Island, New York. Everything about its appearance was clean, modern, professional, and inviting. A large and round blue sign with the Volkswagen "VW" logo on it decorated the front of the building. We can't think of another dealership in town at that time that was as customer-friendly as the Volkswagen franchise.

1959

Volkswagen swung into its twentieth year of production in 1959 on a high note. It celebrated by turning out 575,407 cars and 119,899 of those were registered in the United States. At this point, the company claimed to have built nearly 2.5 million cars. Volkswagen was also the largest seller of imported cars in the United States and the fourth-largest automaker in the world.

The February 1959 edition of *Motor Trend* highlighted Volkswagen-Porsche

LEFT: A new Volkswagen Beetle made the cover of the April 1958 issue of *Motor Trend* to highlight a story about the best buy among cars in the $1,500 to $2,000 economy class. The German car won praise for its simple and functional design. *Archives/TEN: The Enthusiast Network Magazines, LLC*

RIGHT: *Motor Trend*'s "World Show Issue" in 1959 mentioned that much of the Beetle's popularity was built on its resistance to change. After the change to a big rear window in 1958, Volkswagen's keep-it-like-it-is tradition continued in 1959. *Archives/TEN: The Enthusiast Network Magazines, LLC*

distributor Johnny von Neumann of Hollywood Sports Cars. The thirty-seven-year-old businessman was the head of the Volkswagen distributorships in Southern California, Southern Nevada, and all of Arizona. His comments to the magazine shed light on the reasons why Volkswagen was catching on with American motorists, as well as consumers all over the world.

"People are getting tired of driving multiple-100-horsepower cars around with ¼ throttle," von Neumann told the magazine. "With the VW, you can drive flat-out most of the time, maneuver quickly and easily in any kind of traffic, and get real fun out of driving. People who don't have fun driving should stay home."

The 1959 model-year officially began on August 1, 1958. By the following September 19, changes were already being made. On that date, the handle that operated the engine cover was relocated to a spot nearer the steering column. Also, a larger outside rearview mirror was used on German Volkswagens.

Quite a few additional technical changes were put into effect during calendar-year 1959, though the overall appearance of the car still changed very little. Starting in January 1959, the tool kit included a hubcap-removing hook.

Inside the Beetle, a new padded inside sun visor replaced the old see-through plastic type. Volkswagen also began using a covered and padded dashboard for improved safety in Beetle Cabriolets. Another safety feature, a front passenger grab handle, was added at the same time.

The Honest Car

DE LUXE SEDAN

In ten short years the Volkswagen has risen from total obscurity to become a household word on every continent, an accepted international yardstick for judging an automobile. The Volkswagen has the highest export figures of any car in the world.

The Volkswagen has an ideal sales force — more than two million happy owners. No wonder the constantly increasing output at Wolfsburg never catches up with demand.

Why is it that the imagination of more than two million Volkswagen owners has been fired by this amazing car?

Because it possesses a combination of performance and economy never before known in automobile design.

Because of its sensible engineering and sturdy construction.

Because it does not pretend to be anything but what it is — an honest car.

Because there has been a consistent policy unswayed by whims of fashion, holding fast to what has proved itself, yet constantly improving the car and so raising it to an internationally admired pitch of perfection.

The plainest and most gratifying proof of this is the high resale value of a Volkswagen. Buying one is a sound and a secure investment.

SUN ROOF SEDAN

Quite a few additional technical changes were put into effect during the calendar year of 1959, though the overall appearance of the car still changed very little. Starting in January 1959, the tool kit included a hubcap-removing hook.

The tie rod lengths were shortened on the left and lengthened on the right to improve the steering geometry. The fuel tank ventilation system was modified and a new 80mm cap was used. Starting February 23, 1959, some five thousand cars received carburetor modifications, including a double vacuum unit and a vacuum-advance-only-type distributor. New No. 175 spark plugs were used in the VW engine starting in April 1959. In May, the heat exchangers and associated parts were redesigned. A new cork seal was also used on the fuel tap. Silencer-to-tailpipe joints were improved and the silencer stub pipes were shortened. In July, a heat-resistant V-belt was used and fewer pulley spacers were required.

As if to support Johnny von Neumann's claim that Volkswagens were fun-to-drive cars, the performance charts for a stock 1959 Beetle (*Motor Trend*, April 1958) listed a top speed of 75 miles per hour and fuel economy of 35–40 miles per gallon. According to an article in the same magazine's July issue, a stock Volkswagen Beetle did 0-to-60 miles per hour in 31.4 seconds and covered the quarter-mile in 24.9 seconds at 51 miles per hour. *Motor Trend* then tested a Beetle equipped with a Weber stroker kit. It did 0-to-60 in 12.7 seconds and took 20.6 seconds for the quarter-mile at 58 miles per hour.

1960

Holy cow! Volkswagen manufactured 739,443 cars in 1960 and *Ward's* said that 159,995 of them were registered in the United States. Sales of imported cars in the United States fell in 1960, after several American automakers brought out compact-sized economy cars. However, Germany's share of imported car registrations climbed to 44.4 percent, up from 33.7 percent.

"Close to half of the 498,785 new foreign cars sold in the US during 1960 had been shipped in from West Germany, a phenomenon attributable to Volkswagen, the mainstay of the import market," said *Ward's*. "Among the 15 German makes imported, Volkswagen accounted for 72.2 percent of the cars

This 1960 Beetle sedan features new door handles that were grab handles with thumb buttons instead of the old style with levers that pulled out to unlatch the door. A radio antenna was mounted on left side body panel. *Archives/TEN: The Enthusiast Network Magazines, LLC*

TOP LEFT: The 1960 Beetle had curved seat backrests, rear-seat heel boards, a front passenger footrest, five-section rubber floor mats, two-piece floor coverings, and better soundproofing. A plastic headliner replaced the "mouse hair" fabric type. *Archives/TEN: The Enthusiast Network Magazines, LLC*

TOP MIDDLE: As illustrated by this 1960 Volkswagen Beetle, the front luggage compartment cover opened in "alligator" fashion, but the front body side panels were fixed. A front "towel rack" guardrail ran fully across the front of the car. *Archives/ TEN: The Enthusiast Network Magazines, LLC*

TOP RIGHT: In 1960, the dipstick markings were made easier to read and the oil drain plug was moved from the crankcase to the sump plate. A carburetor modification tested on 5,000 cars starting in late February 1959 was extended to all models. *Archives/TEN: The Enthusiast Network Magazines, LLC*

RIGHT: Quite a few additional technical changes were put into effect during 1960, but the external appearance of the car still changed very little. Seven colors were offered for Sedans and ten colors for the Cabriolet. *Archives/TEN: The Enthusiast Network Magazines, LLC*

of German origin registered in the US." Volkswagen built 32.1 percent of all imports sold here in 1960. *Ward's* said this was "reminiscent of earlier years."

On June 15, 1960, the five hundred thousandth Volkswagen was exported to the United States and, in Wolfsburg, West Germany, the one millionth person toured the Volkswagen factory since 1949, which was highlighted in corporate press releases. In November, the Volkswagen Foundation was organized to support scientific and technological research. A French marketing branch was also set up this year.

In 1960, the German auto industry employed fifty thousand people to make three thousand vehicles per day—one every nineteen seconds. *One out of three of these cars was a Volkswagen.* In Germany, it was possible to buy a Volkswagen Standard Sedan with no options for as little as $911 (the Export Sedan went for $1,109).

August 1959 brought Volkswagen's initial 1960 product changes. The dipstick markings were changed to make them easier for owners to read and the oil drain plug was moved from the crankcase to the sump plate to ease serviceability. The carburetor modification that had been tested on five thousand cars starting in late February 1959 was extended to all models. A new two-spoke steering wheel with a deep-set hub and a bright horn ring was used and the steering column design was changed. A number of new body colors also arrived.

Inside the Beetle new push-button door handles were introduced.

The right-hand door armrest was redesigned with an open grip and the door striker plates were improved for security. Many interior upgrades were made, including curved seat backrests, rear seat heel boards, a front passenger footrest, five-section rubber floor mats, two-piece floor coverings, and better soundproofing. A plastic headlining replaced the earlier "mouse hair" fabric type of headliner.

The 1960 Beetle had a number of electrical system upgrades. The front turn-signal indicator lamps were now mounted on the tops of the front fenders in chrome housings. At the rear, the blinkers were integrated into the taillights.

In its October 1959 "Overseas News Reports" column, *Motor Trend* listed Volkswagen changes in 1960: "For roadability, the transmission is mounted differently and the front has a stabilizer bar. Also, defroster pipes are bigger, steering hub is recessed." In January 1960, the valve-clearance adjusting nut was slightly enlarged and resistor-type ignition leads were adopted. In March, several modifications were made to the front trailing arm and the steering damper. Plastic warm air ducts, designed to reduce noise, went into production in May 1960.

Motor Trend (March 1960) did another comparison test of a stock Volkswagen Beetle sedan against two similar cars with aftermarket performance kits installed. Petersen Publications, which owned *Motor Trend*, was big on this type of thing

in its sister publication *Hot Rod* and often repurposed that magazine's Volkswagen hop-up article to fill the pages of *Motor Trend*.

Harry Weber of Los Angeles manufactured the first kit. It featured a half-inch stroker crankshaft, domed pistons, a wild cam, a special exhaust system, and twin Solex carbs. The second car was a 1954 Volkswagen with a well-known kit made by European Motor Products, Inc. (EMPI) of Riverside, California. It had special Okrasa manifolding and heads, large EMPI valves, stiffer valve springs, a 6mm stroker crank, twin Solex carburetors, and Porsche brakes.

The stock Volkswagen did 0–60 miles per hour in thirty-two seconds and the quarter-mile in 24.9 seconds at 52 miles per hour. It had a 68-mile-per-hour top speed. The Weber-tuned Volkswagen did 0–60 miles per hour in seventeen seconds and the quarter-mile in 20.9 seconds at 66 miles per hour. It had a 91-mile-per-hour top speed. The EMPI VW did 0–60 miles per hour in 18.8 seconds and the quarter-mile in 21.4 seconds at 63 miles per hour. It also had a 91-mile-per-hour top speed.

In a May 1960 article, *Motor Trend* indicated that the Beetle's fuel economy level had decreased a bit from the 35–40 miles per gallon figure that had been published for several years. The magazine recorded 28–36 miles per gallon. A Volkswagen Beetle also came in first in Class C (1,100–1,599cc) in the 1960 Mobil Gas Mileage Rally and it registered 34.77 miles per gallon.

Volkswagen manufactured 807,488 cars worldwide in 1961, and 177,308 new Volkswagens were registered in the United States in the calendar year. That total represented a whopping 46.8 percent of the imported car market in the United States. This was Volkswagen's highest share of the market since 1956, when it had stood at 50.9 percent. Sales rose 10.8 percent from 1960.

Despite the fact that Volkswagen registrations in the United States moved steadily upward, by the end of 1961, automotive market experts could see trouble brewing in the future. Volkswagen's success was based on the Beetle and the vehicles the company was building were not keeping up with the times. To buyers throughout the world, the Beetle was an antique car. Antique car collectors were already scooping up Beetles. In the May 1951 issue of *Motor Trend*, D. E. Richards of Hopkins, Minnesota, advertised a "rare" early Volkswagen convertible (no year was mentioned) for $1,395.

In his "Memo From the Editor" in the October 1961 *Motor Trend*, Don Werner noted, "Five years ago, out of every 10 imported cars sold, six were Volkswagens. Latest figures show the ratio is now down to about four VWs out of every 10. If the current VW starts to slip, the new 1500—soon to be introduced—probably will be imported to justify the (company's) more than 600 VW dealers and the $100 million investment in facilities." Werner went on to say that the 1500

had not impressed industry executives on either side of the Atlantic.

If Werner's view of the car's future was gloomy, his magazine still liked the latest Beetle with the larger and more powerful engine, which debuted August 1960. "The 1961 Volkswagen sedan provides the kind of happy surprise that comes when an excellent motor car is made even better," *Motor Trend* said. "And inclusion of the rugged, higher-horsepower transporter engine in this new Volkswagen provides a real surprise, even to long time owners of previous models of this marque. Four more horsepower at first seem like just too little to talk about, but the boost from 36 horsepower at 3,700 rpm to today's output of 40 horsepower at 3,900 revs makes a world of difference in this 1,631-pound (dry weight) automobile."

The new engine had basically the same specs as the older engine except that it was listed as 69 cubic inches instead of 72. It was, as usual, a horizontally opposed, overhead-valve four-cylinder, air-cooled engine with a light alloy block, heads, and finned cylinder with cast-iron cylinder liners. Displacement was 69 cubic inches or 1,192cc. It had a 3.03- x 2.52-inch (77mm x 64mm) bore and stroke. With a 7.0:1 compression ratio, it developed 40 horsepower (US) at 3,900 rpm and 61.0 pounds-feet of torque at 2,000 rpm. The new engine continued with four main bearings and solid valve lifters. It used a 28 PICT Solex single-barrel carburetor.

In addition to the new powerplant, the 1961 Beetle had a full-synchronized four-speed manual transmission that also made a world of difference to US motorists. The previous four-speed had a non-synchro first gear. *Motor Trend* suggested that people who drove 1955 and earlier Volkswagens would have "difficulty realizing this is the same automobile." That may have been a bit of an exaggeration, but it was obvious the "Bug" was winning over fans in America.

The Volkswagen factory promoted twenty-seven changes in the new model, though some were quite minor. The more important alterations included an automatic choke, an anti-icing carburetor heater, a redesigned fuel tank that increased luggage space, an external gas tank vent (to keep fuel odors out of the car), a concave washer on the third gear drive pinion (to reduce transmission noise), softer transmission mountings, a transparent brake fluid reservoir, a front passenger grab handle, standard windshield washers, and a new ignition switch that prevented jamming the starter into action when the engine was running.

All electrical connections in the Beetle were now of the push-on or plug-in type. The electrical fusebox was relocated below the instrument panel, to the right-hand side of the steering column. A passenger side inside sun visor was a new provision. Other improvements included a quieter air intake pipe, new paint colors, color-keyed running boards, new leatherette upholstery, color-coordinated fender

TOP: In 1961, the Beetle got a boost from 38 to 40 horsepower, and the four-speed transmission gained a synchro first gear. Jason Cody's sunroof sedan sports optional whitewall tires for a spiffy look.

BOTTOM LEFT: On the inside of Jason Cody's 1961 Beetle, you can see the new passenger grab handle. Volkswagen also went to an automatic choke, eliminating the choke on the dashboard.

BOTTOM RIGHT: Wilhelm Karmann of Osnabrück was a long-established German coachbuilder who got the job of assembling Volkswagen's Cabriolet. Bryan Campbell's 1961 model carries a body builder's badge from Karmann on its cowl.

beading, a colored steering wheel, and a 90-mile-per-hour speedometer.

Side marker lights and a nonrepeating starter switch were also new. Key slots in the doors were now horizontal instead of vertical. Mechanical parts receiving minor revisions included the air cleaner (with a new heating duct), the automatic-choke carburetor, and the fuel pump. The spark generated by the distributor was now controlled only by vacuum advance. Also new was a detachable generator support that eliminated the threat of casting fractures.

This year the Beetle's economy seemed to dwindle a little bit more, with *Motor Trend* publishing 28–32 miles per gallon as what it wound up with in its road test. The magazine said that a stock 1961 VW Beetle did 0–30 miles per hour in 6.5 seconds, 0–45 miles per hour in 12.5 seconds, and 0–60 miles per hour in 22 seconds. The Beetle's weight-power ratio was 40.8 pounds per horsepower. Horsepower per cubic inch was .550.

1962

Volkswagen's surge continued in 1962 with 876,255 cars leaving the assembly line and 192,570 being registered by Americans. Volkswagen's market share was 56.8 percent of the imported cars sold in the United States. New models such as the 1500, covered elsewhere in this book, were partly responsible for the worldwide increase. The 1500 was not yet available in the United States, but the tiny Beetle was still a big winner for the German company in America.

Most 1962 Volkswagen changes went into production at the Wolfsburg factory on July 31, 1961. A conventional fuel gauge was installed in the dashboard of new models. No longer would Beetle owners need to rely on a tap lever and reserve tank if they ran out of fuel like some motorcycle riders did. The fuel gauge was located between the speedometer and radio (if a radio was ordered).

A worm-and-roller steering system was first introduced for Beetle Cabriolets and Karmann

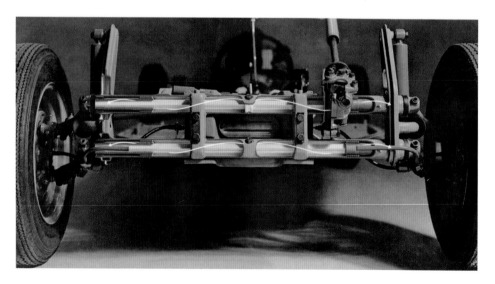

LEFT: A worm-and-roller steering system was first introduced for 1962 Beetle Cabriolets and Karmann Ghias. A month later, it was used in Type 1 Beetle sedans as well, replacing the former spindle arrangement. Adjustable, permanently lubricated tie rods were used at both sides of the steering linkage. The front suspension featured king pins with transverse torsion bars and upper/lower trailing arms.

RIGHT: The air-cooled four-cylinder engine pushing the '62 Beetle down American highways was a 1,192cc, 40-horsepower, horizontally opposed overhead-valve powerplant with a light alloy block and head, and finned cylinders with cast-iron liners.

Ghias. A month later it was used in Type 1 sedans as well, replacing the former spindle arrangement. Larger new, two-section taillights were used. A pair of spring-loaded rods now supported the hood.

Inside new three-point seat belt mountings were provided on both sides of the car in the front compartment. The front heater outlets now had sliding covers to regulate airflow. New air outlets were in the heel boards. New door retainers replaced the old stay-rod type and the door hinges were improved to make opening and closing the doors easier. Longer adjustment rails were used for the front seats, which also had new backrests with an improved adjustment system. Also new was a compressed air–operated windshield washer system.

Adjustable, permanently lubricated tie rods were used at both sides of the steering linkage. New paint and interior trim choices were seen as usual. For increased security against car thieves, a steering-starter lock was a new option. This was the first year that semaphore turn signals were not used on any Beetles anywhere in the world. In previous years, the United States and some other countries required blinker lights, but the use of these fender-mounted turn signals was not universal until 1962. The 1962 taillights incorporated a blinker light lens.

1963

J. Stuart Perkins was now general manager for Volkswagen in the United States. And he kept things on an upward track. The German automaker had a firm grip on the US imported car niche with a 62.3 percent share of the market. The company registered 240,143 new cars in the United States, about twice the 1959 total. That was even up 24.7 percent from 1962. A strong 3.2 percent of all new cars sold in the United States were Volkswagen models, beating both foreign competitors and the new US-built compact cars.

Building on its image in America, Volkswagen ran advertisements poking fun at itself and its hardly-ever-changed Beetle sedan. Due to factory limitations, Volkswagen postponed the US introduction of the 1500 model until 1965. During 1963, Volkswagen increased its dealer count from 687 stores to 744. The company reported that it employed 20,000 Americans and had made a total investment of some $200,000,000 in the US economy.

The Volkswagen Type 1 (or Beetle) received a number of 1963 changes that were introduced at the factory level on July 30, 1962. The oil filter was now fitted with an air filter. Some engine manifolding was slightly enlarged and the housing surrounding the cooling fan was redesigned. Larger-diameter cylinder head induction ports were another change to the 40-horsepower Beetle engine.

Cars with sunroofs got a flatter inside crank handle that was hinged to fold flush into the headliner. The headliner and window guides were now made of plastic. "Volkswagen" lettering replaced the Wolfsburg crest that had decorated the hoods of all Volkswagens since 1951. The VW logo emblem in the center of the hubcaps was no longer trimmed with black paint.

Foam insulation was added to the floorboards. Fresh-air heating was a new addition as well. Shortly after the 1963 calendar year started, the crankcase vent was modified to incorporate a new sludge-draining pipe with a rubber vent. In April 1963, a new plastic (instead of rubber) seal was used around the bumper bracket and the front seat backrest adjustment was changed.

By 1963, the Volkswagen 1,200cc engine in the Beetle was considered one of the most reliable small powerplants around. The cooling fan, however, was loud and annoying to rear-seat passengers. *Archives/TEN: The Enthusiast Network Magazines, LLC*

1964

Volkswagen built 1,216,390 Beetles in 1964. The company also continued to hold the lion's share of the market for imported cars in the United States. For 1964, more than six out of every 10 imported cars sold in the nation were Volkswagen Beetles. However, the company's growth rate was starting to level off a bit and it went up by just 1.1 percent during the 1964 calendar year.

The company continued to run humorous ads highlighting the bug-like shape of its most popular model, as well as its design simplicity and ease of repair. The ads created by the Doyle, Dane & Bernbach advertising agency were very popular and even helped to increase the company's dealer count as they spurred sales higher and higher. During 1963, the number of US dealerships grew from

From the underside of the 1964 Beetle, the most noticeable item was the dual exhaust system. An accessory stabilizer bar ran forward from the outer ends of the rear axles. *Archives/TEN: The Enthusiast Network Magazines, LLC*

750 to 845. The company estimated that approximately 1,600,000 Volkswagens were on American highways. Volkswagen's 307,173 unit sales in the United States in 1964 amounted to 63.4 percent of the market.

The date for the 1964 model changeover at the Wolfsburg factory was August 5, 1963. In the Beetle, perforated vinyl upholstery replaced the former nonporous leatherette material, and a sliding steel sunroof (with a crank) replaced the familiar fold-back fabric unit, except on the Standard Beetle models. The rear license-plate light grew larger, and dual thumb horn push buttons on the steering wheel replaced the chrome-plated horn half-ring used previously.

A new Silver Beige finish color was used on the control knobs and steering wheel, which were previously black. The circular Volkswagen emblem on the hubcaps was all chrome, with no background color behind the criss-crossed letters. This made it much more difficult to see the logos on the hubcaps.

Rear tire pressure specifications were modified. A new synthetic seat covering material was used and foam door seals were adopted. Minor alterations were made to the curved part of the engine cover and the license plate fastening holes. Effective February 5, the old aluminum running board moldings were replaced with chrome-steel moldings. In March 1964, the oil filter cover plate was sealed with cap nuts, and copper washers and a new gasket material was used in that location. The front turn-signal lights also increased in size.

1958

VOLKSWAGEN SEDAN

PAINT COLORS

L41 Black
L225 Jupiter Gray (Standard Sedan only)
L240 Agave Green
L243 Diamond Gray

L245 Light Bronze
L334 Glacier Blue
L335 Capri Blue
L351 Coral Red

INTERIORS

FLOOR MATS
Black mats were in Jupiter

Gray cars; Gray mats in other cars

VOLKSWAGEN CABRIOLET

PAINT COLORS

L41 Black
L241 Bambo Green
L243 Diamond Gray
L244 Moss Green

L358 Inca Red
L329 Shetland Gray
L338 Atlas Blue
L473 Alabaster Gray

INTERIORS

FLOOR MATS Gray mats in all cars

MODEL AVAILABILITY	Deluxe 2-door Sedan ($1,545)
	Deluxe 2-door Sunroof Sedan ($1,625)
	2-door Cabriolet Convertible ($2,045)
WHEELBASE	94.5 inches
LENGTH	160.2 inches
WIDTH	60.6 inches
HEIGHT	(sedan) 59.1 inches
WEIGHT	(sedan) 1,609 lbs.
TREAD	(front/rear) 50.8/49.2 inches
TIRES	(sedan) 5.60 x 15
BRAKES	hydraulic, front/rear drum
WHEELS	steel disc
FUEL TANK	8.8 gallons
FRONT SUSPENSION	king pins with transverse torsion bars and upper/lower trailing arms
REAR SUSPENSION	swing axles with trailing arms and torsion bars
STEERING	worm and cap nut
ENGINE	1,192cc 36-hp horizontally opposed four-cylinder, overhead valve, air cooled, light alloy block and head, finned cylinders with cast-iron liners
TRANSMISSION	four-speed manual
FINAL DRIVE RATIO	4.40:1

1959

VOLKSWAGEN SEDAN

PAINT COLORS

L14 Mignonette Green
L41 Black
L225 Jupiter Gray (Standard Sedan only)
L243 Diamond Gray

L335 Capri Blue
L343 Kalahari Beige
L344 Rush Green
L358 Garnet Red
L434 Fjord Blue

INTERIORS

FLOOR MATS
Black mats in Jupiter Gray

cars; Gray mats in other cars

VOLKSWAGEN CABRIOLET

PAINT COLORS

L41 Black
L241 Bamboo Green
L258 Inca Red

L329 Shetland Gray
L333 Pearl Blue
L473 Alabaster Gray

INTERIORS

FLOOR MATS Gray mats in all cars

MODEL AVAILABILITY	Deluxe 2-door Sedan ($1,545)
	Deluxe 2-door-door Sunroof Sedan ($1,625)
	2-door Cabriolet Convertible ($2,045)
CHASSIS NUMBERS	2007616–2528667
WHEELBASE	94.5 inches
LENGTH	160.6 inches
WIDTH	60.6 inches
HEIGHT	(sedan) 59.1 inches
WEIGHT	(sedan) 1,609 lbs.
TREAD	(front/rear) 50.8/49.2 inches
TIRES	(sedan) 5.60 x 15
BRAKES	hydraulic, front/rear drum
WHEELS	steel disc
FUEL TANK	8.8 gallons
FRONT SUSPENSION	king pins with transverse torsion bars and upper/lower trailing arms
REAR SUSPENSION	swing axles with trailing arms and torsion bars
STEERING	worm and cap nut
ENGINE	1,192cc 36-hp horizontally opposed four-cylinder, overhead valve, air cooled, light alloy block and head, finned cylinders with cast-iron liners
TRANSMISSION	four-speed manual
FINAL DRIVE RATIO	4.40:1

1960

VOLKSWAGEN SEDAN

PAINT COLORS

L41 Black
L391 Pastel Blue
L456 Ruby Red
L478 Beryl Green

L380 Turquoise
L87 Pearl White
L390 Gulf Blue

VOLKSWAGEN CABRIOLET

PAINT COLORS

L41 Black
L54 Poppy Red
L391 Pastel Blue
L456 Ruby Red
L478 Beryl Green

L380 Turquoise
L87 Pearl White
L390 Gulf Blue
L10009 Yukon Yellow
L10018 Brunswick Blue

MODEL AVAILABILITY	Deluxe 2-door Sedan ($1,565)
	Deluxe 2-door Sunroof Sedan ($1,665)
	2-door Cabriolet Convertible ($2,055)
CHASSIS NUMBERS	2528668–3192506 (Sedan and Karmann Ghia)
WHEELBASE	94.5 inches
LENGTH	160.6 inches
WIDTH	60.6 inches
HEIGHT	(sedan) 59.1 inches
WEIGHT	(sedan) 1,631 lbs.
TREAD	(front/rear) 51.4/50.7 inches
TIRES	(sedan) 5.60 x 15
BRAKES	hydraulic, front/rear drum
WHEELS	steel disc
FUEL TANK	8.8 gallons
FRONT SUSPENSION	king pins with transverse torsion bars and upper/lower trailing arms
REAR SUSPENSION	swing axles with trailing arms and torsion bars
STEERING	worm and cap nut
ENGINE	1,192cc 36-hp horizontally opposed four-cylinder, overhead valve, air cooled, light alloy block and head, finned cylinders with cast-iron liners
TRANSMISSION	four-speed manual
FINAL DRIVE RATIO	4.375:1

1961

VOLKSWAGEN SEDAN

PAINT COLORS

L41 Black
L391 Pastel Blue
L456 Ruby Red
L478 Beryl Green

L380 Turquoise
L87 Pearl White
L390 Gulf Blue

ADDITIONAL BEETLE CABRIOLET PAINT COLORS

L54 Poppy Red
L398 Pacific Blue

L10009 Yukon Yellow
L10018 Brunswick Blue

MODEL AVAILABILITY	Deluxe 2-door Sedan ($1,565)
	Deluxe 2-door Sunroof Sedan ($1,655)
	2-door Cabriolet Convertible ($2,055)
CHASSIS NUMBERS	3192507–4010994 (Sedan and Karmann Ghia)
WHEELBASE	94.5 inches
LENGTH	160.6 inches
WIDTH	60.6 inches
HEIGHT	(sedan) 59.1 inches
WEIGHT	(sedan) 1,631 lbs.
TREAD	(front/rear) 51.4/50.7 inches
TIRES	(sedan) 5.60 x 15
BRAKES	hydraulic, front/rear drum
WHEELS	steel disc
FUEL TANK	10.6 gallons
FRONT SUSPENSION	king pins with transverse torsion bars and upper/lower trailing arms
REAR SUSPENSION	swing axles with trailing arms and torsion bars
STEERING	worm and cap nut
ENGINE	1,192cc 40-hp horizontally opposed four-cylinder, overhead valve, air cooled, light alloy block and head, finned cylinders with cast-iron liners
TRANSMISSION	four-speed manual (full synchromesh)
FINAL DRIVE RATIO	4.375:1

1962

VOLKSWAGEN SEDAN

PAINT COLORS

L41 Black	**L87** Pearl White
L456 Ruby Red	**L390** Gulf Blue
L478 Beryl Green	**L469** Anthracite
L380 Turquoise	

ADDITIONAL BEETLE CABRIOLET PAINT COLORS

L54 Poppy Red	**L10009** Yukon Yellow
L398 Pacific Blue	**L10018** Brunswick Blue

MODEL AVAILABILITY	Deluxe 2-door Sedan ($1,595)
	Deluxe 2-door Sunroof Sedan ($1,685)
	2-door Cabriolet Convertible ($2,095)
CHASSIS NUMBERS	4010995–4846835
	(Sedan and Karmann Ghia)
WHEELBASE	94.5 inches
LENGTH	160.6 inches
WIDTH	60.6 inches
HEIGHT	(sedan) 59.1 inches
WEIGHT	(sedan) 1,565 lbs.
TREAD	(front/rear) 51.4/50.7 inches
TIRES	(sedan) 5.60 x 15
BRAKES	hydraulic, front/rear drum
WHEELS	steel disc
FUEL TANK	10.6 gallons
FRONT SUSPENSION	king pins with transverse torsion bars and upper/lower trailing arms
REAR SUSPENSION	swing axles with trailing arms and torsion bars
STEERING	worm and cap nut
ENGINE	1,192cc 40-hp horizontally opposed four-cylinder, overhead valve, air cooled, light alloy block and head, finned cylinders with cast-iron liners
TRANSMISSION	four-speed manual (full synchromesh)
FINAL DRIVE RATIO	4.375:1

1963

VOLKSWAGEN SEDAN

PAINT COLORS

L41 Black	**L87** Pearl White
L456 Ruby Red	**L390** Gulf Blue
L478 Beryl Green	**L469** Anthracite
L380 Turquoise	

ADDITIONAL BEETLE CABRIOLET

PAINT COLORS

L54 Poppy Red	**L10009** Yukon Yellow
L398 Pacific Blue	**L10018** Brunswick Blue

MODEL AVAILABILITY	Deluxe 2-door Sedan ($1,595)
	Deluxe 2-door Sunroof Sedan ($1,685)
	2-door Cabriolet Convertible ($2,095)
CHASSIS NUMBERS	(Beetle Sedan) 4846836–5677118
	(Beetle Convertible) 4765156–up
WHEELBASE	94.5 inches
LENGTH	156.0 inches
WIDTH	60.6 inches
HEIGHT	(sedan) 59.1 inches
WEIGHT	(sedan) 1,565 lbs.
TREAD	(front/rear) 51.4/50.7 inches
TIRES	(sedan) 5.60 x 15
BRAKES	hydraulic, front/rear drum
WHEELS	steel disc
FUEL TANK	10.6 gallons
FRONT SUSPENSION	king pins with transverse torsion bars and upper/lower trailing arms
REAR SUSPENSION	swing axles with trailing arms and torsion bars
STEERING	worm and roller
ENGINE	1,192cc 40-hp horizontally opposed four-cylinder, overhead valve, air cooled, light alloy block and head, finned cylinders with cast-iron liners
TRANSMISSION	four-speed manual (full synchromesh)
FINAL DRIVE RATIO	4.375:1

VOLKSWAGEN SEDAN

PAINT COLORS

L41 Black
L456 Ruby Red
L360 Sea Blue
L87 Pearl White

L469 Anthracite
L518 Java Green
L519 Bahama Blue
L1009 Yukon Yellow

ADDITIONAL BEETLE CABRIOLET

PAINT COLORS

L54 Poppy Red
L398 Pacific Blue

L10018 Brunswick Blue

MODEL AVAILABILITY	Deluxe 2-door Sedan ($1,595)
	Deluxe 2-door Sunroof Sedan ($1,685)
	2-door Cabriolet Convertible ($2,095)
CHASSIS NUMBERS	5677119–6502399 (Beetle)
WHEELBASE	94.5 inches
LENGTH	160.6 inches
WIDTH	60.6 inches
HEIGHT	(sedan) 59.1 inches

WEIGHT	(sedan) 1,609 lbs.
TREAD	(front/rear) 51.4/50.7 inches
TIRES	(sedan) 5.60 x 15
BRAKES	hydraulic, front/rear drum
WHEELS	steel disc
FUEL TANK	10.6 gallons
FRONT SUSPENSION	king pins with transverse torsion bars and upper/lower trailing arms
REAR SUSPENSION	swing axles with trailing arms and torsion bars
STEERING	worm and roller
ENGINE	1,192cc 40-hp horizontally opposed four-cylinder, overhead valve, air cooled, light alloy block and head, finned cylinders with cast-iron liners
TRANSMISSION	four-speed manual (full synchromesh)
FINAL DRIVE RATIO	4.375:1

We've done it again: built another VW.

Actually, we've built more than 6,500,000 of them to date. All of them designed to be serviced easily and economically. (Otherwise, a Volkswagen wouldn't be a Volkswagen.)

For example, the engine can be removed and replaced in just 90 minutes. A fender can be replaced without removing half the car. (It takes just 10 bolts.)

When and if your VW needs parts and/or service (it has a remarkable reputation for staying out of the repair shop) your VW dealer is the man to see. He's the one who has the parts on hand or on tap. 5,008 of them, to be exact. And he's the one who knows how to service your VW for you. Properly. His mechanics are factory-trained; his equipment and tools are specially designed to take care of just one make of car: the VW.

Here, you see the VW Sedan and Sunroof and Convertible at your VW dealer's. The service booklet's been put inside with the VW guarantee (6 months or 6,000 miles, parts and labor and two free maintenance services). And the cars have been given a final road test and tune-up and cleaning.

Got the picture?

CHAPTER 5

SLIM PILLAR

In Germany in 1965, a total of 1,174,687 Volkswagen passenger cars left the assembly line at the factory in Wolfsburg.

Volkswagen continued to hold the lion's share of the market for imported cars in the United States. However, the competition from America's domestic manufacturers was growing keener. During the year, the number of Volkswagen dealers dropped from 968 to 908. Volkswagen's 383,978 unit sales in the United States for calendar-year 1965 amounted to 67.4 percent of the US imported car market. Including tourist deliveries of 14,078 cars and 37,796 trucks, the leading German automaker sold 371,222 vehicles to Americans this year.

A mother leans into her Volkswagen Beetle sedan to talk to her young slugger. The Beetle was a perfect second car for many American families.

1965

The 1965 Volkswagen Beetle went into production on August 3, 1964. It boasted a larger windshield and windows thanks to the A-pillars being slimmed down. The new windshield and windows gave the Beetle a total of 15 percent more glass area, also resulting in an airy look that was much more modern. With more glass to clean, the windshield wipers had to be made longer, and a more powerful wiper motor was required to make them sweep effectively. The windshield wiper blades now "parked" on the left side instead of the right side.

A fold-down rear seat and increased legroom were new conveniences inside the Beetle. A push-button mechanism replaced the former T-type handle on the engine lid. The front seat backs were now slightly thinner and more contoured, while the rear seat folded almost flat in a manner that formed an extended luggage compartment. Twin levers operated the heater, which delivered greater heating volume due to the use of four thermostatically controlled flaps at the fan housing instead of the former throttle ring. This redesign

allowed heated air to flow immediately after the engine was started.

A pair of pivoting sun visors was also installed in 1965 Beetles. Cable-operated window risers replaced the previous single-arm type. The efficiency of the hydraulic braking system was also improved and a new maintenance-free sealed steering system was introduced. A new jack with two levering points was also provided with the cars. Anthracite body finish was discontinued, but Panama Beige and Fontana Gray were added. Additional technical changes were made to the

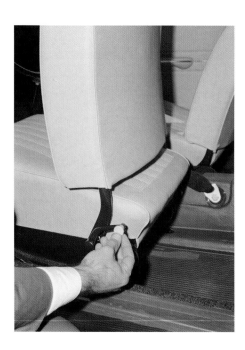

LEFT: Novel latches prevented the front seat backrests from flying forward in 1966. The vinyl seats used in 1966 were also a bit plusher. Front seat belts were anchored to the small tunnel between the bucket seats. *Archives/TEN: The Enthusiast Network Magazines, LLC*

MIDDLE: For 1966, new ball joints replaced the trailing arms previously used. The ball joints doubled chassis lubrication intervals to 6,000 miles between grease jobs. *Archives/TEN: The Enthusiast Network Magazines, LLC*

RIGHT: New for 1966 was a lighted knob for the four-way flashers located just above the ignition switch. The dimmer was on the turn signal. An AM radio ($69.95) and an AM/FM radio ($120.00) were optional. A cigar lighter cost $4.50. *Archives/TEN: The Enthusiast Network Magazines, LLC*

OPPOSITE: A nose view of the Beetle shows its new flat hubcaps, which were the major styling change for model year 1966. Whitewall tires were optional for $35 extra that year. *Archives/TEN: The Enthusiast Network Magazines, LLC*

SLIM PILLAR

It comes in 7 colors.

rear wheel bearings, heater operation, and the engine distributor cam.

According to contemporary sources, the 1965 Beetle had a top cruising speed of 72 miles per hour. Moving from 0–60 miles per hour took 32 seconds and the Bug did the quarter-mile in 23.9 seconds with a terminal speed of 56 miles per hour. Volkswagen Beetle owners could expect 28 to 35 miles per gallon of gasoline.

1966

It took nerve to put out a sales brochure that said "The '66 VW: You won't see any improvement" right on the cover, but that's exactly the kind of self-confidence that Volkswagen reflected in its advertising and promotional material that year. In Volkswagen's case, this made perfect sense since it was the company's quality and consistency that attracted customers. Buyers seemed to understand that "planned obsolescence" was not part of Volkswagen's program. This attitude helped the company build 1,168,146 cars worldwide in 1966.

On another page of the sales catalog, Volkswagen pointed out that it had made 132 major product improvements in the five years since 1961. Photos showed seven of those improvements and the years that they were adopted. Fourteen other improvements were specified in the text at the bottom of the two-page spread. "Every year we improve the Volkswagen to make it work better," said the last paragraph. "So, it's only natural that the '66 VW works best of all."

Images and words like that had high impact to the Volkswagen buyers in America. They flocked to the automaker's 2,272 dealers scattered across the country, most of which were east of the Mississippi. Volkswagen's unit sales in the United States for 1966 amounted to 420,018 vehicles. When tourist deliveries of 15,738 cars and 35,439 trucks were included, the leading German automaker sold 471,195 vehicles in the continental United States.

A more deluxe 1966 sales brochure did a great job outlining the features and benefits of the latest Beetle—from starting well in cold weather, to smooth

ABOVE: *Motor Trend* joked that the 1966 Volkswagen 1300 Beetle held the title for Top Gas Eliminator because of its fuel economy. The magazine added, "Within its family it will place on any freeway," and showed it going by a 1964 Chevy. *Archives/TEN: The Enthusiast Network Magazines, LLC*

RIGHT: The 1967 VW 1600 had upholstery that was serviceable and practical. The seats were reasonably comfortable. The steering wheel and small hand controls were well located, as were the instruments. The pedals were too close. *Archives/ TEN: The Enthusiast Network Magazines, LLC*

OPPOSITE: This 1965 Volkswagen art points out that there were seven colors for Beetles that year. Anthracite body finish was discontinued, but Panama Beige and Fontana Gray were added. More colors were added later.

ABOVE: A new 1500 engine was found in the 1967 Beetle. By this time, the base price was up to $1,717. With 53 horsepower, the car was flexible in traffic but far from competitors in its class, such as the Datsun 1600 or Fiat 124, in performance. *Archives/TEN: The Enthusiast Network Magazines, LLC*

PREVIOUS PAGES: *Motor Trend* said it never experienced dangerous over-steer or uncontrollability in crosswinds with its 1967 Beetle test car. Stability was excellent and the magazine thought the drum brakes were discs. *Archives/TEN: The Enthusiast Network Magazines, LLC*

all-synchromesh gear shifting, to a uniquely smooth-riding all-independent suspension system, to passing by more gas stations. One photo showed a Beetle driving out on a sandy beach, while various domestic cars and trucks had to stay in a parking lot.

Another showed a service technician repairing front fender collision damage by simply bolting on a brand new fender. "You arrive at the conclusion there's no car like a Volkswagen," the copywriters pointed out.

Of course, Volkswagen introduced some significant changes again in 1966 and a larger, more powerful engine was one of them. The "Spotlight on Detroit" column in the October 1965 edition of *Motor Trend* highlighted the annual revisions in the Volkswagen

Beetle sedan. It said that the car boasted "all sorts of changes, but you'll barely be able to tell it by looking." *Motor Trend* also wrote up a "Drivescription" of the Volkswagen 1300 (and the new Volkswagen 1600 fastback) in its February 1966 issue. These articles did not include actual performance numbers, other than top speed, but they gave many details about the two models.

The newly introduced larger, stronger engine was again a four-cylinder, four-stroke powerplant with two pairs of cylinders that were horizontally opposed. It had overhead valves. A 3.03 x 2.72-inch bore and stroke gave displacement of 1,285cc or 78.42 cubic inches. It had a 7.3:1 compression ratio and developed 50 horsepower at 4,600 rpm. Piston speed was 1,811 feet per minute at 4,000 rpm. The new engine weighed 249 pounds. The carburetor was a Solex downdraft-type Model PICT 1 with an automatic choke. With this new engine, the Beetle did 0-to-60 miles per hour in 20.6 seconds and had a top cruising speed of 75

miles per hour. Fuel economy was written up as 30.6 miles per gallon.

The 1300 engine wasn't the only change seen this year. A third defroster outlet for the windshield was added and the headlight dimmer switch was moved to the turn signal lever. Also new were front seat backrests that had safety latches that locked them in the upright position. The Beetle also had a more sensitive accelerator pedal designed to enhance throttle response.

Along with its new 1300 engine, the Beetle also had a 1300 emblem placed on the engine lid. Its newly designed pressed steel wheels had vent slots, and flat hubcaps (with VW logos, of course) were fitted to them. Inside the car, the half horn ring that had been deleted two years earlier was reinstated. A new ball-joint front suspension replaced the old trailing arms type for a smoother ride. Also added was a lighted, four-way flasher knob positioned above the ignition switch.

Some Volkswagen dealers such as Concours Motorcars, Inc.; Fred Howe Motors, Inc.; and Walter

Laev, Inc. of Milwaukee, Wisconsin, included a heater, a defroster, turn signals, a leatherette interior, bumper guards, a windshield washer system, dual inside visors, a fuel gauge, and whitewall tires in their advertised prices and offered seat belts for $21.90 additional. Extra-cost options listed in the factory sales catalog included the leatherette interior, a radio, a radio antenna, hinged rear windows, a side view mirror, and the whitewall tires.

Other factory-approved options and accessories included an AM/FM radio for $120 (the standard AM radio cost $69.95), a cigar lighter for $4.50, a parcel shelf for $14.15, a roof luggage rack for $29.95, vent shades for $6.50, front armrests for $4.95, Cocoa mats for $16.95, and the steel sliding sunroof for $90.

During 1966, Volkswagen publicized a plan to establish "mom and pop" dealerships in towns with populations of 25,000 people. The company said that it hoped to establish 100 such outlets during the first year of the program.

1967

Volkswagenwerk GmbH completed its eighteenth straight year of increasing US sales in 1967, and the increase was a healthy 8.7 percent. However, the company's share of the import market declined to 57 percent, compared to 62.6 percent a year earlier. This was largely due to the fact that American automakers were selling more and more "captive imports." Buick dealers, for instance, were selling

the German-built Opel and Chrysler purchased Britain's Rootes Group.

J. Stuart Perkins remained president of Volkswagen of America. The United States had fourteen Volkswagen distributors. Volkswagen continued to hold the lion's share of the market for imported cars in the United States.

The company's total worldwide output was 1,921,013 Volkswagens. Unit sales in the United States for

calendar-year 1967 amounted to 409,263 units. Including tourist deliveries of 11,294 cars and 34,247 trucks, the grand total of vehicles sold stateside was 454,804 vehicles.

Volkswagen was proud of the fact that it didn't change its cars much from year to year in this era, so it's likely the company was also proud of its 1967 sales brochure, which looked practically identical to the last year's. In fact, the

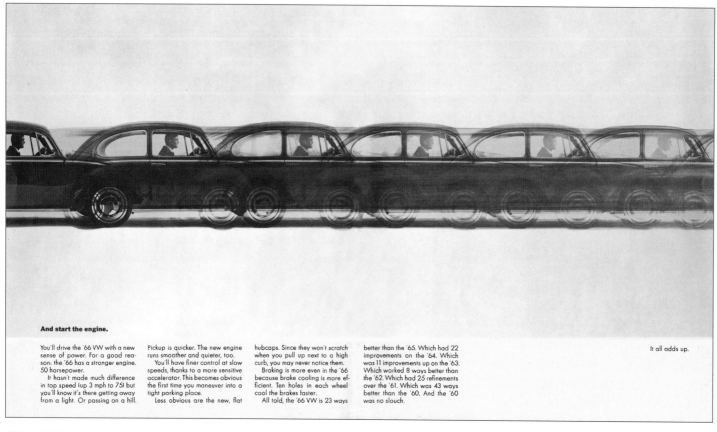

This 1966 Beetle advertisement was meant to project the idea that the German compact was getting faster. The copywriters pointed out that its top speed was up to 75 miles per hour. And better brake cooling stopped it faster too.

four-flap centerfold that pictured a black 1961 Beetle at the top of the first flap and a red 1967 Beetle on the top of the next flap looked identical to the 1966 art, except that the red car changed from a 1966 model to a 1967 model. At least the company said it did . . .

There was new copy at the bottom of the flap with the red car. It read:

New in 1967: a stronger 53-horsepower, 1493-cc. engine, dual brake system. More effective sealed beam headlights, 2-speed windshield wipers, pushbutton door locks, auxiliary rear axle spring for softer ride, driver armrest, recessed door and ashtray handles,

flattened dashboard switches, two back-up lights. Left hand outside mirror. If you own a Volkswagen and one of these features is missing, then you don't own a 1967 Volkswagen. But it can be arranged.

It is apparent that some of these changes were required to meet new US federal safety standards that were going into effect in 1967. The removal of the old glass headlight covers fell into this category, as did the twin reservoir master cylinder, the back-up lights, the safer handles, the flattened switches, and the driver's side rearview mirror. A "Volkswagen"

script now decorated the rear engine cover, which held the license plate in a new vertical position. The electrical system was switched to 12 volts, after two decades of 6-volt operation.

The larger, stronger engine was of similar architecture to the previous one. It had a larger 3.27-inch bore, while the stroke remained at 2.72 inches. This gave it 1,493cc (91.10 cubic inches). It also had a higher 7.5:1 compression ratio and developed 53 horsepower at 4,200 rpm. Piston speed was 1,811 feet per minute at 4,000 rpm. The new engine weighed 252 pounds. The mechanically operated carburetor was a Solex downdraft type with an automatic choke. The new 12-volt battery put out 36 amps.

TOP: Starting in 1967, glass headlight covers were no longer used and the front parking lamps were integrated into the directional signal lights. Karen Carey of Wisconsin owns this delightful Bug.

LEFT: This 1967 Beetle owned by Karen Carey illustrates interior features such as the locking glove box and passenger grab handle.

MIDDLE: Other 1967 improvements that Karen Carey enjoys in her Beetle are two-speed windshield wipers and a 12-volt electrical system. New "soft" control knobs were adopted to meet new Federal Motor Vehicle Safety Standards that went into effect in the United States.

RIGHT: Karen Carey's 1967 Beetle carries its spare tire in the front luggage compartment. Note how the center of the Volkswagen wheel has a wide opening with five wheel bolt holes.

1968

Probably the biggest Volkswagen news of 1968 was the death of Heinz Nordhoff. The man who had engineered Volkswagen's rise from the ashes of World War II passed away on April 12. The sixty-nine-year-old Nordhoff suffered a heart attack following a long illness. Nordhoff—who was affectionately known as the father of the Volkswagen—was replaced by Kurt Lotz in September 1968.

The passing of Heinz Nordhoff had little, if any, effect on worldwide sales of Volkswagens, although total output did drop a noticeable amount to 1,191,854 vehicles. In the United States, however, Volkswagen completed its nineteenth straight year of increasing sales, amounting to 564,956 units. With tourist deliveries of 12,717 cars, 582,009 more Volkswagens came to America in 1968.

That year it was reported that the US imported car market would soon reach one million units and that 550,000 of them would be Volkswagens. That could help explain why the German automaker started the year off with 1,003 dealers and closed the year with 1,064. It was quite amazing to think that twenty years earlier, not even one Volkswagen had yet arrived in the United States! Reading between the lines, it was easy to see that Volkswagen was making improvements in its product to satisfy the demands of American buyers. The engines kept getting larger and more powerful, the styling became slightly more modern, additional safety and convenience features were engineered into the cars, and the ride quality had been improved. Now, it was time to work on gearshifting. The July 1968 issue of *Motor Trend* had an article by Eric Dahlquist on the new Volkswagen Beetle fitted with an automatic transmission.

During 1968, Volkswagen expanded its world market reach by acquiring a 25 percent interest in Industries del Motor, SA (Imosa), a Spanish manufacturer of small commercial vehicles. Industries del Motor, SA (Imosa) then took over the national distribution of Volkswagens in Spain. Volkswagen made an appeal to Spanish dictator Francisco Franco to allow the construction of a new automobile factory capable of building 125,000 cars per year.

"Why do so many people buy Volkswagens?" was the question asked on the cover of a 1968 sales brochure showing a new Beetle sedan in a showroom. The next page pictured a red 1966 Beetle that Ed Coady of Lake Stevens, Washington, used to deliver *The Everett Herald* newspaper and then came Coady's testimonial: "Economy. That was the thing that sold me. This paper route is 17.5 miles long. If I'm going to make the grade on it, I've got to watch all my nickels and dimes. And driving a Volkswagen cut my expenses in half."

SLIM-PILLAR FACTS

▌▌ A series of famous advertisements created by the Doyal, Dane & Bernbach Agency made history in this era. One depicted the Beetle in the dark with only headlights glowing behind it and the headline, "Sometimes we get the feeling we're being followed." Another showed six cars made in 1949: a Tucker, a Packard, a DeSoto, a Studebaker, a Hudson, and a Volkswagen Beetle. "Where are they now?" asked the headline.

▌▌ In his "Used Cars" column in the January 1969 issue of *Motor Trend*, Mike Lamm mentioned Volkswagen's factory-sanctioned used-car warranty program. It covered running gear, brakes, front axle assemblies, and electrical equipment at 100 percent for 30 days or 1,000 miles and the car (sold by a VW dealer) did not have to be a Volkswagen.

▌▌ In 1969, *Motor Trend* carried a mention of the fact that Volkswagens converted into dune buggies were becoming a common sight on the highways. "In California alone, daily registrations at DMV have reached about 150 dune buggies a day," noted "Trends in Travel" columnist V. Lee Oertle.

▌▌ During 1969, race driver Emerson Fittipaldi raced a twin-engine Beetle sedan in Brazil. At the 1,000-kilometer race in Rio de Janeiro, he qualified on the outside pole ahead of a Chevy-Lola and a Ford GT40.

▌▌ In January 1970, *Motor Trend* featured a limousine made from two Volkswagen Beetles. Tony Nancy, a custom upholsterer in Southern California, created it. The magazine called this 131-inch-wheelbase Beetle the 35 Grand Bug, based on its cost of 126,000 Deutschmarks.

The brochure said that Coady had owned six Beetles. At the bottom of the page was a photo of a new Beetle and this caption: "The 1968 Volkswagen Sedan. It gets up to 27 miles per gallon on regular gas—just like Ed Coady's '66 Volkswagen on the left. In fact, every time you run it, it makes an economy run." Coady's feedback showed the practicality of Volkswagen ownership in dollars and sense, as did the following catalog copy: "Because we don't change the way our car looks every year and because of the way it holds up year to year, it often brings more in the end than cars that cost more in the beginning."

The same sales catalog featured positive testimonials from other typical Beetle users in Greenwich, Connecticut; Pacific, Missouri; and Mansfield, Ohio. However, also featured were three untypical Volkswagen owners. They were Ray McMahon, a member of a research expedition in Antarctica who praised his Beetle's cold-weather starting; Rahmatullah Asifi of the Royal Afghan Embassy in Washington, D.C., who liked his car's interior room; and well-known actor Paul Newman, who said he bought his first Volkswagen in 1953, when he was a struggling actor. By the way, his pictured Cabriolet was an older 1963 model.

Of course, the latest models had several of the unseen product changes that Volkswagen was getting famous for. The 1968 improvements included a switch to one-piece single-bar bumpers without overriders (bumper guards). This slightly decreased the Beetle's overall length to 158.7 inches from the previous 160.2 inches. The new bumpers, front and rear, were also raised higher to—as Volkswagen put it—rise "to the level of the big boys on the block." In addition to this, the new bumpers featured strengthened mounting points on the frame.

Other revisions included larger taillights with integrated back-up lights and flatter door handles with trigger-type releases. Beetle owners no longer had to open the front hood to fill the gas tank, because the filler neck and spring-loaded filler cap were moved to an outside location above the right front fender. The rear engine cover also had a slightly bigger bulge. The car now had a cowl air inlet with separate controls, and the hood release was moved to the outside of the car. A collapsible steering column became standard equipment, while the Autostick automatic transmission that *Motor Trend* had tried became optional. The semi-automatic unit could be shifted from low to driving range simply by moving the gearshift lever and without using the clutch. Sarcophagus seat backs were now used, with integrated head restraints. A certification sticker on the doorpost advised that the car met US federal safety standards.

1969

This year Volkswagen's total production rose a bit to 1,241,580 passenger cars of all models, but its US sales slid for the first time in twenty years. The company blamed the decline on a dock strike that took place during the early part of the year. That might be true, because apparently other imports also slipped and Volkswagen still continued to hold the lion's share of the import market. During 1969, Volkswagen sales in the United States included 403,016 Type 1 models (Beetle and Karmann Ghia), 50,361 Type 2 models (Transporters), and 95,527 Type 3 models (Fastbacks and Squarebacks).

The company's US sales for the calendar year amounted to 548,904 units. There were also 14,990 deliveries of cars to American tourists, bringing the grand total to 566,356 vehicles. The number of Volkswagen dealers, which stood at 1,064 at the beginning of 1969, was up to 1,111 by the beginning of 1970.

A short, one-page history of the 1938–1969 Volkswagen "Bug" by Eric Dahlquist appeared in the February 1969 issue of *Motor Trend*. "Today's Beetle is not a fantastically refined copy of

MOTOR TREND
TEST CAR

1946," Dahlquist said. "It is not even the same car, although the qualities that made it the greatest success story of all times of things automotive, glitter as brightly as ever from Wolfsburg."

A long interview with Volkswagen's new chairman and president Dr. Kurt Lotz ran in the August 1969 issue of *Motor Trend*. The magazine described him as, "The man who thinks beyond the Bug." Lotz was a farmer's son who became a Luftwaffe general staff major during World War II. After the war, he worked as a clerk for the German branch of a Swiss electrical company and rose to chairman. He invested in a small computer company, but it lost money and he and his Swiss bosses parted ways. By the time Lotz replaced Nordhoff at Volkswagen, he was thought of as a business whiz kid who rose quickly to the top of the heap.

During the spring of 1969, Volkswagen gained control of NSU. Volkswagen wanted to merge NSU with Audi. A new front-wheel-drive NSU model, the K

ABOVE: The 1971 Beetle interior was not flashy, but it was quite functional. The seats shown here have the optional leatherette trim. They were firm, but the seatbacks were adjustable. All controls were within the driver's reach and all of the instruments were grouped in a single dial. *Archives/TEN: The Enthusiast Network Magazines, LLC*

OPPOSITE: The 1971 *Motor Trend* test car was a 1600 Beetle with the four-speed, all-synchromesh transmission. It actually had a quicker zero-to-sixty run than the Ford Pinto, but Chevy's Vega beat both of them. *Archives/TEN: The Enthusiast Network Magazines, LLC*

This color photo of an earlier Volkswagen Beetle sedan appeared in the July 1973 edition of *Motor Trend* that featured the magazine's nominations for Hall of Fame recognition. The car looks like a 1960s model. *Archives/TEN: The Enthusiast Network Magazines, LLC*

70, had already been publicized and was on its way to the Geneva Auto Show at the time. It was viewed as a competitor to the existing Audi 100 and was supposed to be dropped. However, near the end of 1969, rumors began to fly that the K 70 would become a new Volkswagen model, since Lotz was convinced front-wheel-drive cars would soon dominate the European market.

For the first time in 1969, the Beetle had a truly independent rear suspension with a double-jointed rear axle and semi-trailing arms replacing the previous swing axles. After being moved to the outside a year earlier, the front hood release was again relocated. This time it was in the glove box. Warm air outlets were moved from the bases of the doors to a new location at the rear of the interior. An electric rear-window defogger and defroster was installed, as was an inside fuel-door release, a new steering wheel, and a day/night mirror. Later in the year, the Beetle odometer added readings in tenths of a mile.

Volkswagen sent 1,193,853 new cars into the world in 1970 and also established a new US sales record of 567,602 cars. This included 403,521 Type 1 Beetle models. Volkswagen was America's biggest car importer again. The total number of cars coming to the United States was 582,573 units, which included 12,887 tourist deliveries. In August 1970, Stuart Perkins, the long-reigning president of Volkswagen of America, sat down for an interview with *Motor Trend*. The focus of the article was on his German bosses' reaction to new American subcompact cars, such

as the Chevrolet Vega, Ford Pinto, and AMC Gremlin. Perkins said, "We are still advanced in many respects, quite different from the rest of the pack."

The Beetle 1500 was quietly turned into the Beetle 1600 in 1970. The cylinders in the air-cooled "pancake" engine were bored out to 3.36 inches, while the stroke remained at 2.72 inches. The actual piston displacement was 1,585cc. The horsepower was boosted from 53 brake horsepower to 57 brake horsepower. Despite the increase to 1.6 liters, the Beetle was still referred to as the Type 1 1500 sedan.

The Beetle's front turn signals grew larger and were combined with the side marker lights. The engine lid added air-intake slots (introduced earlier on the convertible), and reflectors were added to the rear bumper and tail lamp housings. Inside the car, the head restraints were smaller and a lock was added to the glovebox. Remote-control knobs for the warm air outlets were dropped. A buzzer now went off when the door was opened with the key still in the ignition. Volkswagen's diagnosis and maintenance program was introduced this year.

1949   **1970**

No matter how you cut it, the design and character of the Type 1 Beetle sedan hadn't changed much over the twenty years between when the blue 1949 model on the left and the red 1970 model on the right were built.

ABOVE: The 1970 Beetle could still be backed into a tight parking space even though the sports car behind it was a little over the line on the road. The 94.5-inch wheelbase Beetle had an overall length of just 158.6 inches or just over 13 feet.

OPPOSITE: Volkswagen's 1970 sales catalog was titled "Presenting the Car of the Future," and this futuristic photo fantasized what it would be like gassing up a Beetle ten years in the future, when gas prices might be higher. "The cost of driving will rise," said the ad copy. "The higher it rises, the more your VW will save."

1965

VOLKSWAGEN BEETLE

PAINT COLORS

L41 Standard Black	**L472** Beige Gray
L87 Pearl White	**L518** Java Green
L19K Yukon Yellow	**L519** Bahama Blue
L360 Sea Blue	**L572** Panama Beige
L456 Ruby Red	**L595** Fontana Gray

MODEL AVAILABILITY	Deluxe 2-door Sedan ($1,563)
	Deluxe 2-door Sunroof Sedan ($1,653)
	2-door Cabriolet Convertible ($2,053)
CHASSIS NUMBERS	11-5000001–11-5979202 (Beetle)
WHEELBASE	94.5 inches
LENGTH	160.6 inches
WIDTH	60.6 inches
HEIGHT	(sedan) 59.1 inches
WEIGHT	(sedan) 1,609 lbs.
TREAD	(front/rear) 51.4/50.7 inches
TIRES	(sedan) 5.60 x 15
BRAKES	hydraulic, front/rear drum
WHEELS	steel disc
FUEL TANK	10.6 gallons
FRONT SUSPENSION	king pins with transverse torsion bars and upper/lower trailing arms
REAR SUSPENSION	swing axles with trailing arms and torsion bars
STEERING	worm and roller
ENGINE	1,192cc 40-hp horizontally opposed four-cylinder, overhead valve, air cooled, light alloy block and head, finned cylinders with cast-iron liners
TRANSMISSION	four-speed manual (full synchro)
FINAL DRIVE RATIO	4.375:1

1966

VOLKSWAGEN SEDAN

PAINT COLORS

L41 Black	**L459** Anthracite
L456 Ruby Red	**L518** Java Green
L360 Sea Blue	**L519** Bahama Blue
L87 Pearl White	**L1009** Yukon Yellow

ADDITIONAL VOLKSWAGEN CABRIOLET PAINT COLORS

L54 Poppy Red	**L10018** Brunswick Blue
L395 Pacific Blue	

MODEL AVAILABILITY	Deluxe 2-door Sedan ($1,585)
	Deluxe 2-door Sunroof Sedan ($1,675)
	2-door Cabriolet Convertible ($2,075)
CHASSIS NUMBERS	116-000001–116-1021298 (Beetle and Karmann Ghia)
WHEELBASE	94.5 inches
LENGTH	160.6 inches
WIDTH	60.6 inches
HEIGHT	(sedan) 59.1 inches
WEIGHT	(sedan) 1,720 lbs.
TREAD	(front/rear) 51.4/51.2 inches
TIRES	(sedan) 5.60 x 15 tubeless
BRAKES	hydraulic, front/rear drum
WHEELS	disk-type with drop-center rim 4J x 13
FUEL TANK	10.6 gallons
FRONT SUSPENSION	Independent suspension of both wheels through equal upper and lower trailing arms, 2 transverse torsion bars protected in tubes, and an anti-sway bar. Double-acting telescopic shock absorbers.
REAR SUSPENSION	Independent suspension of wheels through swing-axle shafts with trailing arms; one torsion bar on each side mounted and protected in transverse tube. Double-acting telescopic shock absorbers.
STEERING	worm and roller steering and divided tie rod; hydraulic steering damper; 2.6 turns of steering wheel lock to lock
ENGINE	1,285cc 50-hp horizontally opposed four-cylinder, overhead valve, air cooled, light alloy block and head, finned cylinders with cast-iron liners
TRANSMISSION	four-speed manual (full synchro)
FINAL DRIVE RATIO	4.375:1

1967

VOLKSWAGEN SEDAN

PAINT COLORS

L41 Black	**L595** Fontana Gray
L282 Lotus White	**L620** Savanna Beige
L456 Ruby Red	**L633** VW Blue
L518 Java Green	**L639** Zenith Blue

ADDITIONAL VOLKSWAGEN CABRIOLET PAINT COLORS

L19K Yukon Yellow

MODEL AVAILABILITY	Deluxe 2-door Sedan ($1,639)
	Deluxe 2-door Sunroof Sedan ($1,729)
	2-door Cabriolet Convertible ($2,075)
STARTING SERIAL NUMBER	117-000001 (Beetle)
WHEEL BASE	94.5 inches
LENGTH	160.2 inches
WIDTH	60.6 inches
HEIGHT	(sedan) 59.1 inches
WEIGHT	(sedan) 1,764 lbs.; (Cabriolet) 1,852 lbs.
TREAD	(front/rear) 51.4/53.4 inches
TIRES	(sedan) 5.60 x 15
BRAKES	hydraulic, front/rear drum
WHEELS	disk-type with drop-center rim 4J x 13
FUEL TANK	10.6 gallons
FRONT SUSPENSION	Independent suspension of both wheels through equal upper and lower trailing arms, 2 transverse torsion bars protected in tubes, and an anti-sway bar. Double-acting telescopic shock absorbers.
REAR SUSPENSION	Independent suspension of wheels through swing-axle shafts with trailing arms; one torsion bar on each side mounted and protected in transverse tube. Double-acting telescopic shock absorbers.
STEERING	worm and roller steering and divided tie rod; hydraulic steering damper; 2.6 turns of steering wheel lock to lock
ENGINE	1,493cc 53-hp horizontally opposed four-cylinder, overhead valve, air cooled, light alloy block and head, finned cylinders with cast-iron liners
TRANSMISSION	four-speed manual (full synchro)
FINAL DRIVE RATIO	4.125:1

1968

VOLKSWAGEN SEDAN

COLORS	CLOTH & LEATHERETTE	LEATHERETTE
L41 Black	Platinum	India Red
L282LOTUS White	India Red	Black
L30A Royal Red	Platinum	Black
L610 Delta Green	Platinum	Platinum
L620 Savanna Beige	India Red	Gazelle
L633 VW Blue	Platinum	Platinum
L639 Zenith Blue	Water Blue	Black

VOLKSWAGEN CABRIOLET

COLORS	CLOTH & LEATHERETTE	LEATHERETTE
L41 Black	Black	India Red
L282 Lotus White	Black	Black
L30A Royal Red	Black	Black
L54K Poppy Red	Black	Black
L620 Savanna Beige	Black	Gazelle
L633 VW Blue	Silver Gray	Platinum
L639 Zenith Blue	Black	Black
L19 Yukon Yellow	Black	Black

MODEL AVAILABILITY	Deluxe 2-door Sedan ($1,699)
	Deluxe 2-door Sunroof Sedan ($1,78)
	2-door Cabriolet Convertible ($2,099)
SERIAL NUMBERS	118-000001–119-1016098 (All Beetles)
WHEELBASE	94.5 inches
LENGTH	158.7 inches
WIDTH	61.0 inches
HEIGHT	(sedan) 59.0 inches
WEIGHT	(sedan) 1,808 lbs.; (Cabriolet) 1,918 lbs.
TREAD	(front/rear) 51.6/53.1 inches
TIRES	(sedan) 5.60 x 15 tubeless
BRAKES	hydraulic, front/rear drum
WHEELS	disk-type with drop-center rim 4J x 15
FUEL TANK	10.6 gallons
FRONT SUSPENSION	Independent suspension of both wheels through equal upper and lower trailing arms, 2 transverse torsion bars protected in tubes, and an anti-sway bar. Double-acting telescopic shock absorbers.

continued on page 90

continued from page 89

REAR SUSPENSION Independent suspension of wheels through swing-axle shafts with trailing arms; one torsion bar on each side mounted and protected in transverse tube. Double-acting telescopic shock absorbers.

STEERING worm and roller steering and divided tie rod; hydraulic steering damper; 2.6 turns of steering wheel lock to lock

ENGINE 1,493cc 53-hp horizontally opposed four-cylinder, overhead valve, air cooled, light alloy block and head, finned cylinders with cast-iron liners

TRANSMISSION four-speed manual (full synchro)

FINAL DRIVE RATIO 4.125:1

OPTIONAL EQUIPMENT Leatherette interior, whitewall tires, hinged rear side windows, sunroof.

ACCESSORIES Radio and antenna, rear speaker, underdash parcel shelf, air conditioner, cigarette lighter, luggage rack, vent shades, gravel guards, tissue dispenser, and more.

The window sticker indicates this 1968 Beetle has the autostick transmission that could be used as a full automatic or shifted through the gears. The torque converter was a small BorgWarner unit. *Archives/TEN: The Enthusiast Network Magazines, LLC*

1969

VOLKSWAGEN SEDAN

PAINT COLORS

L41 Black	**L90C** Toga White
L50B Diamond Blue	**L620** Savannah Beige
L60B Peru Green	**L630** Cobalt Blue

ADDITIONAL VOLKSWAGEN CABRIOLET PAINT COLORS

L54K Poppy Red	**L19K** Yukon Yellow (Old L10009)

MODEL AVAILABILITY Deluxe 2-door Sedan ($1,799)
Deluxe 2-door Sunroof Sedan ($1,899)
2-door Cabriolet Convertible ($2,209)

SERIAL NUMBERS 119-000001–119-1093704 (All Beetles)

WHEELBASE 94.5 inches

LENGTH 158.7 inches

WIDTH 61.0 inches

HEIGHT (sedan) 59.0 inches

WEIGHT (sedan) 1,808 lbs.; (Cabriolet) 1,918 lbs.

TREAD (front/rear) 51.6/53.1 inches

TIRES (sedan) 5.60 x 15 tubeless

BRAKES hydraulic, front/rear drum

WHEELS disk-type with drop-center rim 4J x 15

FUEL TANK 10.6 gallons

FRONT SUSPENSION Independent suspension of both wheels through equal upper and lower trailing arms, 2 transverse torsion bars protected in tubes, and an anti-sway bar. Double-acting telescopic shock absorbers.

REAR SUSPENSION Independent suspension of wheels through swing-axle shafts with trailing arms; one torsion bar on each side mounted and protected in transverse tube. Double-acting telescopic shock absorbers.

STEERING worm and roller steering and divided tie rod; hydraulic steering damper; 2.6 turns of steering wheel lock to lock

ENGINE 1,493cc 53-hp horizontally opposed four-cylinder, overhead valve, air cooled, light alloy block and head, finned cylinders with cast-iron liners

TRANSMISSION four-speed manual (full synchro)

FINAL DRIVE RATIO 4.125:1

1970

VOLKSWAGEN BEETLE SEDAN

PAINT COLORS

L20D Clementine Orange
L30A Royal Red
L41 Black
L50B Diamond Blue
L60D Elm Green

L70F Chinchilla
L90D Pastel White
L620 Savanna Beige
L630 Cobalt Blue

VOLKSWAGEN BEETLE CABRIOLET

PAINT COLORS

L20D Clementine Orange
L19K Yukon Yellow
L30A Royal Red
L41 Black
L50B Diamond Blue
L54 Poppy Red

L60D Elm Green
L66B Deep Sea Green
L70F Chinchilla
L90D Pastel White
L620 Savanna Beige
L630 Cobalt Blue

MODEL AVAILABILITY	Deluxe 2-door Sedan ($1,839)
	Deluxe 2-door Sunroof Sedan ($1,929)
	2-door Cabriolet Convertible ($2,249)
STARTING SERIAL NUMBER	1102000001 (Beetle)
WHEELBASE	94.5 inches
LENGTH	158.6 inches
WIDTH	61.0 inches
HEIGHT	(sedan) 59.1 inches
WEIGHT	(sedan) 1,808 lbs.; (Cabriolet) 1,918 lbs.
TREAD	(front/rear) 51.6/53.1 inches
TIRES	(sedan) 5.60 x 15 tubeless

BRAKES	hydraulic, front/rear drum
WHEELS	disk-type with drop-center rim 4J x 15
FUEL TANK	10.6 gallons
FRONT SUSPENSION	Independent suspension of both wheels through equal upper and lower trailing arms, 2 transverse torsion bars protected in tubes, and an anti-sway bar. Double-acting telescopic shock absorbers.
REAR SUSPENSION	Independent suspension of wheels through swing-axle shafts with trailing arms; one torsion bar on each side mounted and protected in transverse tube. Double-acting telescopic shock absorbers.
STEERING	worm and roller steering and divided tie rod; hydraulic steering damper; 2.6 turns of steering wheel lock to lock
ENGINE	1,585cc 57-hp horizontally opposed four-cylinder, overhead valve, air cooled, light alloy block and head, finned cylinders with cast-iron liners
TRANSMISSION	four-speed manual (full synchro)
FINAL DRIVE RATIO	4.125:1

CHAPTER 6

BEETLES & SUPER BEETLES

In 1971, the addition of new models and a larger Type 1 Super Beetle helped Volkswagen increase total production to 1,284,928 vehicles, but it was also the second year running that sales in the United States slid. They were still large and included 352,549 Type 1 models (Beetle, Super Beetle, and Karmann Ghia), 63,025 Type 2 models (Transporters), 80,186 Type 3 models (Fastbacks and Squarebacks), and 24,870 Type 4 models (411s). Including tourist deliveries of 10,249 cars, the German carmaker sold 532,904 units to Americans during 1971.

The new Super Beetle was a reaction to the cars like the Vega, Pinto, and Toyota Corolla. It had a 95.3-inch wheelbase and an overall length of 161.8 inches.

This is the red Beetle sedan that appeared on the cover of *Motor Trend* in January 1971 in an article that compared the Volkswagen to Chevy's Vega and Ford's Pinto. "Two Car of the Year Nominees Take on the Car of the Decade," wrote author A. B. Shuman. *Archives/TEN: The Enthusiast Network Magazines, LLC*

The "Import Report" in *Motor Trend*'s January 1971 issue said that Volkswagen was the only import carmaker to respond favorably to new US government safety programs. Kurt Lotz was quoted as saying, "Being Europe's leading manufacturer and exporter, we have to contribute as much as possible to the improvement of safety in every respect. Our US experience taught us that American safety rules are the only valid base for unified European regulations."

In a *Motor Trend* article that compared the latest Beetle to the Pinto and the Vega, writer A. B. Shuman concluded, "But, for the non-enthusiasts, those desiring to have the simplest, least expensive transportation, the VW will continue to be the answer." That statement showed Volkswagen's experience in the entry-level market, but the niche was getting crowded with new competitors.

The numbers made it clear the Beetle was facing competitive pressures in the United States in 1971. No longer did the person in the market for a small car have only the Beetle and a Renault to choose from. AMC, Chevy, and Ford were in the market, along with Subaru, Peugeot, Fiat, Honda, and Datsun. In fact, more than forty cars sold in America were now priced below $2,500 and not all were foreign.

Still, on a worldwide basis, Volkswagen remained near the top of the automobile industry. In August 1971, *Motor Trend* reported on the world's largest automakers. They were, in order, Fiat, Toyota, Ford, Volkswagen, and GM. These rankings were a clear indication the automotive world was changing and that manufacturers in the United States were being challenged by imports.

Late in 1971, Dr. Kurt Lotz resigned from the helm of Volkswagen under severe criticism and political pressure (the German government and the Land of Niedersachsen owned 36 percent of VW stock and once the Social Democrats came into power, Lotz, who was a Christian Democrat, lost his political clout). Lotz resigned rather than have the company board members vote him out.

"Lotz's departure will not change VW's problems much," noted *Motor Trend* (November 1971 "International Report"). "The Wolfsburg outfit still depends too heavily on the aging Bug and on the US market, where Japanese competition and Nixon's protective measures might put it into trouble."

Rudolf Leiding succeeded Lotz. In the December *Motor Trend*, Karl Ludvigsen gave an excellent summary of the German auto industry at the time, including a good explanation of the management shake-up at Wolfsburg.

The regular Beetle continued in production in 1971, looking much the same as it did in 1970 (and for more than thirty years in fact). Computer-analysis plugs were installed in models built during the second half of the 1971 model year. This was the last year for the Model 1511 Cabriolet, as all future Beetle ragtops built from 1972 through early 1980 would be Super Beetles (convertibles only after 1977).

The new Super Beetle was mainly a reaction to the cars such as the Vega, Pinto, and Toyota Corolla. A comparison road report that *Road and Track* published concluded that the Corolla was a better and cheaper car than the Beetle. The Beetle's only plus in the article was its "lovable personality" and management was upset. Volkswagen was working on the Golf/Rabbit at the time, but the company was not ready to launch the new water-cooled, front-wheel-drive model.

Someone in Germany decided that the "Love Bug" could be made a little more lovable if it was upgraded to match up better with the Corolla. However, Volkswagen did not want to give up the regular Beetle's hold on the entry-level buyer, so the plan was to keep it in the lineup as a price leader. Then, the new Super Beetle could be sold to customers who wanted more features.

The focus with the Super Beetle was on more luggage space and

The focus with the new-for-1971 Super Beetle was on more luggage space and greater overall comfort and ride. It looks like this ball team got everything in the car except the last pitch.

greater overall comfort and ride quality, but Volkswagen knew that the improvements would require the biggest ever investment in the Beetle. An entirely new suspension was to be part of the package and that required a completely new platform and extensive front body panel alterations, such as fenders with a more rounded shape and a wider front hood. New inner fenders were designed to allow

MacPherson struts to be mounted. A new spare tire well was required too.

Volkswagen designated the Super Beetle Model Number 1302. Both 1,300cc and 1,600cc engines were offered in European versions of the car (the 1600 was dubbed the 1302S), but in the United States, only the larger 60-horsepower engine was utilized. Volkswagen's sales catalog emphasized that it was,

"The most powerful, most exciting and most comfortable Beetle ever."

The Super Beetle looked like a Beetle, but there were plenty of differences. Its spare tire was horizontal in a recessed wheelwell under the cargo area in the floor of the still-up-front trunk. The jack was stowed under the rear seat and a vacuum-operated windshield washer bottle was on the right inner fender. This added up to an 80 percent increase of storage space in the trunk.

Both new engines featured dual-port cylinder heads. An external oil cooler was added. A bigger engine cover was needed for the larger engine. The cover had five wide louvers on each side. A flow-through ventilation system included air vents behind the rear windows. A passenger side vanity mirror was also added.

The Super Beetle's new front suspension combined MacPherson struts and coil springs with transverse control arms. The rear trailing arms were improved. These changes resulted in a better turning radius and more precise steering geometry. Ride comfort was increased too. The inner fenders were heavier and a larger anti-roll bar was fitted. At the rear, double-jointed half shafts were used.

The first 1971 Super Beetle was finished on August 11, 1970. By year's end, workers at Volkswagen plants in two German cities—Wolfsburg and Emden—had built around 700,000. Although Beetle fanatics found faults with the Super Beetle, the public scooped them up. Buyers especially took to the $267 extra air-conditioning system and the $139 semi-automatic transmission.

Volkswagen promoted the fact that the car had eighty-nine improvements, including the power boost to 60 horsepower. The Super Beetle had chrome trim around its side windows and the body width and front tread dimensions both grew wider. Yet the turn radius was shorter. These cars also received computer-analysis plugs.

While top speed and quarter-mile times were never a very important selling point for Beetles and Super Beetles, it is interesting to note how the performance characteristics changed at certain points in the cars' histories. In 1971, the Beetle figures were as follows: 0–30 miles per hour: 4.5 seconds, 0–60 miles per hour: 16 seconds, 0–75 miles per hour: 36.3 seconds. Quarter-mile: 19.8 seconds at 65 miles per hour. Passing speeds: 40–60 miles per hour: 9.1 seconds, 50–70 miles per hour: 14.5 seconds. Fuel economy: 25.3 miles per gallon.

1972

In 1972, for the second straight year, Volkswagen had fewer US sales as total deliveries fell to 491,774 for the model year. To make matters worse, the company's worldwide sales dropped to 1,082,098 passenger cars of all models.

In America, 360,449 Type 1 Beetles, Super Beetles, and Karmann Ghias found owners. In addition, Volkswagen sold 49,235 Type 2 trucks and buses, 49,528 Type 3 Fastbacks and Squarebacks, and 32,562 Type 4 model 411s in the United States. Including tourist deliveries, 491,774 vehicles were sold

to Americans during 1972. Calendar-year sales by US dealers (not counting tourist deliveries) came to 485,645 units compared to 520,830 in 1971.

Many factors impacted the German automaker's American business in 1972, including a rise in imported car prices and increased competition from other imported marques and domestic subcompacts. A skidding US dollar and the threat of increased tariffs were other factors that VW management had to contend with. In its February 1972 issue, Motor Trend published

an "Investigative Report" titled "Volkswagen Marches to a Different Drummer." It was the true, behind-the-scenes story of the company's crisis and management shake-up.

Writer Edouard Seidler concluded, "What's good for VW is obviously good for Germany, and what's good for Germany is also good for Europe. This is why former mechanic Rudolf Leiding has suddenly become the most important man, industrially and economically, on the continent. A man to watch. Nine hundred thousand

The original Type 1 Beetle soldiered on in 1972. It was smaller than the new Super Beetle and had a flatter windshield and a less-rounded front end. The regular Beetle's bumper also looked heavier and blunter.

stockholders, 190,000 employees, the German chancellor and a few hundred million Europeans are watching."

In March 1971, *Motor Trend* predicted that Volkswagen would have to find new markets for its cars, such as in Red China, if its sales in the United States kept slipping and losing ground to Japanese automakers. A company representative joined a Mexican trade delegation visiting Red China in 1972. In April 1972, *Motor Trend* reported that "Volkswagen is presently operating at a loss." A drop of 10–15 percent in 1972 home-market sales was projected. US sales were expected to bounce back, but not enough to improve the overall profit picture.

Not helping Beetle sales was its inclusion in a June 1972 *Motor Trend* article entitled, "Twenty Auto Defects That Could Kill You." A close read revealed that the defect was heater fumes in pre-1963 Beetles and this may actually have inspired sales of newer, replacement cars. Volkswagen continued to focus on safety in 1972. One system being worked on was a foam-filled tubular seat belt setup that might have been an alternative to the airbag.

Volkswagen marked a historic milestone in 1972 when the Volkswagen Beetle became the most-produced car in history. It replaced the Model T Ford, which previously held the production-total record of 15,007,033. This took place on February 17, when the 15,007,034th Beetle came off the assembly line in Wolfsburg. Changes to the 1972 Beetle

Some things change. Some things never change Volkswagen does both.

were modest. They included installation of a four-spoke energy-absorbing safety steering wheel and new inertia-reel seat belts. The rear window grew 11 percent larger for improved rear vision and a hinged parcel shelf covered the luggage well. There were more louvers in the rear deck lid. Some control and instrument refinements were also provided.

The Super Beetle returned for its second year in 1972. In fact, it was actually a Super Beetle that took the

"most-made" title away from the Model T Ford. Volkswagen donated that 15,007,034th car to the Smithsonian Institution for permanent display in its industrial history section. To memorialize this milestone, Volkswagen painted six thousand of its 1972 Super Beetles with a unique metallic blue color and bolted special ten-spoke pressed-steel wheels on the cars. These VWs were called Marathon Beetles and they were only sold to customers in Europe.

1973

In 1973, 1,128,784 Volkswagens were produced, a modest increase. But not in America, where sales were down for the third year in a row. The total was 476,295 (excluding tourist deliveries). That included 371,097 Type 1 (Beetles, Super Beetles, and Karmann Ghias). That gave Volkswagen a 27.5 percent share of the US market. In addition, 4,307 tourist deliveries were made. Volkswagen had 1,206 US dealers at the start of 1973, but 12 would leave by year's end.

In the spring of 1973, Volkswagen Chairman Rudolf Leiding said he planned to treat the American and European markets differently. The VW executive described this revolutionary concept as his "double policy." He turned to designers such as Giorgio Guigiaro of Turin, Italy, to try to give future Volkswagen models a modern new design image, but the 1973 Beetle looked very familiar.

As usual, the Type 1 had only minor revisions for the new model year starting in August 1972. They included new front seats, larger more visible taillights, 5-mile-per-hour bumpers, a computer diagnosis socket, better cold-start performance, brighter headlights, and a 24-month/24,000-mile warranty.

Volkswagen built some factory-customized versions of the Beetle and Super Beetle for certain markets. A run of 2,500 Beetle GTs were made for the British market and German buyers were offered 3,500 Beetles with an S version of a 1,600cc engine, 5½-inch wheels, special 175/70SR15 radial tires, Saturn Yellow body finish with black front and rear lids, a racing-type steering wheel, fully

BELOW: "The 1973 Super Beetle's new 'bubble' windshield sticks out like a 1957 Firesweep Plymouth," said *Motor Trend*. This Volkswagen model also featured improved ventilation and non-glare windshield wipers. *Archives/TEN: The Enthusiast Network Magazines, LLC*

NEXT PAGE: Volkswagen's 1973 sales brochure gave potential buyers the features and specifications of the Super Beetle sedan and then announced, "Now that you know what we put into it, here's what you can put into it."

Now that you know what we put into it, here's what you can put into it.

LEFT: Perhaps the easiest way to distinguish the 1973 Volkswagen Beetle from previous models was by the change to this type of taillight. *Motor Trend* thought they were large enough to use on a Mack truck. *Archives/TEN: The Enthusiast Network Magazines, LLC*

RIGHT: The windshield for a 1973 Super Beetle was 42 percent larger than before. *Motor Trend* said it was large enough to wrap around Senior Editor Eric Dahlquist. *Archives/TEN: The Enthusiast Network Magazines, LLC*

OPPOSITE: This page from the 1973 Volkswagen sales catalog emphasized the Beetle's traditional selling points, such as easy parking, water tightness, fuel economy, an outstanding and rugged suspension, and great utility use.

reclining sports seats, and a heated rear window for just $240 extra.

The standard 1973 Super Beetle had a new curved, panoramic windshield with greater glass area and an improved flow-through ventilation system. To go along with the new wraparound windshield was a redesigned safety dashboard with added padding and relocated gauges that appeared to be adaptable to airbags. It also had new, face-level blower-assisted air vents. Like all 1973 Beetles, the Super Beetle featured black windshield-wiper arms, larger "elephant's feet" taillights designed especially to meet US safety standards, and 5-mile-per-hour bumpers. The new front seats could be adjusted seventy-seven ways!

Improved intake-air preheating was intended to deliver quicker starts in cold weather. Other improvements included the computer diagnosis socket, brighter headlights, and a 24-month/24,000-mile guarantee. For better engine cooling, the rear deck lid was redesigned and now had four stacks of horizontal louvers spread across the engine cover just above the license plate light. The outer stacks had seven louvers and the inner ones had six. A row of forty-two short vertical louvers ran across the panel that the engine cover was hinged to.

John Pashdag tested the Super Beetle Convertible in the May 1973 issue of *Motor Trend*. He described the latest ragtop as "a genuine hot rod compared to the earlier convertibles" and pointed out the car's 17.9-second 0-to-60 time was much better than the 22.9 seconds that the 1971

Volkswagen Cabriolet took. He also noted that the handling and braking of the Super Beetle were improved.

A limited-edition 1303 Super Beetle Sports Bug was featured in *Motor Trend*'s June 1973 issue. Costing $250 more than a Super Beetle sedan, it included distinctive red and black stripes around the car and tapered tailpipe tips. The trim, door handles, wipers, and bumpers were matte black. Five-and-a-half-inch-diameter silver Lemmertz GT wheels with radial tires were supplied. The Sport Bug sales catalog showed black headlamp doors, but some cars had chrome ones. Inside were sports bucket seats, a leather sports steering wheel, and a leather gearshift knob. The Sports Bug had a $2,669 port-of-entry price.

The 1973 Volkswagen lineup consisted of the Beetle, the Karmann Ghia, the Fastback/Squareback models, the Super Beetle, the 412 (an updated 411), and the venerable Bus. *Archives/TEN: The Enthusiast Network Magazines, LLC*

1974

Ten years earlier Bob Dylan had sung "Times They Are A-Changin'" and, in 1974, Volkswagen management was likely to agree. Annual worldwide sales were under a million units for the first time since 1967. Panic was setting in.

Stuart Perkins, president, and Alexander E. Breckwoldt, vice president, continued at the helm of Volkswagen US and again saw declining US sales. In fact, they saw the largest (9.3 percent) decline since 1964. US sales were a relatively miserable 243,664 Type 1 models, of which most were Beetles and Super Beetles, since Karmann Ghias trickled out of the factory.

Even with tourist deliveries, Volkswagen moved just 336,257 vehicles in America during 1974. Total dealer sales were only 334,515 units. Surprisingly, though, the number of dealers rose from 1,194 at the start of 1974 to 1,201 by the start of 1975. Volkswagen knew that

TOP: Featured in *Motor Trend* in 1974 were (left to right) Rolls-Royce, 1940 Ford Woody, and 1939 Ford sedan restyling packages designed to fit the Volkswagen Beetle. *Archives/TEN: The Enthusiast Network Magazines, LLC*

BOTTOM: This Volkswagen modified with the 1940 Ford Woody body kit also has a rear-mounted "continental" tire and "gangster" whitewalls. All three kits were available in the Volkswagen aftermarket. *Archives/TEN: The Enthusiast Network Magazines, LLC*

BEETLES & SUPER BEETLES FACTS

▌▐ In 1971, Volkswagen began work on a so-called safety car that *Motor Trend* dubbed the "Safety Bug."

▌▐ The "Books" column in the February 1973 issue of *Motor Trend* reviewed "Is Your Volkswagen a Sex Symbol?"—a new book by Dr. Jean Rosenbaum published by Hawthorn Books.

▌▐ A group in Paris, France, voted the 1973 Volkswagen Cabriolet "Most Snobbish Car of the Year."

▌▐ Eric Dahlquist wrote an article entitled "Factory Tour: The Building of the People's Car" in the July 1973 issue of *Motor Trend*. It touched on VW history, but focused mostly on the then-modern operation of the Wolfsburg plant. "Every worker in America ought to just get a picture of what he's up against," suggested Dahlquist.

▌▐ In July 1973 issue, *Motor Trend* selected the Volkswagen to be among its automotive Hall of Fame nominees. "The VW somehow symbolized a return to traditional values—a movement triggered to lessor and major degrees by clever advertising, outstanding dealer service and solid craftsmanship," said the magazine.

▌▐ During 1973, VW ran an advertisement headlined "They got the bug again." It featured testimonials from previous Beetle owners who switched to other cars and came back to the Bug for its economy and dependability.

▌▐ A special Beetle that did 0-to-60 miles per hour in 7.2 seconds and had a top speed of 130 miles per hour was featured in the March 1974 issue of *Road Test* magazine. The VW Nordstadt was made by a German tuner company and required 2,000 hours of labor to create. The car used a VW/Porsche 914 chassis and a 2,687cc 210-horsepower flat-six Carrera engine. It carried a base price of $23,000.

▌▐ On the cover of the 1974 Beetle sales catalog was a red car floating in the ocean. "The VW Beetles. Built better than ever" was the sales pitch.

if it had more stores in the States, it could eventually sell more of the new models that were coming.

The Beetle was still the most popular Volkswagen, but this was the final year for the original Type 1. The new Volkswagen Rabbit was expected to soon pass it by and become the company's sales leader. Stuart Perkins predicted that he would sell 130,000 to 140,000 Rabbits in 1975 compared to 100,000 Beetles. The 1974 Beetle had energy-absorbing bumpers, new wheels, and a seatbelt-ignition interlock system. The front seat headrests were smaller than in 1973.

The Super Beetle received a number of changes. In the United States, new federal safety standard went into effect mandating that cars sold in the country had to be able to withstand a 5-mile-per-hour front end impact and a 2½-mile-per-hour rear end impact without suffering injury-causing damage. To meet these regulations, Volkswagen added "self-restoring energy absorbing bumpers." What amounted to shock absorbers were added to heavier steel bumpers to meet the rules.

An ignition interlock was another new feature designed to force front seat occupants to buckle up. For better handling during panic stops, the Super Beetle used a new kingpin angle. And Volkswagen finally adopted an AC alternator. Also new in the engine compartment was a cylinder head made of a better alloy.

Road Test magazine (April 1974) said that the Super Beetle "had a heavy feeling, sits high and gives a cramped feeling to one used to more spacious cars. (The) chair-high seats might be right for some. Performance is not startling." The magazine noted that the only instrument was a large, center speedometer. The fuel gauge was inside the one circular dial. The seats were high and firm. There was little room for the driver's left foot and not much rear legroom.

The test driver noted a blind spot to the left, but good vision to the rear. The steering was hard. The car was subject to crosswinds and gave a choppy, bouncy ride. *Road Test* said riders could feel the road surfaces. The magazine did admit that the car had "a good performance feel" and advised that the brakes worked well. It had a high overall noise level, but only light wind noise was heard. The Super Beetle was rated seventh among nine imports for fuel economy.

To sell Beetles, more and more special edition packages were created. One of these was the 1974 Sun Bug assortment that could be added to sedans or cabriolets. Sun Bugs had a Hellas Metallic Gold finish and lots of other extras, such as silver sport wheels, a sedan sunroof, a Kamei tunnel console, and wood dash trim. Nut Brown upholstery was used inside. There was a Sun Bug gearshift knob logo and a logo intended for dealer installation on the engine cover.

This year 904,005 Volkswagen passenger cars were built worldwide, down about 51,000 from 1974. In the United States, with a mere 268,751 deliveries, Volkswagen relinquished its first place in US imported car sales to Toyota, which had 278,103 deliveries. The German automaker's US sales included 92,037 Type 1 models, which now meant the same as 92,037 Super Beetles. Total sales by 1,201 US dealers, which did not include tourist deliveries, were 267,730 units. That meant 1,021 tourist deliveries were made. Volkswagen's sales slid downhill very quickly in the second half of 1975 as a result of pressure from labor, financial, and political problems in Germany.

Total worldwide Beetle sales for 1975 came in at nearly half what they had been, with only 441,116 customers buying them. Management changes were happening and soon Toni Schmücker took over as chairman of Volkswagen in Germany. One of his first moves was to cut the Beetle line back to the Super Beetle Cabriolet Convertible and one Standard Beetle Sedan for the world market.

A Bosch L-Jetronic electronic fuel-injection system replaced the

Updating a theme used earlier in 1970, Volkswagen pictured a 1949 Beetle and a current Beetle in its 1975 catalog and asked if people could spot the 30,000 changes made to the car over twenty-six years.

We've been making the Volkswagen long enough to know better.

Take a look at the 1949 Volkswagen. Now take a look at the 1975 model. The one on the right. If you can spot the nearly 30,000 changes we've made, you're good. And if you can't, don't feel bad. That's the way we like it.

Way back when we first started making the Volkswagen, we designed it not necessarily to look good, but to run good.

So we didn't have to bend ourselves out of shape bending last year's car into this year's shape.

In fact, it was precisely because we didn't force ourselves to make changes that we could spend more time hunting up what really had to be changed.

So, over the years, we've increased the life of the car and the number of horses that drive it. In fact, though today's Beetle isn't the fastest animal in the world, it's certainly no snail.

We've improved the braking and then improved the improvements.

We've added another synchromesh speed to our transmission, bringing it to a grand total of four.

Maybe we don't make much noise about how quiet our car now rides, but listen closely sometime.

While we've gotten rid of excess baggage, we've also added room for your baggage. And for legs. And heads.

The seats in a Volkswagen are contoured to hug your contours in cornering.

And here's something else you'll have to take sitting down. Our inertia reel seat belts. They'll allow you complete freedom of movement except when you shouldn't be moving freely. That's when they spring into action, locking you securely in place.

We've added dash to the dash. Lights have grown and doors have grown easier to open and close. Windows have grown larger. And clearer. Thanks to our optional electrical defrosting system.

Today, you can even get a Beetle without a clutch pedal and get what you got from a Beetle with one. Great gas mileage.

What's more, things have happened under the hood we couldn't even begin to tell you about. Except to tell you it's made for a better car.

We've even added a VW to the hub caps. As if you couldn't tell it's a VW by the fact that it always looks the same.

Even though we make about 1,000 changes a year.

Super Beetle's carburetor this year. To broadcast the change, a Fuel Injection logo was affixed to the engine cover in place of the previous Volkswagen script. The computerized fuel-injection system upped gas mileage from 25 to 33 miles per gallon, but also required the use of unleaded fuel that the computer was programmed for.

Among other improvements to the 1975 Super Beetles was the addition of rack-and-pinion steering. The rear suspension was reworked with geometry improvements. A new AS21 aluminum alloy was used in the construction of the engine case, and there was now only one tailpipe for the first time since the 1955 Beetle. Federal Clean Air regulations spurred other product changes. A catalytic converter was a mandatory addition to cars sold in the California market.

Of course, there was a special edition package. This year it was called the La Grande Bug. "You don't drive in it, you arrive in it," said the sales brochure copy. The accompanying art had a photo of a chauffeur outside a mansion with a pair of La Grande Bug Beetles. One of the cars had a sliding steel sunroof.

This Nepal Orange 1975 convertible has the Formula Vee dealer option conversion kit that included 4.5 x 15 Sprinster Star sports wheels, overriders on Euro bumpers, Super Vee stripes, a Super Vee deck lid badge, and a tunnel tray.

Our convertible. Room with a view.

It may come as a surprise to you to learn that the solid, practical, hard-headed Volkswagen can also lose its head.

At the drop of a hat.

Introducing the 1975 Volkswagen Convertible. With an easy to open flip top that's vinyl on top. Which means it's waterproof and windproof, but not cleaning proof.

An inch thick middle layer of insulation separates the top of the top from the bottom of the top, which is handsome leatherette. So when you're not getting a view of the sky above, at least you're not getting a view of the struts and crossbars below.

The rear window also offers some clear advantages. Because it's glass, it won't yellow with age or split from the cold. It's also been raised, lowered and widened. So not only can you see better, you can see higher, lower, and wider.

But in addition to being a convertible, the Beetle Convertible, being a Beetle, offers you the scrupulous inspections, the attention to detail, the economy and the guarantee that you'd get in a Beetle.

Plus something that'll give your gas mileage a shot in the arm — electronic fuel injection — and something that'll make it easier on your arm — rack and pinion steering.

All of which means that even while you're riding around with your nose in the air, at least your head's not in the clouds.

The Classic Volkswagen.

1976

Volkswagen had total worldwide sales of about $10,711,500,000 in 1976 and net earnings of $502,000,000. Net earnings in Germany were $1,436,000 and in the United States $730,000. Worldwide production rose to 1,436,000 units. Total factory sales came to 1,561,506 cars. Volkswagen had 183,000 workers.

Volkswagen sales in the United States slid 24.5 percent in 1976. Worse yet, it marked the sixth straight year of declines for the former King of the Imports. Most of the loss was due to declining sales of the Beetle, which fell 70.6 percent. The German automaker's US sales included just 27,009 Beetles.

Volkswagen now owned a 13.56 percent share of the imported-car market. Toyota had 23.24 percent and Datsun had 18.10 percent. By the beginning of 1977, the factory dealer count would fall to 1,052 from 1,175.

Sporty new wheels were used on the 1976 Beetle. A rear window defogger was also installed. The Super Beetle Cabriolet was one of the only convertibles offered in America in this era, so demand for it took a leap. Coachbuilder Karmann in Osnabrück, Germany, built Cabriolet bodies. Volkswagen asked that firm to up its output from thirty-three to fifty bodies daily.

As for special editions, this was the year of the Triple White Super Beetle Convertible. It had Alpine white finish, opal-white upholstery, and a white convertible top. US ragtop sales increased by more than five thousand each year after 1974.

1977

The Beetle was nearly gone, the Rabbit grew in popularity, and Volkswagen continued importing the Scirocco, the Dasher, and the van or "Microbus." Sales climbed 29.4 percent in 1977, reversing a long seven-year decline. The US sales included 164,706 Rabbits, 25,857 Dashers, 26,108 Type 2 buses, 24,786 Sciroccos, 2,230 Tourist Deliveries, and just 19,245 Type 1 Beetles. Total dealer sales (not including tourist deliveries) stood at just 260,702 units.

The German automaker sold 262,932 vehicles to Americans during 1977. The company was still third overall in imported car sales with a 12.6 percent market share versus 23.9 percent for Toyota and 18.8 percent for Datsun.

Volkswagenwerk AG had total worldwide sales of $12,076,000,000 in 1977 and net earnings of $209,500,000. Net earnings in Germany were about $1,561,000 and in the United States about $658,000. Worldwide production was counted at 2,219,000 units and total factory sales came to 1,687,053 vehicles.

This was the Beetle sedan's last year in the US market. As *Ward's Automotive Yearbook 1978* put it, "This year also marked the demise of the Beetle, the familiar car that started off the import boom in the 1950s and 1960s." The company had built 19.3 million Beetles since the model was first marketed in 1945 and 5 million were sold in the United States since it first came to the country in 1949. The convertible was still in production in 1978.

This year was thus one of historic change for the company that was, in many American minds, the archtypical importer. Probably more than any other car, the Beetle established overseas makes as basically reliable, economical transportation that provided a bit of style with their austerity. Change had overcome the Beetle, however, as the rising price of the Deutsche Mark pushed its price ever upward. Its unusual design, with its air-cooled, rear-mounted engine, also gave the car some tricky handling characteristics, and it was not as economical as newer designs.

A Champagne Edition Super Beetle Cabriolet was Volkswagen's latest special edition package. It was finished in Alpine white and came with opal-white upholstery. The convertible top was ivory colored. A gold stripe appeared on the lower body perimeter. The Champagne Edition also had a rosewood dash insert, sports wheels, and white sidewall tires. These late Super Beetle Convertibles featured a long list of standard equipment, and in 1977 a rear window defroster and adjustable front headrests were added to the list. Also a good number of options and accessories could be dealer installed.

OPPOSITE: Sporty new wheels were used on the 1976 Beetle. A rear-window defogger was also installed. The Super Beetle Cabriolet was one of the only convertibles offered in America in this era, so demand for it took a leap.

NEXT PAGE: This 1977 catalog art showed a red Super Beetle Convertible and pictures of ten different options owners could have, from mag-style wheel covers to a lockable ski rack.

It leaves many

This year, Volkswagen offers, among other options, the sun, the moon, and the stars. Which come your way courtesy of the 1977 Beetle Convertible.

Ours is the most inexpensive 4-seater convertible you can find today. But that doesn't mean we cut any corners. Take our top, for example. On the outside it's top-quality vinyl, windproof, waterproof and easy to clean. On the inside it's insulated and fully upholstered. (Even the metal braces are covered.) It flips up and down with the flick of a wrist. (There are

ptions open to you.

no complicated motorized devices to get stuck when you're stuck in a rainstorm.)

In addition, the rear window is a real window. Made of glass, not plastic.

And because it's glass, we're able to offer an electric rear window defogger as standard equipment—something no other convertible has.

Underneath it all, the same dependable and economical Volkswagen you get when you buy a regular Beetle. Which means that this year, you can definitely afford not to have a roof over your head.

You can also afford to choose from many accessories. Like mag-type wheel covers (1). Floor mats (2). Fog lamps and a front spoiler (3).

Bumper overriders (4). Vent shades (5). Even a tunnel console and a sports gearshift lever (8).

A luggage rack (6), lockable ski rack (10) or trailer hitch (7) can help you bear a heavy load.

An AM/FM radio (9) is a sound investment. As is optional air conditioning (9).

After all, when you own an economy car like the Beetle, you can afford the luxury of adding on to it.

1971

VOLKSWAGEN BEETLE

PAINT COLORS

12D Shantung Yellow
20D Clementine Orange
31F Berian Red
41 Black
50D Sapphire Blue
54D Marine Blue
60D Elm Green

66B Deep Sea Green
90D Pastel White
91D Kansas Beige
96D Silver Metallic
96E Gemini Metallic (blue)
97D Colorado Metallic (red)

MODEL AVAILABILITY	2-door Sedan ($1,780)
	2-door Sunroof Sedan ($1,989)
	2-door Cabriolet Convertible ($2,299)
SERIAL NUMBERS	1112000001–1113200000
WHEELBASE	94.5 inches
LENGTH	158.6 inches
WIDTH	61.0 inches
HEIGHT	(sedan) 59.1 inches
WEIGHT	(sedan) 1,786 lbs.; (Cabriolet) 1,896 lbs.
TREAD	(front/rear) 51.6/53.1 inches
TIRES	(sedan) 5.60 x 15 tubeless
BRAKES	hydraulic, front/rear drum
WHEELS	disk-type with drop-center rim 4J x 15
FUEL TANK	10.6 gallons
FRONT SUSPENSION	Independent suspension of both wheels through equal upper and lower trailing arms, 2 transverse torsion bars protected in tubes and an anti-sway bar. Double-acting telescopic shock absorbers.
REAR SUSPENSION	Independent suspension of wheels through swing-axle shafts with trailing arms; one torsion bar on each side mounted and protected in transverse tube. Double-acting telescopic shock absorbers.
STEERING	worm and roller steering and divided tie rod; hydraulic steering damper; 2.6 turns of steering wheel lock to lock
ENGINE	1,585cc 57-hp horizontally opposed four-cylinder, overhead valve, air cooled, light alloy block and head, finned cylinders with cast-iron liners
TRANSMISSION	four-speed manual (full synchro)
FINAL DRIVE RATIO	4.125:1

1971

VOLKSWAGEN SUPER BEETLE

PAINT COLORS

12D Shantung Yellow
20D Clementine Orange
31F Berian Red
41 Black
50D Sapphire Blue
54D Marine Blue
60D Elm Green

66B Deep Sea Green
90D Pastel White
91D Kansas Beige
96D Silver Metallic
96E Gemini Metallic (blue)
97D Colorado Metallic (red)
11E Lemon Yellow

MODEL AVAILABILITY	2-door Sedan ($1,899)
SERIAL NUMBERS	1112000001–1113200000
WHEELBASE	95.3 inches
LENGTH	161.8 inches
WIDTH	62.3 inches
HEIGHT	(sedan) 59.1 inches
WEIGHT	(sedan) 1,874 lbs.
TREAD	(front/rear) 54.3/53.1 inches
TIRES	(sedan) 5.60 x 15 tubeless
BRAKES	hydraulic, front/rear drum
WHEELS	disk-type with drop-center rim 4J x 15
FUEL TANK	10.6 gallons
FRONT SUSPENSION	MacPherson struts with coil springs
REAR SUSPENSION	swing axles with trailing arms and torsion bars
STEERING	worm and sector
ENGINE	1,585cc 60-hp horizontally opposed four-cylinder, overhead valve, air cooled, light alloy block and head, finned cylinders with cast-iron liners
TRANSMISSION	four-speed manual (full synchro)
FINAL DRIVE RATIO	spiral bevel

1972

VOLKSWAGEN BEETLE

PAINT COLORS

10B Texas Yellow	**90D** Pastel White
20B Brilliant Orange	**91D** Kansas Beige
30B Kasan Red	**95B** Turquoise Metallic
41 Black	**96D** Silver Metallic
51B Gentian Blue	**96E** Gemini Metallic (blue)
54D Marina Blue	**97D** Colorado Metallic (red)
61B Sumatra Green	

MODEL AVAILABILITY	Deluxe 2-door Sedan ($1,780)
	Deluxe 2-door Sunroof Sedan ($1,999)
SERIAL NUMBERS	1112000001–1113200000
WHEELBASE	94.5 inches
LENGTH	158.6 inches
WIDTH	61.0 inches
HEIGHT	(sedan) 59.1 inches
WEIGHT	(sedan) 1,786 lbs.; (Cabriolet) 1,896 lbs.
TREAD	(front/rear) 51.6/53.1 inches
TIRES	(sedan) 5.60 x 15 tubeless
BRAKES	hydraulic, front/rear drum
WHEELS	disk-type with drop-center rim 4J x 15
FUEL TANK	10.6 gallons
FRONT SUSPENSION	Independent suspension of both wheels through equal upper and lower trailing arms, 2 transverse torsion bars protected in tubes, and an anti-sway bar. Double-acting telescopic shock absorbers.
REAR SUSPENSION	Independent suspension of wheels through swing-axle shafts with trailing arms; one torsion bar on each side mounted and protected in transverse tube. Double-acting telescopic shock absorbers.
STEERING	worm and roller steering and divided tie rod; hydraulic steering damper; 2.6 turns of steering wheel lock to lock
ENGINE	1,585cc 57-hp horizontally opposed four-cylinder, overhead valve, air cooled, light alloy block and head, finned cylinders with cast-iron liners
TRANSMISSION	four-speed manual (full synchro)
FINAL DRIVE RATIO	4.125:1

1972

VOLKSWAGEN SUPER BEETLE

PAINT COLORS

10B Texas Yellow	**95B** Turquoise Metallic
20B Brilliant Orange	**96D** Silver Metallic
30B Kasan Red	**96E** Gemini Metallic (blue)
41 Black	**96M** Marathon Metallic (blue)
51B Gentian Blue	**97D** Colorado Metallic (red)
54D Marina Blue	**13M** Saturn Yellow
61B Sumatra Green	**21E** Blood Orange
90D Pastel White	**63K** Willow Green
91D Kansas Beige	

MODEL AVAILABILITY	2-door Sedan ($2,159)
	2-door Cabriolet Convertible ($2,599)
SERIAL NUMBERS	1112000001–1113200000
WHEELBASE	95.3 inches
LENGTH	161.8 inches
WIDTH	62.3 inches
HEIGHT	(sedan) 59.1 inches
WEIGHT	(sedan) 1,874 lbs.; (Cabriolet) 1,896 lbs.
TREAD	(front/rear) 54.3/53.1 inches
TIRES	(sedan) 5.60 x 15 tubeless
BRAKES	hydraulic, front/rear drum
WHEELS	disk-type with drop-center rim 4J x 15
FUEL TANK	10.6 gallons
FRONT SUSPENSION	MacPherson struts with coil springs
REAR SUSPENSION	swing axles with trailing arms and torsion bars
STEERING	worm and sector
ENGINE	1,585cc 60-hp horizontally opposed four-cylinder, overhead valve, air cooled, light alloy block and head, finned cylinders with cast-iron liners
TRANSMISSION	four-speed manual (full synchro)
FINAL DRIVE RATIO	spiral bevel

1973

VOLKSWAGEN BEETLE

PAINT COLORS

10B Texas Yellow	**91D** Kansas Beige
20B Brilliant Orange	**95B** Turquoise Metallic
30B Kasan Red	**96B** Alaska Metallic (blue)
41 Black	**96M** Marathon Metallic (blue)
52B Biscay Blue	
54D Marina Blue	**98A** Maya Metallic (brown)
61B Sumatra Green	**21E** Blood Orange
90D Pastel White	**65K** Ravenna Green

MODEL AVAILABILITY	Deluxe 2-door Sedan ($1,780)
	Deluxe 2-door Sunroof Sedan ($2,299)
STARTING SERIAL NUMBER	(Beetle) 1132000001
WHEELBASE	94.5 inches
LENGTH	159.8 inches
WIDTH	61.0 inches
HEIGHT	(sedan) 59.1 inches
WEIGHT	(sedan) 1,742 lbs.
TREAD	(front/rear) 51.6/53.1 inches
TIRES	(sedan) 6.00 x 15L
BRAKES	hydraulic, front/rear drum
WHEELS	disk-type with drop-center rim 4J x 15
FUEL TANK	10.6 gallons
FRONT SUSPENSION	Independent suspension of both wheels through equal upper and lower trailing arms, 2 transverse torsion bars protected in tubes and an anti-sway bar. Double-acting telescopic shock absorbers.
REAR SUSPENSION	Independent suspension of wheels through swing-axle shafts with trailing arms; one torsion bar on each side mounted and protected in transverse tube. Double-acting telescopic shock absorbers.
STEERING	worm and roller steering and divided tie rod; hydraulic steering damper; 2.6 turns of steering wheel lock to lock
ENGINE	1,585cc 46-hp horizontally opposed four-cylinder, overhead valve, air cooled, light alloy block and head, finned cylinders with cast-iron liners
TRANSMISSION	four-speed manual (full synchro)
FINAL DRIVE RATIO	4.125:1

1973

VOLKSWAGEN SUPER BEETLE

PAINT COLORS

10B Texas Yellow	**91D** Kansas Beige
20B Brilliant Orange	**95B** Turquoise Metallic
30B Kasan Red	**96B** Alaska Metallic (blue)
41 Black	**96M** Marathon Metallic (blue)
52B Biscay Blue	
54D Marina Blue	**98A** Maya Metallic (brown)
61B Sumatra Green	**21E** Blood Orange
90D Pastel White	**13M** Saturn Yellow
	65K Ravenna Green

MODEL AVAILABILITY	2-door Sedan ($2,499)
	2-door Convertible ($3,050)
STARTING SERIAL NUMBER	(Super Beetle) 1332000001
	(Convertible) 1532000001
WHEELBASE	95.3 inches
LENGTH	161.8 inches
WIDTH	62.4 inches
HEIGHT	(sedan) 59.1 inches
WEIGHT	(sedan) 1,911 lbs.; (Cabriolet) 1,979 lbs.
TREAD	(front/rear) 54.6/53.6 inches
TIRES	(sedan) 5.60 x 15 tubeless (6.00 x 15 Cabriolet)
BRAKES	hydraulic, front/rear drum
WHEELS	disk-type with drop-center rim 4J x 15
FUEL TANK	10.6 gallons
FRONT SUSPENSION	MacPherson struts with coil springs
REAR SUSPENSION	swing axles with trailing arms and torsion bars
STEERING	Recirculating ball
ENGINE	1,585cc 60-hp horizontally opposed four-cylinder, overhead valve, air cooled, light alloy block and head, finned cylinders with cast-iron liners
TRANSMISSION	four-speed manual (full synchro)
FINAL DRIVE RATIO	spiral bevel

1974

VOLKSWAGEN BEETLE

PAINT COLORS

- **10A** Rallye Yellow
- **20B** Brilliant Orange
- **31A** Senegal Red
- **41** Black
- **54D** Marina Blue
- **60A** Tropical Green
- **61A** Cliff Green
- **80Z** Sahara Beige
- **91Z** Atlas White
- **95C** Moss Metallic (green)
- **96M** Marathon Metallic (blue)
- **96B** Alaska Metallic (blue)
- **98C** Helias Metallic (beige)

MODEL AVAILABILITY	2-door Sedan ($2,625)
SERIAL NUMBERS	1112000001–1113200000
WHEELBASE	94.5 inches
LENGTH	163.4 inches
WIDTH	61.0 inches
HEIGHT	(sedan) 59.1 inches
WEIGHT	(sedan) 1,831 lbs.
TREAD	(front/rear) 51.6/53.1 inches
TIRES	(sedan) 6.00 x 15L
BRAKES	hydraulic, front/rear drum
WHEELS	disk-type with drop-center rim 4J x 15
FUEL TANK	10.6 gallons
FRONT SUSPENSION	Independent suspension of both wheels through equal upper and lower trailing arms, 2 transverse torsion bars protected in tubes and an anti-sway bar. Double-acting telescopic shock absorbers.
REAR SUSPENSION	Independent suspension of wheels through swing-axle shafts with trailing arms; one torsion bar on each side mounted and protected in transverse tube. Double-acting telescopic shock absorbers.
STEERING	worm and roller steering and divided tie rod; hydraulic steering damper; 2.6 turns of steering wheel lock to lock
ENGINE	1,585cc 46-hp horizontally opposed four-cylinder, overhead valve, air cooled, light alloy block and head, finned cylinders with cast-iron liners
TRANSMISSION	four-speed manual (full synchro)
FINAL DRIVE RATIO	4.125:1

1974

VOLKSWAGEN SUPER BEETLE

PAINT COLORS

- **10A** Rallye Yellow
- **20B** Brilliant Orange
- **31A** Senegal Red
- **41** Black
- **54D** Marina Blue
- **60A** Tropical Green
- **61A** Cliff Green
- **80Z** Sahara Beige
- **91Z** Atlas White
- **95C** Moss Metallic (green)
- **96M** Marathon Metallic (blue)
- **96B** Alaska Metallic (blue)
- **98C** Helias Metallic (beige)
- **31M** Ibiza Red
- **95M** Ontario Metallic (blue)
- **99M** Ischia Metallic (green)
- **97A** Diamond Silver Metallic
- **32K** Phoenix Red

MODEL AVAILABILITY	2-door Sedan ($2,849)
	2-door Cabriolet ($3,475)
SERIAL NUMBERS	1112000001–1113200000
WHEELBASE	95.3 inches
LENGTH	164.8 inches
WIDTH	52.3 inches
HEIGHT	(sedan) 59.1 inches
WEIGHT	(sedan) 1,955 lbs.; (Cabriolet) 2,043 lbs.
TREAD	(front/rear) 54.9/53.2 inches
TIRES	(sedan) 6.00L x 15
BRAKES	hydraulic, front/rear drum
WHEELS	disk-type with drop-center rim 4J x 15
FUEL TANK	10.6 gallons
FRONT SUSPENSION	MacPherson struts with coil springs
REAR SUSPENSION	swing axles with trailing arms and torsion bars
STEERING	worm and sector
ENGINE	1,585cc 60-hp horizontally opposed four-cylinder, overhead valve, air cooled, light alloy block and head, finned cylinders with cast-iron liners
TRANSMISSION	four-speed manual (full synchro)
FINAL DRIVE RATIO	spiral bevel

VOLKSWAGEN BEETLE

91Z Atlas White		**61A** Cliff Green	
20A Marino Yellow		**32K** Phoenix Red	
13H Ceylon Beige		**96M** Marathon Metallic (blue)	
51C Miami Blue		**97B** Acona Metallic (blue)	
61H Lofoten Green		**98C** Hellas Metallic (bege)	
31A Senegal Red		**98B** Viper Green Metallic	
41 Black		**28N** Orange	
10A Rallye Yellow			

MODEL AVAILABILITY	Deluxe 2-door Sedan ($2,999)
	2-door Cabriolet Convertible ($2,299)
SERIAL NUMBERS	(Sedan) 1152000001–1152600000
WHEELBASE	94.5 inches
LENGTH	158.6 inches
WIDTH	61.0 inches
HEIGHT	(sedan) 59.1 inches
WEIGHT	(sedan) 1,831 lbs.
TREAD	(front/rear) 51.6/53.1 inches
TIRES	(sedan) 600L x 15
BRAKES	hydraulic, front/rear drum
WHEELS	disk-type with drop-center rim 4J x 15
FUEL TANK	10.6 gallons
FRONT SUSPENSION	Independent suspension of both wheels through equal upper and lower trailing arms, 2 transverse torsion bars protected in tubes, and an anti-sway bar. Double-acting telescopic shock absorbers.
REAR SUSPENSION	Independent suspension of wheels through swing-axle shafts with trailing arms; one torsion bar on each side mounted and protected in transverse tube. Double-acting telescopic shock absorbers.
STEERING	worm and roller steering and divided tie rod; hydraulic steering damper; 2.6 turns of steering wheel lock to lock
ENGINE	1,585cc 48-hp horizontally opposed four-cylinder, overhead valve, air cooled, light alloy block and head, finned cylinders with cast-iron liners
TRANSMISSION	four-speed manual (full synchro)
FINAL DRIVE RATIO	4.125:1

VOLKSWAGEN SUPER BEETLE SEDAN

PAINT COLORS

91Z Atlas White	**10A** Rallye Yellow
20A Marino Yellow	**61A** Cliff Green
13H Ceylon Beige	**32K** Phoenix Red
51C Miami Blue	**96M** Marathon Metallic (blue)
61H Lofoten Green	**97B** Acona Metallic (blue)
31A Senegal Red	**98C** Hellas Metallic (bege)
41 Black	**98B** Viper Green Metallic

VOLKSWAGEN SUPER BEETLE CABRIOLET

PAINT COLORS

11D Berber Yellow	**41** Black
13K Sunshine Yellow	**50C** Lagoon Blue
20C Nepal Orange	**80E** Light Ivory
30C Malaga Red	**95K** Palma Metallic (green)
31M Ibiza Red	**97A** Diamond Silver Metallic
41 Black	**97B** Ancona Metallic (blue)

MODEL AVAILABILITY	2-door Sedan ($3,295)
	2-door Cabriolet ($3,595)
SERIAL NUMBERS	(Sedan) 1352000001–1352600000
	(Cabriolet) 15552000001–1552600000
WHEELBASE	95.3 inches
LENGTH	161.8 inches
WIDTH	52.3 inches
HEIGHT	(sedan) 59.1 inches
WEIGHT	(sedan) 1,831 lbs.; (Cabriolet) 1,955 lbs.
TREAD	(front/rear) 54.3/53.1 inches
TIRES	(sedan) 5.60 x 15 tubeless
BRAKES	hydraulic, front/rear drum
WHEELS	disk-type with drop-center rim 4J x 15
FUEL TANK	10.6 gallons
FRONT SUSPENSION	MacPherson struts with coil springs
REAR SUSPENSION	swing axles with trailing arms and torsion bars
STEERING	worm and sector
ENGINE	1,585cc 60-hp horizontally opposed four-cylinder, overhead valve, air cooled, light alloy block and head, finned cylinders with cast-iron liners
TRANSMISSION	four-speed manual (full synchro)
FINAL DRIVE RATIO	spiral bevel

1976

VOLKSWAGEN
SUPER BEETLE SEDAN

PAINT COLORS

91Z Atlas White	**10A** Rallye Yellow
20A Marino Yellow	**32K** Phoenix Red
61H Lofoten Green	**97A** Diamond Silver Metallic
57H Ozeanic Blue	**96N** Viper Green Metallic
31A Senegal Red	**99D** Topaz Metallic
041 Black	

VOLKSWAGEN
SUPER BEETLE CABRIOLET

PAINT COLORS

13K Sunshine Yellow	**50C** Lagoon Blue
20C Nepal Orange	**80E** Light Ivory
30C Malaga Red	**97A** Diamond Silver Metallic
31M Ibiza Red	**97B** Ancona Metallic (blue)
41 Black	**96N** Viper Green Metallic

MODEL AVAILABILITY	2-door Sedan ($3,499)
	2-door Cabriolet ($4,545)
SERIAL NUMBERS	(Sedan) 1162000001–1162200000
	(Cabriolet) 1562000001–1562200000
WHEELBASE	95.3 inches
LENGTH	161.8 inches
WIDTH	52.3 inches
HEIGHT	(sedan) 59.1 inches
WEIGHT	(sedan) 1,720 lbs.; (Cabriolet) 2,106 lbs.
TREAD	(front/rear) 54.3/53.1 inches
TIRES	(sedan) 5.60 x 15 tubeless
BRAKES	hydraulic, front/rear drum
WHEELS	disk-type with drop-center rim 4J x 15
FUEL TANK	10.6 gallons
FRONT SUSPENSION	MacPherson struts with coil springs
REAR SUSPENSION	swing axles with trailing arms and torsion bars
STEERING	worm and sector
ENGINE	1,585cc 60-hp horizontally opposed four-cylinder, overhead valve, air cooled, light alloy block and head, finned cylinders with cast-iron liners
TRANSMISSION	four-speed manual (full synchro)
FINAL DRIVE RATIO	spiral bevel

1977

VOLKSWAGEN
SUPER BEETLE SEDAN

PAINT COLORS

12A Panama Brown	**31B** Mars Red
13A Dakota Beige	**62A** Bali Green
32A Brocade Red	**95D** Bronze Metallic
41 Black	**96N** Viper Green Metallic
51C Miami Blue	**97A** Diamond Silver Metallic
63Y Manilla Green	**97F** Timor Brown Metallic
90A Polar White	**99F** Bahama Blue Metallic
11A Riyad Yellow	

VOLKSWAGEN
SUPER BEETLE CABRIOLET

PAINT COLORS

20A Marino Yellow	**96F** Brazill Brown Metallic
30C Malaga Red	**96N** Viper Green Metallic
41 Black	**97A** Diamond Silver Metallic
52K Barrier Blue	**97B** Acona Metallic
90A Polar White	**98F** Black Metallic
31B Mars Red	**90B** Alpine White

MODEL AVAILABILITY	2-door Sedan ($3,699)
	2-door Cabriolet ($4,799)
SERIAL NUMBERS	(Sedan) 1172000001–1173200000
	(Cabriolet) 1572000–1572200000
WHEELBASE	95.3 inches
LENGTH	161.8 inches
WIDTH	52.3 inches
HEIGHT	(sedan) 59.1 inches
WEIGHT	(sedan) 1,905 lbs.; (Cabriolet) 2,030 lbs.
TREAD	(front/rear) 54.3/53.1 inches
TIRES	(sedan) 5.60 x 15 tubeless
BRAKES	hydraulic, front/rear drum
WHEELS	disk-type with drop-center rim 4J x 15
FUEL TANK	10.6 gallons
FRONT SUSPENSION	MacPherson struts with coil springs
REAR SUSPENSION	swing axles with trailing arms and torsion bars
STEERING	worm and sector
ENGINE	1,585cc 60-hp horizontally opposed four-cylinder, overhead valve, air cooled, light alloy block and head, finned cylinders with cast-iron liners
TRANSMISSION	four-speed manual (full synchro)
FINAL DRIVE RATIO	spiral bevel

CHAPTER 7

CABRIOLETS & O-LAYS

In Germany, Volkswagen built 1,177,106 cars in 1978, but many of them were Golf/Rabbit, Dasher, and Scirocco models. The popularity of the air-cooled Beetle was at a low. However, the Type 2 air-cooled Transporter— affectionately known as the Volkswagen bus—was still holding its own for now. In fact, the air-cooled Transporter—redubbed the Vanagon—would survive for three more years after the Beetle disappeared from most VW factories in 1979.

On January 19, 1978, European production of the standard Beetle sedan ended. Production of Super Beetle Cabriolets at the Karmann factory in Osnabrück was projected to continue a few years. In the US, only the Super Beetle Cabriolet remained. *Archives/TEN: The Enthusiast Network Magazines, LLC*

In the United States, James W. McLernon took over as the new president of Volkswagen of America in 1978. Richard L. Mugg was vice president of the Volkswagen division. US sales for 1978 can be a little tricky to understand, since Rabbits made at a plant in Pennsylvania were not counted as imported cars. VW's imported-car sales were down 16.5 percent. Total US sales included 126,343 imported Rabbits, 23,017 domestically built Rabbits, 28,739 Dashers, 23,322 Type 2 buses, and 28,137 Sciroccos. Only 9,932 Type 1 Super Beetle Cabriolets were sold, excluding any purchased among 2,941 tourist deliveries. Total dealer sales were 219,414 units, but Super Beetles Cabriolets were rare.

The German automaker dropped to fourth place in United States imported car sales with a 10.9 percent market share versus 22.2 percent for Toyota, 17 percent for Datsun, and 13.8 percent for Honda. Volkswagen still had 1,058 US dealers at the start of 1978, but this dropped to 1,026 at the beginning of 1979.

Nevertheless, in spite of the declining popularity of the Beetle, there was an overall resurgence of the US imported car market and that meant added sales and a highly successful year for Volkswagen on a worldwide basis. The company recovered almost fully from the near bankruptcy of 1974 and 1975 and managed to pile up cash reserves of about $3 billion in fiscal 1978. With money in the bank, Volkswagen started looking for nonautomotive businesses to buy.

BELOW: In 1978, production of the Super Beetle Cabriolet, at the Karmann factory in Osnabrück, was expected to continue a few years. At Volkswagen dealerships in the United States, only Super Beetle Cabriolets were being sold as new cars.

OPPOSITE: Volkswagen stated that the 1978 Super Beetle Convertible was "one of the best Convertibles we've ever built." It delivered 30 mpg on the highway and 21 mpg around town.

THE SUN, THE MOON AND THE STARS
ARE YOURS TO ENJOY.

CONTROL 5 FUNCTIONS
FROM THE STEERING COLUMN.

LUXURIOUSLY UPHOLSTERED,
SPACIOUS SEATING.

THE ONLY SMALL FOUR-PASSENGER
CONVERTIBLE IN PRODUCTION TODAY.

On January 19, 1978, European production of the Standard Beetle Sedan closed out forever. No longer would the Volkswagen factory crank out "Love Bugs." Production of the Super Beetle Cabriolet at the Karmann factory in Osnabrück was projected to continue on for a few years. At Volkswagen dealerships in the United States, only Super Beetle Cabriolets remained for sale.

Car and Driver magazine declared that the top-down Beetle "can be one of the world's finest convertibles." The writer added, "Though terribly slow . . . the flat-out driving style required to keep it moving compensates for a lot of flaws." With so few weaknesses remaining, the writers suggested that the Beetle should be regarded "as an institution rather than an automobile."

"Once again, Volkswagen promises you the sun, the moon and the stars," boasted the sales catalog for the 1978 Super Beetle Cabriolet, but rumors were flying that the Beetle convertible would soon go the way of the Cadillac Eldorado ragtop. As happened in the case of some 1973–1976 US-made convertibles, such talk spurred customers to buy while they could. The Champagne edition was continued as the Champagne II and now featured a standard Blaupunkt AM/FM radio, a quartz clock, and a burled elm dashboard appliqué.

Of the 9,932 Super Beetle Cabriolets sold in the United States in 1978, all had a four-cylinder engine, a four-speed manual transmission, radial tires, reclining bucket seats, and a rear defogger. Steel wheels were on 30.7 percent.

1978 BEETLE CONVERTIBLE SPECIFICATIONS.

ENGINE:

	Type	Air-cooled, rear mounted
	Cylinders	4 cylinders, opposed
	Displacement	96.66 cubic inches (1584 cc)
	SAE Net HP	48 @ 4200 rpm
	Fuel/Air Supply	AFC fuel injection

TRANSMISSION & DIFFERENTIAL:

	Type	Fully synchronized, transaxle rear
	No. Speeds	4 forward, 1 reverse
	Final Drive	Rear wheel drive, double-jointed axles
	Clutch	Single disc, dry

CHASSIS & SUSPENSION:

	Frame	Semi-unitized body/chassis, platform with center tube
	Front Suspension	Independent coil/shock absorber struts negative steering roll radius
	Rear Suspension	Independent, torsion bars with trailing and diagonal arms
	Service Brake	Dual circuit, drums front and rear
	Parking Brake	Cable operated on rear wheels
	Rim Size	4½J x 15
	Tire Size	6.00 x 15
	Steering	Rack and pinion

ELECTRICAL SYSTEM:

	Rated Voltage	12 Volt, 50 Amp alternator
	Battery	12 Volt, 45 Amp/hour

DIMENSIONS:

	Wheelbase	94.5 inches
	Length	164.8 inches
	Width	62.4 inches
	Height (Unloaded)	59.1 inches
	Ground Clearance (Loaded)	5.9 inches
	Turning Circle	29.5 feet (curb to curb)

PERFORMANCE:

	Top Speed	80 mph
	Fuel Consumption*	Highway: 30 mpg City: 21 mpg

*Based on 1978 EPA estimated mileage with manual transmission. Your actual mileage may vary, depending on where and how you drive, your car's condition and optional equipment. Ask your local dealer for a free copy of the EPA/FEA Gas Mileage Guide for New Car Buyers.

Printed in U.S.A. 63-11-86010   Specifications subject to change without notice.

The specifications table for the 1978 Super Beetle Convertible didn't have much that was new on it. Of the 9,932 Super Beetle Cabriolets sold in the United States in 1978, all had a four-cylinder engine, a four-speed manual transmission, radial tires, reclining bucket seats, and a rear defogger.

The 1979 VW Beetle Convertible

The 1979 VW Beetle Convertible.

Treat yourself to one of life's little pleasures.

After 29 years, millions of Beetles, and countless improvements, the 1979 Convertible is still a very sensible way to flip your lid.

In fact, it's the only small four-passenger convertible in production today. And the only one that's built like a Beetle.

As you discover the sheer fun of owning and driving this sporty convertible, you'll also discover a dependable Bug underneath it all. With a bottom that's completely sealed with steel to keep out water, salt and dampness. And a body protected from the environment by three coats of paint.

The proven, 1.6 liter fuel injected engine delivers great performance. And according to E.P.A. estimates*, our Beetle Convertible delivers 30 mpg highway, 21 mpg city. So you can clip along with the sun on your face and fun in your heart, without getting clipped at the pump.

There's a top-quality top made of windproof, waterproof, easy-to-clean vinyl. And inside, it's fully insulated and upholstered to completely conceal the metal braces. The rear window, by the way, is a real window—glass embedded with electric heating elements to keep off snow and ice.

Go ahead. Raise the roof and let a little sunshine in.

1979 BEETLE CONVERTIBLE SPECIFICATIONS.

ENGINE:		
	Type	Air-cooled, rear mounted
	Cylinders	4 cylinders, opposed
	Displacement	96.66 cubic inches (1584 cc)
	SAE Net HP	48 @ 4200 rpm
	Fuel/Air Supply	AFC fuel injection
TRANSMISSION & DIFFERENTIAL:	Type	Fully synchronized transaxle, rear
	No. Speeds	4 forward, 1 reverse
	Final Drive	Rear wheel drive, double-jointed axles
	Clutch	Single disc, dry
CHASSIS & SUSPENSION:	Frame	Semi-unitized body/chassis, platform frame with center tube
	Front Suspension	Independent, coil/shock absorber struts, negative steering roll radius
	Rear Suspension	Independent, with trailing and diagonal arms, torsion bars
	Service Brake	Dual circuit, drums front and rear
	Parking Brake	Mechanical, operated on rear wheels
	Rim Size	4½Jx15 Sports wheel
	Tire Size	165 SR 15 White wall, steel belted
	Steering	Rack and pinion
ELECTRICAL SYSTEM:	Rated Voltage	12 Volt, 50 Amp alternator
	Battery	12 Volt, 45 Amp/hour
DIMENSIONS:	Wheelbase	94.5 inches
	Length	164.8 inches
	Width	62.4 inches
	Height (Unloaded)	59.1 inches
	Ground Clearance (Loaded)	5.9 inches
	Turning Circle	29.5 feet (curb to curb)
PERFORMANCE:	Top Speed	80 mph
	Fuel Mileage*	Highway: 30 mpg City: 21 mpg

*Based on 1978 EPA estimated mileage with manual transmission. Your actual mileage may vary, depending on where and how you drive, your car's condition and optional equipment. 1979 EPA data not available at press time. Ask your local dealer for a free copy of the 1979 EPA/FEA Gas Mileage Guide for New Car Buyers.

AUTHORIZED DEALER

TOP: The air-cooled Super Beetle Convertible reached the end of the road in 1979, at least in Europe and the United States. The 1,156,455 cars built in Germany this year did not include many Super Beetle ragtops like this one.

BOTTOM: Specifications for the last air-cooled Volkswagens made for the US market did not change a lot. The chart points out that the EPA mileage figures included are based on 1978 numbers, because 1979 figures were not yet available.

The air-cooled Beetle had reached the end of the road, at least in Europe and the United States. The 1,156,455 vehicles built by Volkswagen in Germany this year did not include many Super Beetle Cabriolets. In all of its formats—from prototype to movie star Herbie "Love Bug" to the Champagne Edition Super Beetle Cabriolet—the world's best-selling car lasted more than four decades and, of course, its history wasn't yet over. Production would continue in Mexico for another twenty-five years.

Contributing to the 1979 discontinuation was the fact that 1979 was a horrible year for the auto industry everywhere in the world. In Detroit, storage lots throughout the city were filled with new cars that no one wanted. At Volkswagen dealers throughout the United States, 1979 sales also plummeted. Statistically, Volkswagen's business fell from 219,224 vehicles in 1978 to 125,070 vehicles in 1979. The latter total included just 10,681 Type 1 Super Beetle Cabriolets.

Volkswagen dropped to sixth place in imported car sales in the United States with a 5.4 percent market share. Volkswagen's worldwide sales in the 1979 fiscal year amounted to about $11,195,000,000 and net income stood at $184,000,000. Worldwide production totaled up to 1,396,916 vehicles.

Industry observers were actually shocked when the Super Beetle Cabriolet returned to the American model lineup in 1979, since new federal safety and pollution guidelines that would virtually outlaw convertibles were expected. Implementation of the new regulations was delayed and that allowed the Beetle to put in a last curtain call before it left the stage.

"After 29 years, millions of Beetles, and countless improvements, the 1979 Convertible is still a very sensible way to flip your lid," said the copy on a single-page sales flyer for 1979 Super Beetles. For its last hurrah, the Super Beetle Cabriolet was marketed with every Champagne Edition feature as *standard* equipment. This was reflected on the very un-Beetle-like $6,495 window sticker.

A new special edition model, the Epilog Cabriolet, was finished in triple black. It featured black paint with a matching interior and matching convertible top. The black paint was a tribute to four shiny black KdF-cars displayed in front of a swastika-decorated curtain at the Volkswagen factory in 1941. Instead of the gray paint that was standard issue when production began, the four prototypes were finished in shiny black with chrome bumpers and chrome moldings around their military blackout-style headlight covers. These Epilog (AKA "Triple Black") ragtops were $200 more than other models.

Car enthusiasts convinced that the 1979 Super Beetle Cabriolet would be the world's truly "last convertible" flooded dealers with orders for the cars. As a result, the Karmann factory wound up with a pile of back orders that kept the production line going from July 31, 1979 (the originally scheduled end-of-production date), until January of 1980. The last car was a white Cabriolet that left the factory assembly line on January

TOP: Operating the top could be accomplished with one person, but having a partner certainly helped. They started by uncovering the folded top and lifting it up off the rear deck. *Archives/TEN: The Enthusiast Network Magazines, LLC*

BOTTOM: Raising the top on a Super Beetle was pretty simple. As the fabric top came up, it had to be guided toward the top of the windshield. With two people, the job was a breeze. *Archives/TEN: The Enthusiast Network Magazines, LLC*

10, 1980. Naturally, it had a white interior and matching white convertible top. Today, it's in the Karmann museum.

O-LAY (MEXICAN BEETLES)

The Volkswagen Beetle had been introduced to the Mexican marketplace in 1954, when three of them and a Type 2 Microbus arrived in Mexico City. Mexicans had never seen anything like the Beetle and could not have believed that the cars would actually be produced in Mexico someday

and continue in production there until 2004, twenty-five years after Germany stopped making them.

Few cars were in Mexico at that time, but many natives had seen the US models that competed in the La Carrera Panamericana events, or Mexican Road Races. Mexican car enthusiast Alfonso de Hohenlohe—who was related to one of Dr. Ferdinand Porsche's friends—entered seven Volkswagen Beetle sedans in the 1954 Mexican Road Race to show that the cars would hold up in a treacherous competition. All of the Beetles finished the grueling course.

This led to the creation of Volkswagen Mexicana, S.A. That same year, Hohenlohe founded Distribuidora Volkswagen Central, S.A. de C.V. (Central Volkswagen Distributor), which opened in 1955 as Mexico's first VW dealership.

Within five years, Beetles were being put together in Mexico through licensing arrangements with Automex (which became Chrysler de Mexico) and with Studebaker-Packard de Mexico. Then, in 1962, a Volkswagen assembly plant was erected in the city of Xalostoc. The manufacturer was PROMMEXA. In January 1964, Volkswagen de México, S.A. de C.V. was formed. The Xalostoc plant was too small to fill the growing demand for Beetles, and a huge new Volkswagen plant started construction in Puebla, Puebla, in 1965. By 1967, Beetle manufacturing began there, and by 1969 the 100,000th unit was built.

German-made Beetles and cars produced in Mexico were different. For instance, the small oval window model remained available in Mexico all the way through 1964. The big window body was not used South of the Border until 1985. Mexican cars also had wheels with a five-bolt pattern like Beetles made in Brazil. The Mexican Beetles and German-made ones had color differences. For instance, when the Mexican plant was assigned manufacture of a new Caribe model, it produced Beetles with Caribe colors. Also, at times changes made in Germany didn't show up on Beetles built in Mexico until several model years later.

As the Beetle grew more and more popular throughout the world, it also

The Volkswagen Super Beetle Convertible was much more fun to drive with the top down. When the top was raised, wind noise increased at high speeds and visibility to the rear of the car was poor. *Archives/TEN: The Enthusiast Network Magazines, LLC*

gained traction in Mexico. By June of 1972, the two hundred thousandth Volkswagen built in Mexico was assembled. Mexican-built cars were also exported to other nations. Some went to South American countries such as Costa Rica. Others were sent to Europe. When sales slowed in the 1970s, Volkswagen tried to increase them by making special edition cars and a few options, such as the Volkswagen Beetle Jeans and Sport Jeans packages, were made in Mexico.

When Beetle production halted in Germany in 1978, Volkswagen knew there was still a market for the car there and in other European countries, so it kept the assembly lines in Mexico set up for Beetle production. However, the cars sent to Europe weren't identical to cars sold in Mexico. They had a 1,200cc engine instead of a 1,600cc engine and a ventless engine cover. In addition, paint colors used on Caribes and Sciroccos were applied on these cars too.

From 1981 on, the Beetles built in Mexico were officially renamed Volkswagen models. To meet new seat safety rules, the Mexican plant used a seat used in late-1960s American Beetles and still later in Type 3 Microbuses. On May 15 of that year, Mexico built the twenty millionth Beetle made since the company started. This led to a Silver Metallic tribute car with Jetta side stripes.

Throughout the 1980s, the Mexican-made Beetles continued the Volkswagen tradition of adapting small changes from year to year, but leaving the basic design alone. It was actually reassuring to know

that the company's classic disapproval of planned obsolescence still had a place in the automotive world. For 1983, the front seats now had adjustable headrests, a handbrake-on light was added to the dash, and limited-edition Aubergine Metallic paint was new.

Volkswagen celebrated three decades of Beetle production in Mexico in 1984 with three commemorative edition packages. A second package was a red car for the West German market. A yellow Volkswagen was the third in the set.

In 1985, Volkswagen stopped exporting Mexican-made Beetles to Europe and released a 50-Years Germany package sold only in European markets. At this time, the Mexican Volkswagen (Beetle) adapted the larger rear window from 1972 and later German Beetles, and the bulged engine cover of the 1975 and later German Beetles.

In mid-1986, a Volkswagen Europa Edition 1 was launched and the Caribe's double-diagonal braking system was used for the car. Metallic paint colors were also discontinued. The Volkswagen Europa Edition 2 was released in 1987. In 1989, the Mexican government instituted pricing and tax controls, so the Mexican Beetle morphed into an entry-level-equipped Volkswagen sedan. To some it seemed like the "People's Car" was going back to its low-cost roots.

The 1990s started with production of the two millionth Mexican Volkswagen. Was it a coincidence that the same car was the one millionth Beetle built South of the Border? A catalytic converter was a mandatory change

the following year. New switches and a new steering wheel were pirated from the Golf parts bin and some rear end sheet metal changes were made to fit the converter in the engine compartment. Mexican cars reverted to a single tailpipe.

New Brazilian wheels were adopted in 1992 and another millionth car was ticked off. Naturally, a commemorative edition model was released at the twenty-one-millionth worldwide mark. For 1993, Mexican Beetles finally adopted fuel injection. Later that year a GL Sedan and a Wolfsburg Edition was introduced. In 1994, Volkswagen celebrated its fortieth anniversary in Mexico and brought out three new Limited Edition cars: the Firebeetle, the Volkswagen Beetle Edition One, and a 40th Anniversary edition.

In 1995, many improvements were made, including seating and seat belt upgrades, front disc brakes, and an alternator in place of the old generator. In all, eighty-seven improvements were introduced that year as well as three new paint colors. A Limited Edition El Volkswagen Beetle Jeans package was also released.

In 1996, Volkswagen went to matte black finish on many parts that had previously been chrome plated. The bumpers and headlight moldings were changed to the body color. A stripper model, the Volkswagen Sedan City, came out in 1997 and deleted a lot of the previous items made standard in 1995. However, a Volkswagen Sedán Clásico model kept most of the equipment and had slightly fancier

CABRIOLET & O-LAY FACTS

- In 1954, former Mexican president Lázaro Cárdenas made a trip from Michoacán, just to see the Volkswagen Beetle. The local press immediately published the news under the title "The People's Man" with "The People's Car."

- Around 1980–1981, the nickname Vocho came into popular usage in Mexico to describe the Volkswagen Beetle.

- In 2003, a group of Mexican Volkswagen dealers chipped in to buy a Sedán Última Edición Bwas that they sent to Vatican City in Italy as a present for Pope John Paul II.

trim. In midyear, the Volkswagen Beetle Harlekin arrived. It had the body panels painted in four different colors.

In 1999, the special model was the Volkswagen Sedán Unificado that blended the City model's upholstery with metallic colors from the Sedán Clásico. This new Volkswagen Beetle was the last regular version and remained unchanged until 2003. In March 2003, the end of the Vocho production was announced (although the last year of production was 2004). The reason given was a gradual and continuous decline in demand for the Beetle. A new Chevrolet model called the Pop took the first place in Mexican sales away from the Beetle.

In June 2003, a Volkswagen Sedán Última Edición was brought out as a throwback car honoring the long history of the Beetle. In Mexico, these cars were also sold as 2004 models along with a limited run of Unified Beetles. The Volkswagen Sedán Última Edición had a production run of 2,999 units. The last one made was sent to the Volkswagen Museum in Wolfsburg.

Several of the Sedán Última Edición Beetles were exported to other countries, primarily North America and Europe. After the Volkswagen Sedán Última Edición went out of stock, standard 2003 and 2004 Beetles continued to sit in many Mexican dealership and some were modified to the same specifications to move them off the sales floors. Today, the real versions remain popular, especially with the many enthusiasts who collect Volkswagen Beetles.

At the rear, the Super Beetle Convertible's top stacked up on the rear deck and a protective cover was provided. Under the trunk lid was a 96.66-cid 60-horsepower flat four. *Archives/TEN: The Enthusiast Network Magazines, LLC*

1978

VOLKSWAGEN
SUPER BEETLE CABRIOLET

PAINT COLORS

20A Marino Yellow   **90E** Alpine White
31B Mars Red   **97B** Ancona Metallic (blue)
52K Barrier Blue

MODEL AVAILABILITY	2-door Cabriolet ($5,695)
SERIAL NUMBER	(Cabriolet) Not available
WHEELBASE	94.5 inches
LENGTH	164.8 inches
WIDTH	63.9 inches
HEIGHT	(sedan) 59.1 inches
WEIGHT	(Cabriolet) 2,059 lbs.
TREAD	(front/rear) 54.9/54.7 inches
TIRES	(sedan) 165SR15
BRAKES	hydraulic, front/rear drum
WHEELS	disk-type with drop-center rim 4J x 15
FUEL TANK	10.6 gallons
FRONT SUSPENSION	MacPherson struts with coil springs
REAR SUSPENSION	swing axles with trailing arms and torsion bars
STEERING	worm and sector
ENGINE	1,585cc 48-hp horizontally opposed four-cylinder, overhead valve, air cooled, light alloy block and head, finned cylinders with cast-iron liners
TRANSMISSION	four-speed manual (full synchro)
FINAL DRIVE RATIO	spiral bevel

1979

VOLKSWAGEN
SUPER BEETLE CABRIOLET

PAINT COLORS

90E Alpine White   **99Y** Colibri Green
A5A Florida Blue   **A3V** Indiana Red Metallic
41 Black   **96F** Brazil Brown Metallic
A1D Lemon Yellow   **98G** Platinum Metallic
31B Mars Red   **94K** Pearl Metallic
97A Diamond Silver   **K6V** River Blue Metallic
Metallic

MODEL AVAILABILITY	2-door Cabriolet ($6,800)
SERIAL NUMBER	not available
WHEELBASE	94.5 inches
LENGTH	164.8 inches
WIDTH	63.9 inches
HEIGHT	(sedan) 59.1 inches
WEIGHT	(Cabriolet) 2,059 lbs.
TREAD	(front/rear) 54.9/54.7 inches
TIRES	(sedan) 165SR15
BRAKES	hydraulic, front/rear drum
WHEELS	disk-type with drop-center rim 4J x 15
FUEL TANK	10.6 gallons
FRONT SUSPENSION	MacPherson struts with coil springs
REAR SUSPENSION	swing axles with trailing arms and torsion bars
STEERING	worm and sector
ENGINE	1,585cc 48-hp horizontally opposed four-cylinder, overhead valve, air cooled, light alloy block and head, finned cylinders with cast-iron liners
TRANSMISSION	four-speed manual (full synchro)
FINAL DRIVE RATIO	spiral bevel

CHAPTER 8

car with room enough to handle things no other car can handle.

The Volkswagen Station Wagon is second to none when it comes to moving people. That's with all its seats in.

With its back seats out, the wagon is second to none when it comes to moving. Period.

A VW Wagon has 176 cu. ft. of carrying space. (You'd have to put 2 conventional wagons together to get more space than that.)

But 2 conventional wagons together still can't handle some of the odd-shaped things a VW can handle. Because they don't have a flat floor, a high ceiling and a big side door that slides out of the way.

Besides, what you can carry in a VW doesn't necessarily have to be inside a VW. You can always open the sunroof and have a 41" x 45" hole on top that will let you keep on loading up.

With the roof open, things that ride best standing up (like a grandfather clock or a tall sapling from the nursery) can ride standing up.

Of course, driving around in a car this huge does have its problems. Like when you come across a big bargain somewhere and find you have no excuse to pass it up.

Simply because you have such a perfect way to get it home.

BUSES

The history of the Volkswagen Transporter dates back to 1947 when Ben Pon drew a sketch for a Leifenwagen (light delivery van) that he saw a market for in his native Holland. The drawing showed a simple boxy vehicle with the driver sitting above the front axle and a pusher Volkswagen engine at the rear.

Volkswagen engineers went to work on the idea and eight Transporters were displayed late in 1949. The first production line models were Panel Vans, designed for commercial use, but it didn't take long for designers to envision other applications for both commercial and personal transportation use. Transporters weren't exported to the United States until 1952, when ten were sold there.

On Transporters, the serial number is on a plate mounted on the firewall in the engine compartment. That engine was the same one used in the 1950 Volkswagen Type 1 Beetle. A total of 1,141 Transporters were produced in 1950.

With 176 cubic feet of room, the interior of the 1970 Volkswagen Station Wagon was 6 cubic feet larger than the interior of the earlier "Split Window" models. These are called "Clippers" or "Bay Window" vans and the 1970–1972 models had the low-mounted amber parking lamps, seen here. A single slide-back passenger side door allowed entry to the rear of the vehicle.

1951

In 1952, production of the boxy Transporter continued with little change. It used the same drivetrain layout as the sedan. Ambulance and Postal versions of the van were early creations. Volkswagen also advised its dealers to work with commercial customers to carry out modifications of the Panel Van for different commercial applications and suggested some possibilities in

a magazine it sent to dealerships in February 1951. It depicted Panel Vans with customized laundry truck and bread van bodywork. Volkswagen dealers also outfitted Transporters with bins and shelving inside and an awning so parts could be sold at events.

In November 1951, some additional commercial applications for the Transporter were promoted in the

Volkswagen dealer magazine. They included a refrigerated milk van, a mobile workshop truck, an early "Wohnwagen" or campmobile, an airplane guide car with "Follow Me" signs, and a Fire Department Van. A total of 3,074 Transporters were built in 1951 and probably many custom commercial versions were produced in single-digit quantities.

1952

Production of the boxy rear-engined Transporter station wagon continued with little change and total output climbed to 5,194 Transporters produced in 1952. Consumer sales of the pioneering *minivan* (Volkswagen bus) began in July 1951 when it showed up in a German language sales brochure. Original Volkswagen literature referred to the vehicle as a "Kleinbus Sonderausführung" or "Small

Bus," but the single word "Microbus" was more commonly used to describe it. Both Standard and Deluxe models were offered. The latter had windows cut into the roof, curved rear corner glass and sometimes an optional sliding roof. It was an Achtsitzer Sonder-Modell (eight-passenger model) and cost a bit more than a standard microbus. The brochure showed a stylized rendering

of this bus with a white-painted sliding-style roof, a Sealing Wax Red lower body and a Chestnut Brown (almost black) V-shaped front panel. A uniformed bus driver was driving it. This version had two "barn-door" style doors in the center of the passenger side and 4-row seating Transporters were officially exported to the United States this year and 10 were sold there.

VW-Kastenwagen

Auto-Handelsgesellschaft M·B·H
GEORG RITTERSBACHER
VOLKSWAGEN-GROSSHANDLER
KAISERSLAUTERN

LEFT: The history of the Volkswagen T1 (Transporter Type 1) dates to 1947, when Dutch importer Ben Pon drew a sketch for a *Leiferwagen* (light delivery van) that he saw a market for in his native Holland. This is a 1950 Kastenwagen (Panel Van) version. Revell of Germany makes a plastic model kit of this truck.

OPPOSITE: This 1951 sales literature shows a Panel Van with double doors on both sides of the vehicle. As you can see from the smaller photos, interior room was good for big loads, but the view to the rear with the tiny window was limited.

Bei einem Minimum an Anschaffungs- und Unterhaltungskosten bietet der VW-Kastenwagen seinem Besitzer alles, was man sich von einem Transportfahrzeug der schnellen Klasse wünscht: überraschend große Geräumigkeit und Tragkraft mit vielen Variationsmöglichkeiten für die Aufteilung des Laderaumes je nach Verwendungszweck, eine gefällige Form mit großen, ungebrochenen Außenflächen für wirkungsvolle Werbebeschriftung und alle Voraussetzungen für einen flinken und wendigen Einsatz im Großstadtgewühl wie auch für zuverlässige Robustheit im Überlandverkehr, selbst auf schlechten Wegen. Die weit zu öffnenden Flügeltüren geben einen sehr bequemen Zugang zum Laderaum frei, der durch einen Ganzstahlaufbau hervorragend geschützt und durch seine Lage zwischen den Achsen bestens gefedert ist.

Motor, Kraftstoffbehälter und Reserverad befinden sich leicht zugänglich in einem geschützten Raum im Heck des Wagens.

Ein ganz nach vorn verlagertes, rundum verglastes Fahrerhaus gewährt freien Blick auf die Fahrbahn bis unmittelbar vor den Wagen; durch ein breites Rückfenster wird auch der Blick nach hinten freigegeben.

Für Wärme und Frontscheiben-Entfrostung sorgt eine sofort wirksame Heizanlage; der Belüftung dienen schwenk- und ausstellbare Seitenfenster.

Auf Wunsch wird der VW-Kastenwagen auch viertürig geliefert, also mit Zugang von beiden Seiten her.

VW-Achtsitzer „Sonder-Modell"

TOP: Offered from 1951–1955, the Volkswagen Achtsitzer Sonder-Modell was a special eight-seater version of the Transporter with four small observation windows (one for each passenger) on each side.

BOTTOM: From 1951 to 1953, the Volkswagen Achtsitzer Sonder-Modell had a 69-cid 25-horsepower flat four. This was changed to 73 cid 30 horsepower for 1954 and 1955. As you can see, it was available with a rollback cloth sunroof as well.

Sonnendach (Bauart Golde), dieses technisch und geschmacklich gleichermaßen erlesene Fahrzeug zu einem gläsernen Aussichtswagen, wie er einem sonst nur bei großen und teuren Luxus-Omnibussen begegnet. Dabei bleibt der „VW-Achtsitzer" doch ein flinkes, ungewöhnlich wirtschaftliches Transportmittel, das sich durch die Serpentinen der Berge wie auch durch den dichtesten Stadtverkehr ebenso rasch und geschickt windet wie irgendein Personenwagen, zu dessen Gattung er hinsichtlich seiner technischen Merkmale, seiner Zulassung und Versteuerung gehört, obgleich er das Antlitz und die Vorzüge eines modernen „Reise-Omnibusses in Kleinformat" hat.

*D*er „VW-Achtsitzer" ist längst zum idealen Fahrzeug für alle Arten der schnellen Personenbeförderung geworden.
Sein noch eleganterer Bruder gar, der VW-Achtsitzer „Sonder-Modell", ist genau das, was anspruchsvolle, auf angenehmes und genußreiches Fahren bedachte Reisende sich wünschen. Seine Rundumverglasung, nur durch schmale Tragleisten unterbrochen, und Plexiglasscheiben im Dachbord machen, in Verbindung mit dem serienmäßig eingebauten

A truck version of the Transporter called the Pick-Up was introduced in August 1951 as a 1952 model. It had the cab and platform of the split-windshield Panel Van with a rear wall added and a long cargo bed with drop-down side doors.

The 1953 Transporters lost the piano-hinged vent window of previous models.

The factory catalog models included the Panel Van, the Kombi, the Microbus, and the Pick-Up. The Kombi had removable center and rear seats so that

it could be used as a passenger car or a cargo van. The cargo area lacked a headliner and interior panels. A few basic changes were made in the van line. The production of Transporters took a small jump to 5,375 units in 1953.

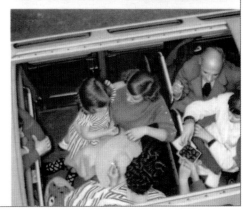

In geschmackvoller Zweifarben-Kombination zeigt sich die Schönheit des Sonder-Modells, zeitlose Zweckform in vollendeter Gestaltung. Doppelte Chromleisten unterstreichen die elegante Linienführung des Aufbaus; Chromleisten zieren auch die vorderen und hinteren Stoßstangen und die Radfelgen. Das Sonder-Modell hat auf jeder Seite des Passagierraumes vier Fenster; dazu kommen die großen Seitenfenster des gleichfalls rundumverglasten Fahrerraumes, der wie eine Flugzeugkanzel freie Sicht nach allen Seiten bietet. Ein breites Aussichtsfenster mit Plexiglasecken bildet den harmonischen Abschluß am Heck. Freien Durchblick nach oben gewähren das geöffnete Sonnendach und der transparente Plexiglas-Dachbord. So wünscht man sich den idealen Reisewagen für kleine Gesellschaften! Diesem Wunsch entspricht auch der geräumige, behaglich eingerichtete Innenraum mit seinen sechs bequemen Sitzen. Der Einstieg durch die breite seitliche Zweiflügeltür zu den hinteren Sitzen wird durch Umklappen der Rücklehne des rechten Vordersitzes bequem gemacht. Auf allen

Plätzen hat man reichlich Kopf-, Bein- und Ellbogenfreiheit. Im VW-Achtsitzer gibt es keine drückende Enge. Raum für viel Gepäck findet man im Wagenheck. Haltestangen, Mantelhaken, Armschlaufen und selbstverständlich auch Ascher vervollständigen die gediegene Innenausstattung. Auf der breiten Polstersitzbank im Fahrerraum haben zwei Personen mehr als reichlich Platz. Eine zusätzliche Annehmlichkeit ist die schnell wirkende, regulierbare Warmluftheizung, die auch die Frontscheiben entfrostet. Die Frischluftzufuhr läßt sich ganz nach Wunsch einstellen, die Seitenfenster des Fahrerraumes sind zu verschieben, in ihrem vorderen Drittel sogar schwenkbar. Für Entlüftung des Innenraumes bei geschlossenem Sonnendach sorgen zwei ausstellbare Seitenfenster. Geschmackvoll ist auch die serienmäßige Armaturentafel in Wagenbreite; sie vereint alle die bekannten VW-Armaturen einschließlich einer Zeituhr in übersichtlicher Weise; auch Einbaumöglichkeit für einen Autosuper wurde geschaffen.

Passengers entered the Volkswagen Achtsitzer Sonder-Modell through double side doors and the right-hand seats folded forward to make it easier to enter or leave the vehicle. The driver sat in an upright position to turn the big wheel.

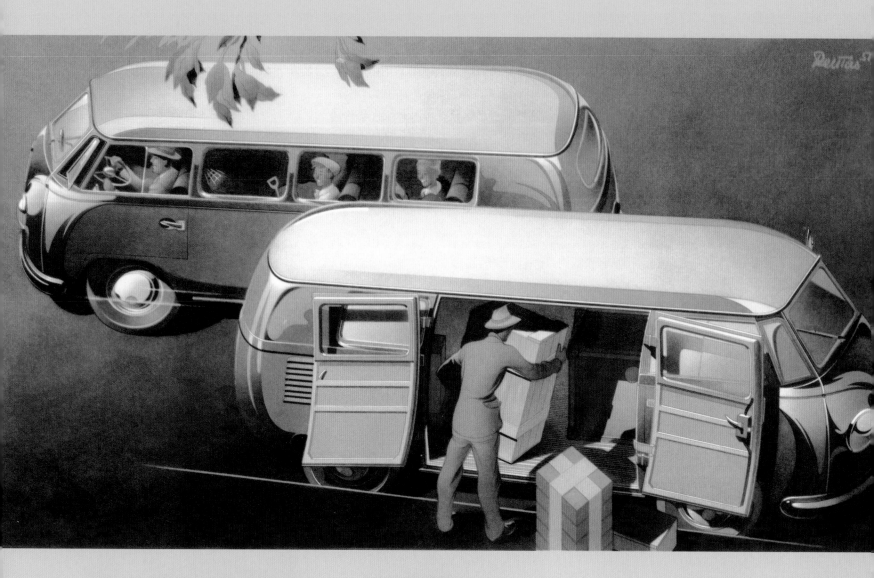

ABOVE: The 1953 Kombi had removable center and rear seats so that it could be used both as a passenger car and as a cargo van. This slightly stylized artistic view of the boxy Volkswagen truck shows each option in action.

RIGHT: The 1953 Volkswagen Transporters lost the piano-hinged vent window of previous editions. The factory-cataloged models of the Transporter included the Panel Van, the Kombi, the Microbus, and the Pick-Up.

THEWS MOTORS
W. WESTERN AVE. RD.
R.R.#3 BOX 146A
SOUTH BEND, INDIANA
The Volkswagen Transporters

The 1954 Transporter had a larger engine. American used-car guides such as *Red Book National Market Reports Official Used Car Evaluations* often listed the Transporter series as simply the Volkswagen Station Wagon series.

The new engine was of the same basic design with a bigger 3.03-inch (77mm) bore, but the same 2.52-inch (64mm) stroke. This boosted displacement from 69.0 to 72.7 cubic inches (1,131cc to 1,192cc). The compression ratio was also upped from 5.8:1 to 6.6:1. This resulted in a horsepower rating of 30 brake

horsepower at 3,400 rpm. The Transporter used the Kübelwagen double reduction axle and had a top speed of around 50 miles per hour. Zero-to-60 times didn't compute. It reached 25 miles per gallon.

The 1954 Transporter sales catalog listed six models, of which three (eight-passenger Microbus, Deluxe Microbus, and Kombi) were passenger vehicles and three (Delivery Van, Pick-Up Truck, and Ambulance) were commercials. The Kombi was offered with or without occasional passenger seats. The seats were removable, but a Kombi could

carry eight to nine passengers with all seats in place. The rear windows pivoted outward for extra ventilation.

The eight-passenger Microbus was again available with a Golde brand sunroof at extra cost. The Deluxe Microbus included the Golde sunroof, windows all around the body, and side observation panels in the roof. Enthusiasts of today identify different models by counting the number of windows. This was a pretty good year for early Transporter sales, which climbed upward to 7,630 units.

In addition to the models shown in this 1954 brochure, the Transporter could be custom-ordered in many commercial variations, from ambulances to airport limousines. Check out that eight-passenger bus with whitewall tires.

The Volkswagen Transporters

The 1955 Transporter series included the same three passenger models and the same three commercial vehicles. A special interiors brochure was put out by Volkswagen to stress the idea of customizing vans for different trades. Different concepts were pictured, such as a mobile movie theater with a projection screen inside and another with a medical van with a life support pod inside.

Inside the Kombi van, the cargo area lacked a headliner and interior sidewall panels. The eight-passenger Microbus was available with or without the optional Golde sunroof. The Deluxe Microbus included the Golde sunroof, windows all around the body, and side observation panels in the roof.

The June 1955 issue of *Motor Trend* stated, "Heavier Microbus uses the same engine [as Beetle], has high, wide compartment for 9 people or much cargo. Deluxe version has roll-back roof. For use as a station wagon where little power needed." Apparently, the vans didn't need anything more than this type of basic promotion, because the annual production total zoomed to 10,152 units.

Amazingly, Volkswagen Pick-Ups, such as this 1955 model, used the same 94.5-inch wheelbase platform as the Beetle. The standard overall length was 165 inches. Binz offered a double-cab model that became a factory option in 1958.

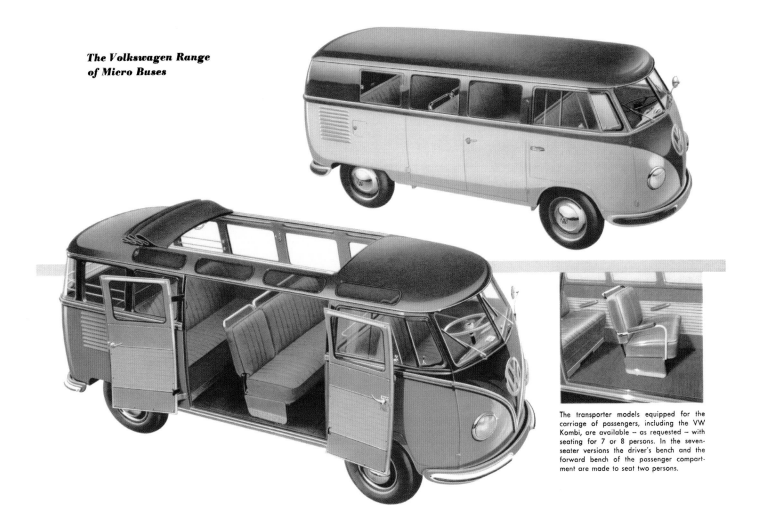

The Volkswagen Range of Micro Buses

The transporter models equipped for the carriage of passengers, including the VW Kombi, are available — as requested — with seating for 7 or 8 persons. In the seven-seater versions the driver's bench and the forward bench of the passenger compartment are made to seat two persons.

The 1955 passenger models of the Transporter—including the Kombi—could be configured for seven- or eight-passenger seating. In eight-passenger versions, a full-width front seat was provided.

1956

In 1956, a new Volkswagen plant in Hanover, Germany, went into operation. The company said it was equipped with "the finest automated machinery" to produce the precision-built Volkswagen station wagon. This is what management had decided to call passenger-carrying versions of the Transporter. By 1959, the Hanover plant was building four hundred trucks and station wagons daily, while over two thousand Beetle sedans per day were made at Wolfsburg.

What *Motor Trend* magazine (October 1956) described as "the ingenious German-made Kamper Kit" was also available for the 1956 Microbus. The Westfalia camper conversion kit included a folding table, a small folding bench, a plaid-covered full-length bench, a cupboard, a camp icebox, a camp stove, a fold-out bed, storage cabinets, a roof transom, an awning, lockers, and curtains.

Volkswagen didn't enlarge the Transporter engine, but managed to squeeze more horsepower out of the existing configuration. *Ward's Automotive Yearbook* said 11,798 Transporters were produced in 1956.

ABOVE: This 1956 Volkswagen Transporter has a German-made "Kamper Kit" option. The wide side doors made entry easy for anyone and an awning mounted on a collapsible framework that stowed under the seat provided shade. *Archives/TEN: The Enthusiast Network Magazines, LLC*

RIGHT: The "Kamper" version of the 1956 Transporter had curtains on all windows and across the back of the front seats for privacy. A table and a jump seat folded out of the wall when in use. The breadbox on wheels got 27 mpg fuel economy. *Archives/TEN: The Enthusiast Network Magazines, LLC*

This was a good year for Transporter sales and production rocketed to 20,711 units. Factory models were very much unchanged. However, one 1957 brochure listed twenty-two SO (Sonderausführungen or special order) commercial conversions, including the SO22 Westfalia Camping Box and the SO23 Westfalia Deluxe camping car. It also listed and SO-coded some of the custom conversions mentioned in previous years, as well as others—such as the SO7 refrigerated freezer van, the SO14 pole-carrying trailer, the SO15 Tipper Truck, and the SO19 display and exhibition van. Some SO models were factory supplied and some came from coachbuilders such as Karosserie Baufirma. The new camper buses were fitted with such extras as a folding table and fold-out beds.

An interesting variant introduced this year was the M16 Binz Pick-Up with double cab. Lorch Binz Karosseriefabrik of Lorch, Worttemberg, Germany, offered it. It was based on a coach-built conversion that company had done back in 1953. A rear cabin was added behind the driver's compartment and the curb-side storage cabinet was eliminated. This became known as the SO16 Binz Double Cab Pick-Up and is a very collectible conversion model today.

TOP: The 1957 Pick-Up was easy to load when the sides of the cargo box and the tailgate were flopped down. There was additional storage room in a lockable, weather-tight compartment with a hatch on the right-hand side of the vehicle.

BOTTOM: A bird's-eye view of the 1957 Pick-Up shows the skid rails on the bottom of the bed. Above it is a Pick-Up with the canvas top; below is a drawing that shows the full-width side storage compartment.

NEXT PAGE: The 1958 Panel Van version of the Transporter could also be ordered in primer so that specific commercial paint schemes, such as those shown at the bottom, could be from paint shops and sign makers.

1958

The Transporter series again included three regular passenger models. The Kombi van was offered with or without occasional passenger seating. The seats were removable, but a Kombi could carry eight to nine passengers with all seats in place. The rear windows pivoted outward for extra ventilation. Since the center and rear seats were removable, the Kombi could be a passenger car or a cargo van. The cargo area lacked a headliner and interior panels.

The Eight-Passenger Microbus was available with a Golde brand sunroof at extra cost. The Deluxe Microbus included the Golde sunroof, windows all around the body, and side observation panels in the roof. Enthusiasts of today identify different models by counting the number of windows. A camper bus was also available and included such extras as a folding table and fold-out beds. *Ward's 1959 Automotive Yearbook* reported that 23,841 Transporters had been produced in 1958.

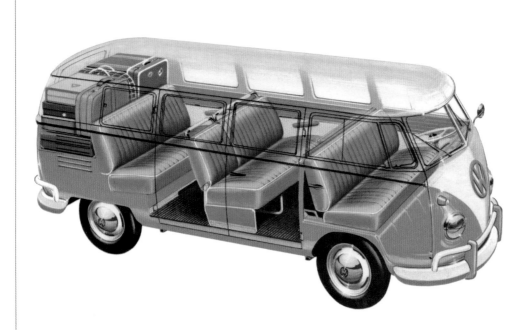

The driver's area is neat and practical. Unusual features are the utility shelf that stretches the full width of the Station Wagon beneath the instrument panel, and the roomy pockets in the doors. The handsome two-spoke steering wheel, the steering column and the instrument knobs are finished in a subdued matching color. Sun visors are standard equipment.

The big trunk area easily takes 16 pieces of average-size luggage. The rear door opens upward und stays in position automatically.

This "X-ray" picture shows the sensible design of the interior. There is plenty of leg room. The wide seats with their comfortable backs and durable leatherette upholstery are very inviting. The upholstery harmonizes tastefully with the colorful trim of the roof, sidewalls and doors. There's a narrow shelf on the partition wall behind the driver's compartment ... a sound-proof floor cover ... practical hand rails ... good-looking ash trays ... and hooks for clothing.

Station wagons were all the rage in America in the late 1950s, so Volkswagen began promoting the passenger van version of the 1957 Kombi as its station wagon. Buyers could choose a two- or three-passenger middle seat. X-ray illustrations in the 1958 Volkswagen Transporter catalog showed different interior configurations. The drawing above shows the Kombi Van fitted with three rows of seats. The cab interior and the luggage compartment above the engine are illustrated in the drawings on the right.

In 1959, the station wagon models were promoted as "The Larger Volkswagen for Large Families and Small Parties." Changes for the year included a light-colored heat-reflecting roof, extra strong bumpers, more attractive interior trim, and wider armrests with smooth, strong foam rubber upholstery. Wide side doors made it easy to get in and to get to the rear seats. Buyers had the choice of a two-person center seat or a three-person center seat with a folding back.

The driver's compartment had a full-width utility shelf and a two-spoke steering wheel. Sixteen pieces of luggage could fit in the trunk area. The trunk had an upward-opening door. The Deluxe Station Wagon had four Plexiglas skylights on each side of the roof. It also had a special roof air-circulating system.

Volkswagen trucks made in the Hanover factory included the Pickup (now written as one word), the Panel Delivery, and the Kombi Station Wagon. The Pickup had a wide-open floor and full-width, lockable weather-tight storage compartment on the curbside, just behind the front wheel. The load bed provided users with 45.2 square feet of load area. Stakes and a cloth canopy or tarpaulin to cover the load bed was available as an option. Sales catalog illustrations showed how the Pickup could be converted into a mobile store or a display vehicle.

The Panel Delivery had a strong steel body, a steel-ribbed floor, and wall guards to protect the interior. Wing-style doors on the right side were fitted. The front door opened toward the front of the truck and the rear one opened toward the rear. The sides of the Panel Van could be used as a billboard. The Kombi was like a Panel Van with three removable seats so that it combined the features of a panel delivery truck and a passenger-carrying van. A new production record of 29,184 Transporters was set and was only the beginning.

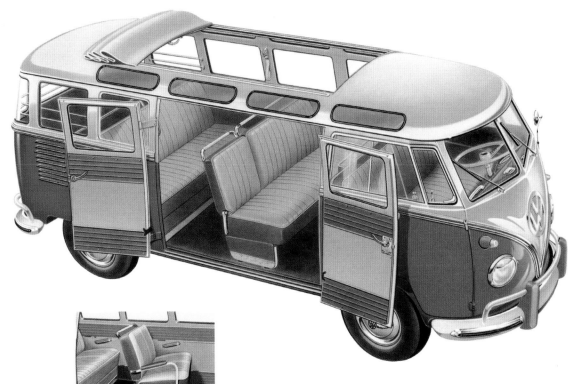

Still available from Volkswagen in the 1959 Transporter line was the eight-passenger Station Wagon with twenty-three windows (including ventipanes and observation windows). There was also a seven-passenger Convertible Station Wagon version with a two-person middle seat, seen in the inset photo.

An X-ray look into a VW Panel Delivery
shows its remarkable distribution of space and loading area.
The VW Panel Delivery
offers valuable billboard or advertising display areas —
four examples are shown.
If you plan to use your own distinctive color treatment,
order your Panel prime coated.

Special Interior Adaptation: Ask for literature offering helpful suggestions
left: Interior space can be inexpensively partitioned with large boards.
center: Cupboard design handles a large number of small parcels.
right: Interchangeable system of boards and posts.

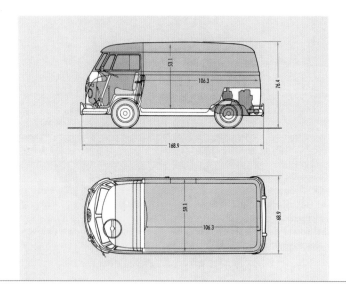

ABOVE: Still available from Volkswagen in the 1959 Transporter line was the eight-passenger Station Wagon with twenty-three windows (including ventipanes and observation windows). There was also a seven-passenger Convertible Station Wagon version with a two-person middle seat, seen in the inset photo.

OPPOSITE: By 1960, Volkswagen Pickups, Panel Deliveries, and Station Wagons were being pushed along by an 1,192cc 36-horsepower engine. The front independent suspension featured two laminated torsion bars.

1960

Effective with serial number 491002, the Volkswagen station wagons and trucks became 1960 models. Volkswagen promoted the station wagons as fun vehicles with catalog art suggesting camping trips, airport and hotel shuttle use, use by clubs to make trips, sightseeing in Paris (through the open roof option), school bus use, and visits to ski resorts. Another panel depicted a van in a neighborhood in the United States. "Thrifty like the famous passenger car, the Station Wagons offer roominess, dependability, safety and all comfort that make a long trip a pleasure . . . summer or winter," said the catalog.

Truck versions of the boxy vehicle were hyped as "money makers for every business." Volkswagen said that the Pickups, Panel Vans, and Kombis could "deliver more goods for less money, with less effort." Sales increased slightly, and 30,350 Transporters were produced in 1960.

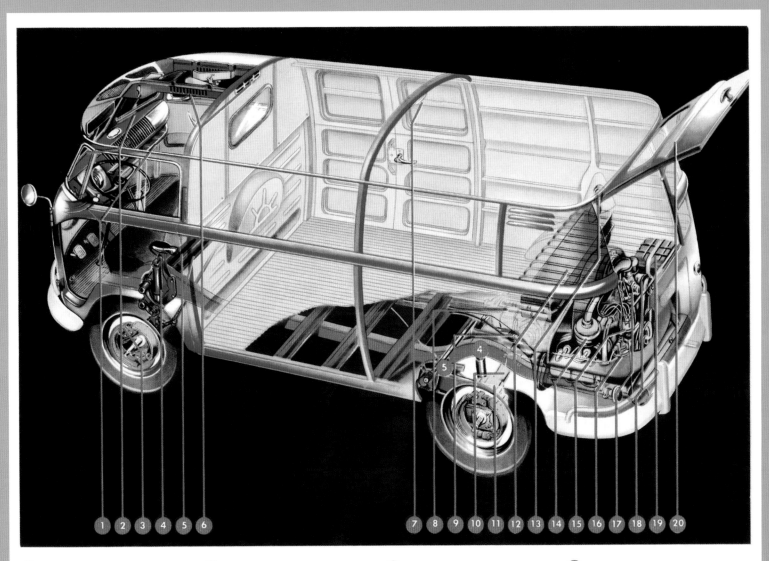

1. Parcel tray
2. Defroster vents
3. Brake wheel cylinder
4. Telescopic shock absorber
5. Torsion bars
6. Ventilator
7. Dome lamp
8. Transmission
9. Flexible heater pipe
10. Rear axle
11. Spur reduction gears
12. Fuel tank
13. Fuel tank filler
14. Oil bath air cleaner
15. Distributor
16. Fuel pump
17. Carburetor
18. Generator
19. Battery
20. Rear loading door

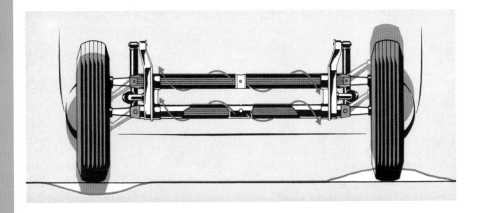

It holds more peop|

Whether you're chauffeuring the brownie troop, the bowling team or your own growing family, everyone will be comfortable inside this Volkswagen.

It comes with 3 rows of seats (for 7 adults) as stand- ard equipment. And if you want seating for 8 or 9, y can get it for a little extra.

The seats are spaced 12″ apart. And there's a foot-wide aisle down the side of the wagon. So no c has to step on or over anyone else.

There's also a compartment behind the rear se that's big enough for a dozen pieces of luggage. So one has to step on them either.

with less crowding.

Of course, roominess isn't the only reason people feel so comfortable in our Wagon. There's a ventilating and heating system with outlets that can be individually adjusted. Coat hooks to keep bulky outer garments out of the way. Soft leatherette upholstery and paneling that wipes clean with a damp cloth. And lots of big windows all around to give everyone a bright, cheerful view of the scenery.

Traveling in a VW Wagon is almost as good as traveling in your own home.

And best of all, no matter where you're going, you'll still feel like having a good time when you get there.

1961

The split windshield Volkswagen Transporter continued to be offered in the 1960s. The Microbuses received a horsepower boost like the Beetle sedan. The series still offered three different passenger transporters, and four trucks were listed in the Volkswagen truck sales catalog: the Panel Delivery, the Kombi Station Wagon, the Pick-Up, and the Double Cab Pick-Up (yes, they returned to hyphenated spelling). The Kombi had seating for eight to nine passengers with all of the removable seats in place. The rear windows pivoted outward for extra ventilation. The cargo area was untrimmed. The Eight-Passenger Station Wagon (the term Microbus seems to have been dropped) was fully trimmed inside and the Golde sunroof cost extra. The Deluxe Station Wagon included the sunroof, windows all around, and side observation windows. A camper was also available and included such extras as a sink, icebox, folding table, and fold-out beds.

The Transporter really was an efficient design for moving passengers or cargo. The sales literature pointed out that it was only 9 inches longer than the Beetle and correspondingly agile, although it could carry a ¾-ton load. Also noted was the fact that the 14-foot-long Pick-Up could load more than a 1-ton truck. The company said it had made 178 improvements to the vehicle in the last twelve years and that it had sold more than 125,000 trucks to American businessmen. Total production in Hanover this year was 33,506 Transporters of all types.

PREVIOUS PAGE: Five members of the Brownie troop, their leaders, and a dog could easily get comfortable in the Volkswagen Station Wagon. With big windows all around, the interior seemed a lot airier than those of the earliest VW buses.

BELOW: The 1961 Deluxe Station Bus with optional Skyview windows is illustrated here with a cutaway view that highlights a dozen important selling points this model offered, from vent wings to a double-insulated warm-air heating system.

OPPOSITE: A gal with period-correct pedal pushers gets ready to camp out in a tent on top of a 1960–1961 Volkswagen Bus owned by the Gainesville Paper Co. We hope she didn't roll out of bed and slide off the top of her vehicle. *Strozier Library; Florida State University*

1. Vent wings
2. Special roof air-circulating system
3. Sliding windows
4. Sun-roof
5. Skylights, glare-resistant
6. Picture windows
7. Trunk room for 16 luggage pieces
8. Volkswagen engine worldapproved in 2 ½ million units.
9. Transmission
10. Double acting telescopic shock absorbers
11. Torsion bar suspension
12. Double insulated warm-air heating system.

1962

Microbuses and related station wagons remained available with the same powertrain as other Volkswagens. The series still offered three different passenger transporters. The Kombi had passenger seating for eight to nine with all of the removable seats in place. The rear windows pivoted outward for extra ventilation. The cargo area was untrimmed. The Eight-Passenger Station Wagon was fully trimmed inside. The Deluxe Station Wagon included the sunroof, windows all around, and side observation windows. A Camper was also available. A new production record was set with 41,179 Transporters being produced in 1962.

Station Bus and Window Van models remained available in 1962, as did the camper conversions. All models continued to use the same powertrain as other Volkswagens. For the year, 41,179 transporters were made—a new record.

ABOVE: Seeing double. A good way to sell the 1962 Volkswagen Double-Cab Pick-Up was to show four examples of this model in the same sales catalog. The rear section of the cab could be set up for hauling people or cargo.

NEXT PAGE: Transporter-based commercial models included the Model 261 Pick-Up and the Model 265 Deluxe Cab Pick-Up. In this era, Volkswagen moved away from stylized renderings and used actual photographs of the trucks in its promotional materials.

1963

Beginning in 1963, larger round front turn-signal indicators were installed on Microbuses. A fresh-air heating system also became available. The series again offered three different passenger transporters. The Kombi had eight- to nine-passenger seating with all of the removable seats in place. The rear windows pivoted outward for extra ventilation. The cargo area was untrimmed.

The Eight-Passenger Station Wagon was fully trimmed inside and its spaciousness was promoted in an interesting fold-out sales brochure this year. A photo presented on a two-page spread showed the moon shining through the open sunroof and the Plexiglas skylights. The photographer made the blue interior look like the inside of a passenger train or maybe a 747. It was fittingly described for the early '60s as a "space vehicle."

Volkswagen said it could fit eight passengers and 1,632 pounds of stuff. Of course, it couldn't do both at once, because you had to remove the center and rear seats to carry that much cargo.

The brochure showed the window version from the rear with the flap-type engine cover raised. It had red paint below the beltline and white above, including around the windows. The Standard Station Wagon was shown with white upper and green lower paint

Patrick Hoffman's 1963 Volkswagen truck is a double-door Panel Delivery. Here we see the front door on the right-hand side of the body swung open. The second door, directly behind it, is closed.

with the wing doors open. In the front, the white upper section dropped down to the bumper in a curved V (resembling a bikini) with a large circular VW emblem in front. The bumpers were white.

Cutaway drawings throughout the brochure showed the technical features of the Transporter and gave example of how much bulky cargo—from telescopes to kid's toys—could be accommodated inside. Of course, the telescope was set up to poke through the open sunroof. Was the user looking for spaceships?

Transporter-based commercial models included the Model 211 Panel Delivery, the Model 261 Pick-Up, and the Model 265 Deluxe Cab Pick-Up. Late in 1962, Volkswagen announced that 10 camper kits would be available for Transporters at various prices, so it was no longer necessary to buy the

expensive Westfalia Camper. However, eight of the kits were still made by that German company. A camper model was no longer listed separately.

An optional new 1500 engine was available in Transporters this year. This 91.1-cubic-inch engine was a bored and stroked version of the previous one with new 3.27 x 2.72-inch specifications. It had a slightly higher 7.2:1 compression ratio that helped boost its output to 50 horsepower at 3,900 rpm. It used a Solex carb with automatic choke. This engine would become the standard powerplant in 1965.

Standard equipment in all models included a tool and jack under the driver's seat and a spare wheel. The Deluxe Station Wagon added many more items, such as the sliding sunroof, glare-absorbing skylights,

electric clock, inside rearview mirror, padded sun visors, chrome-plated door fittings, assist straps and clothes hooks, luggage compartment carpeting, a rear bench rail to secure luggage, chrome front and rear bumpers with protective rubber moldings, chrome-plated beltline moldings, louver moldings, and wheel trim rings. The sliding sunroof and skylights could be deleted from a Deluxe Station Wagon.

Options for all models included whitewall tires, hinged side windows, an electrically operated roof ventilator, a split front seat, a retractable entry step, wing doors on both sides, the sliding sunroof, a sliding window in the roof-high driving cab partition, and a second outside mirror. Production this year was another record, 45,960.

The 1964 Deluxe Station Wagon (left) came with a sliding sunroof, all-around windows, glare-absorbing skylight windows, a carpeted luggage compartment, a luggage rail, and chrome trim. The Standard (right) did not.

1964

Volkswagen didn't have much time or reason to change its station wagon and truck offerings this year as production at the Hanover plant soared to 54,146 Transporters. Volkswagen switched to fatter, but smaller 14-inch tires.

RIGHT: Volkswagen returned to calling this model a Station Wagon (instead of a Station Bus) in 1964. Sales literature stressed that it was only a few inches larger than a Beetle, but offered 170 cubic feet of interior room, far more than a Beetle.

BELOW: Here's a 1964 Westfalia Camper with a framed tent. This is the largest and most colorful of the Westfalia side tents. It has large screened windows on the sides and a freestanding frame that allows the camper to be driven away.

1965

Transporter production continued without major change in 1965, except that the formerly optional 1500 engine was now standard equipment in this model. For the first time, production declined slightly to 50,400 and *Ward's Automotive Yearbook* reported truck sales of 37,796 units in the United States.

"Want to buy a going business?" — that was the tag line on the 1965 Volkswagen trucks sales catalog, which showed a red Panel Van speeding off the cover in a time-lapse photo. The first four inner pages were different lengths so that you first saw the business' "front office" (seat), then the "big backroom" (cargo crates), then

the powerplant (engine and transaxle), and finally the whole Transporter, sans body. Each facing page described business advantages of the Transporter.

The next page showed how the seats and interior space could be arranged to serve a florist, a TV serviceman, a baker, and a dry cleaning shop. There was no actual truck in the photos, just the

The 1965 Volkswagen sales catalog didn't just show its Standard and Deluxe Station Wagon models. Instead, it gave customers, including these musicians, ideas as to how a VW Transporter could be put to work for them.

TV Westerns were popular in the mid-1960s, so Volkswagen decided to show how five cowhands could make good use of a double-cab Pick-Up to carry their lariats and saddles.

goods set up behind several different seating configurations. The florist truck would have had a single driver's seat, the TV repairman's truck would use the 40/60 split bench with a partition behind it, and both other setups used only the 40/60 split bench without partition.

Naturally, the next page showed the various second and third seat installations you could work out in the Kombi for business or pleasure, which included a camper-type interior. Different cargo bed setups for the

drop-side Pick-Up—designed for builders, farmers, electricians, plumbers, and flooring contractors—were shown on the next two-page spread, followed by different Double Cab Pick-Up possibilities for ranchers, gardeners, farmers, utility workers, and contractors. Lastly, different station wagon seating arrangements for road shows, hotels, antique and real estate dealers, and salesmen were shown.

The main lesson here was that Volkswagen didn't show just pretty

pictures of all its models. Instead, it gave customers, including different business owners, ideas as to how the Transporter could be put to work for them. It was all very cleverly planned and all done on heavy paper with outstanding photography. The remaining pages of the catalog showed a cutaway that depicted body features and an unusual photo that almost looked like the pieces of a model car being put together. Different models had slightly different specs because of bumper sizes.

Again, six factory models of the Transporter were offered. This year all six were promoted in one sales catalog, which was the truck catalog. The Standard Station Wagon came in seven- and eight-passenger versions. A 12-volt electrical system was optional. Options for this model included the sliding sunroof, whitewalls, hinged side windows, an electrically operated roof

ventilator, a split front seat, a retractable step, wing doors on both sides, a sliding window in the roof-high driving cab partition, and a second outside mirror. This rig could be ordered with only a single front seat and with either a two- or three-passenger second seat.

The Deluxe Station Wagon was pretty much the same, except that the sunroof was standard (but could be deleted) and

the skylight windows were included. This is what collectors today call a twenty-three-window van. Each side of it has a vent window, a door window, four side windows, and four skylights. The windshield was split and the rear window was one piece, so that adds up to ten pieces of glass on each side, two in front and one large window at the rear.

The Double Cab Pick-Up was a little longer and shorter than other models and could handle a 1,665-pound payload without the optional bows and tarpaulin arrangement (1,610 pounds with it). The upper sides of the load box folded down like flaps. The single cab Pick-Up was the same length and height as the Double Cab. It could only seat two people as opposed to the Double Cab's five-person capacity. It could handle a 1,764-pound payload (1,687 pounds with optional bows and tarpaulin). Other options include lockable storage compartment doors on both sides and an enlarged loading platform. The side panels and tailgate were standard, but this model could be purchased without them for a little less money.

The Kombi and Panel were the same length and height as the station

Sportsmobile
ANDREWS, INDIANA 46702 ● PHONE 219 786-3337

LEFT: Sportsmobile of Huntington, Indiana, is still in business today doing high-quality camper vehicle conversions. The company's first conversions were done in 1961 on Volkswagen buses and Ford vans. This conversion is on a 1968 or later Bay Window or Clipper van.

NEXT PAGE: An optional sunroof added sportiness to the Volkswagen Station Wagon. It also improved the vehicle's already excellent ventilation. Its disc brakes outdid the competition and the sliding side door worked perfectly. *Archives/TEN: The Enthusiast Network Magazines, LLC*

wagons. The Kombi came in seven- or eight-passenger formats. Options included double doors on both sides, split front seats, a swivel seat for the driver, side or roof paneling, a sliding partition window, and the sliding sunroof. Options for the Panel included split front seats, a swiveling driver's seat, double doors on both sides,

and side or roof paneling. Optional equipment for all models included a right-hand outside mirror, a windshield washer, hinged windshields, an electric ventilation system, an 86 amp-hour battery, a 12-volt electrical system, and retractable steps for the side doors. The final drive ratio changed this year.

Volkswagen's unit sales in the United States for calendar-year 1966 amounted to 420,018 units, including tourist deliveries and 35,439 trucks. In Hanover, Germany, the model year production total was 49,557 Transporters.

1967

In the last year of the split-windshield design, Microbus production continued with minimal change. There was a slight boost to 53 horsepower, from the same displacement. The series again

offered three passenger transporters. The Kombi had passenger seating for eight or nine with all removable seats in place. Its rear windows pivoted outward for extra ventilation. The

Eight-Passenger Station Wagon was fully trimmed inside. The Deluxe Station Wagon included a sunroof, windows all around, and side observation windows. A Campmobile was available. *Ward's* reported that 34,247 Volkswagen trucks were sold to Americans on a calendar-year basis. Model-year production was reported as 31,016 Transporters.

In 1967, a dual-circuit braking system was introduced, but Volkswagen encountered problems with it and removed it from the market until it could be improved. Despite this, the 1966 and 1967 models were the ultimate versions of the first-generation Transporter with the split-windshield styling.

Gary Daniels loaned his Titan Red over Lotus White 1967 Transporter Station Wagon—commonly known as a thirteen-window bus—to the Forney Museum of Transportation in Denver, Colorado, for their 2014 Volkswagen exhibit.

From 1973 to 1979, the amber front safety lights were mounted on either side of the fresh air system grille. Enthusiasts call these post-1972 Transporters "high light" models; the earlier ones built before late 1971 are "low light" models.

1968

The Volkswagen Transporters were restyled for 1968, taking on an appearance closer to American vans with a sliding-type side door. Some reference sources of the time called these the Clipper models for 1968. Later, they were simply identified as the Type 22 and the Type 24. The 24 was an L-trim version with bumper guards and equipment that made it a little longer and wider than the standard version. It also came equipped with radial tires.

Both trim levels gained a larger 1600 engine. It had a 3.36 x 2.27-inch bore and stroke and displaced 96.66 cubic inches (1,584cc). It used a 7.5:1 compression ratio. It developed 57 horsepower at 4,400 rpm. These vehicles had the same wheelbase as the older-style station wagons and trucks, but they were 5½ inches longer. They were also about 1 inch wider and higher.

A one-piece wraparound windshield with rounded corners was used. The side windows were longer, larger, nd vented. A sliding door replaced the double swing-out wing doors on the curbside. This reduced the number of doors from four to three. A sunroof was still optional, but it was now made of metal and was smaller than before. New safety features included a deep-dish steering wheel, a padded dashboard and sun visors, impact-absorbing outside mirrors, and rubber-covered interior knobs. The driver had a new vinyl-trimmed seat.

A new fresh air vent system ducted into the front and rear compartment. A new double-jointed rear suspension was used. Cargo volume, without center or rear seats, rose to 177 cubic feet. Station Wagons received a 28-cubic-foot luggage compartment that was accessible via a hinged rear door.

Passenger models included a Kombi, a Station Wagon, and a Campmobile. The redesigned Type 2 series also included a full line of commercial models.

The new Type 2 or T2 Transporters were built in Germany until 1979. In Mexico, the Kombi and Panel were made from 1970 to 1994. The pre-1971s are often called T2a or Early Bay Window versions. The 1972 and

later T2bs are called Late Bay Window models. The redesign and general modernization of the Transporter pushed production at the Hanover factory to 64,411 trucks. Naturally, the new models were tested by automotive publications, which reported that the new 1600 had a top speed of 72 miles per hour and reached 23 miles per gallon fuel economy.

The new Type 2 or T2 Transporters are known as "Clipper" or "Bay Window" models. They were introduced in 1968 and the early versions are often called T2a models. They had the front parking lights below the headlights, as seen on the camper on page 169. Seen here is a 1972 or later T2b model with the parking lights above the headlights. It also has a camper kit.

This is a 1968 Devon Eurovette camper conversion on a Volkswagen Clipper Type 2 Transporter. It looks like Devon supplied just about everything you could want to camp out in the Woodstock era. *Archives/TEN: The Enthusiast Network Magazines, LLC*

1969

Restyled for 1968, Volkswagen's Microbuses and Campmobiles continued without major change in 1969. Passenger models included a Kombi, a Station Wagon, and a Campmobile. The T2a series lasted three years, and these vehicles were characterized by their rounded bumpers incorporating a step for use when the door was open. These would be replaced by indented bumpers without steps on later models. The 1968–1970 models also had 90-degree opening front doors, front bumper guards with no lip, distinctive engine covers, and crescent-shaped air intakes in the roof pillars. Production rose to 64,411 units this year and 50,361 were sold in the United States.

Standard equipment in a model like the Kombi included a padded dash, sun visors, side panels, two-speed electric wipers with windshield washers, an electric rear window defogger, leatherette upholstery, a breakaway rear view mirror, two outside mirrors, back-up lights, seat belts, and a steering ignition lock. Accessories included trailer hitches, aluminum die-cast side steps, a tissue dispenser, AM or AM/FM radios, bumper overriders, a full-width under-dash parcel shelf, and side window vent shades.

The car that comes in a box.

TOP: Skylight windows were gone and Volkswagen's new bay window Station Wagon had a much cleaner and boxier appearance. A large VW emblem remained on the front, and low-mounted amber parking lights were seen.

BOTTOM: Restyled for 1968, Volkswagen's Station Wagon continued without major change in 1969. The automaker described this as a box that seats seven, but a nine-seat setup was optional. The rear seats were removable for cargo carrying.

1970

The Bay Window Bus did a good job reviving Volkswagen's once-steady growth in the truck segment. In 1970, production climbed again to 71,729 Type 2 models. This year Volkswagen promoted "the car that comes in a box." It described Detroit station wagons as "basically sedans with extra carrying space tagged onto the back end." The sales catalog said the Volkswagen station wagon was a "big carrying space" with an air-cooled engine, a solid-steel bottom, four-wheel independent suspension, and some other good things.

Three rows of seats were still part of the station wagon and Kombi Van equipment, but removing four bolts would loosen all the removable seats. A nine-passenger seating option was available and you could still get a sliding sunroof. The sunroof was smaller than before though and in about the center of the roof.

A car you can feel at home in.

The Volkswagen Station Wagon comes with 3 rows of seats and a front-to-back aisle as standard equipment.

Up front, you'll find big, comfortable seats. In back, nice, roomy benches.

The benches, by the way, can be easily rearranged.

So if you have occasion to turn your Wagon into a nursery, you can.

Just remove 4 bolts. Take out the center seat. Put in a play-pen. And turn Junior loose.

Or serve him dinner.

Anything that's spilled or dropped can be washed away with soap and water.

Because the upholstery and the side paneling are leatherette. And the floor mat is rubber.

You don't have to worry about spilling anything on things like tennis rackets or suitcases either.

They can be tucked safely away in a 35.0 cu. ft. baggage compartment in back of the seats.

That way the people get the seats all to themselves.

But everyone needn't just sit there on their seats. There's plenty of room for legs to cross, elbows to bend, papers to be read.

There are also hooks for coats to be hung. A ventilating system and a heating system with outlets that can be individually adjusted.

So that when you get wherever you're going and step out of the car, you'll feel like you just left home.

The bay window van continued to feature three rows of seats, but now there was a front-to-back aisle to lead passengers to their seat. By undoing a couple of bolts, the seating configurations could be rearranged.

Volkswagen dealers did a great job promoting the use of a diagnostic system to troubleshoot the Beetles and Buses. As this photo shows, the rear window of the bay window bus was also large. A spare was mounted inside.

1971

The Transporter continued without major outward change, except that the amber side safety light was now oblong in shape and was positioned farther forward. As on all the early Bay Window vans, the front turn indicators were mounted low on the nose. US sales of Transporters came to 63,025 units and total production was 74,852, so most buses went to the United States.

The 1971 Transporter did get an improved 1,584cc engine with dual intake ports on each cylinder head. It now produced 60 horsepower at 4,400 rpm and 81.7 pounds-feet of torque at 3,000 rpm. Another important mechanical upgrade was the introduction of front disc brakes and new ventilated road wheels. Air flowing through the ventilation holes in the wheels cooled the disc brakes.

Standard equipment included an adjustable driver's seat and backrest, ashtrays, back-up lights, coat hooks, directional signals (wraparound in front), a dished safety steering wheel, dome lights, a cab and cargo area, dual padded sun visors, a vanity mirror on the right sun visor, seven- to nine-passenger seating options, electric two-speed windshield wipers, four-way emergency flashers, a fresh air heater and defroster, a fresh air ventilation system, an electric rear window defogger, a glove box with a door, a breakaway day-and-night inside rearview mirror, left-hand and right-hand outside rearview mirrors, a leatherette headliner in the cab, leatherette upholstery, a nonrepeat ignition/steering/starter lock, a padded dashboard, roll-down cab windows, seat belts for all seats, side safety

reflectors, a sliding loading door on the right-hand side of the body, an early cut-in 540-watt generator, and a windshield washer system.

The Campmobile included sleeping facilities for two adults and two children. It was available with an adjoining free-standing tent with flooring and window netting, a pop-up top and a luggage rack, and any regular Volkswagen station wagon accessories. Campmobile had a separate sales catalog.

Extras and accessories available for Transporters included whitewall tires, a radio and antenna, a rear radio speaker, a cigarette lighter, a luggage rack, and a ladder that owners could attach in order to be able to reach the luggage rack.

In an April 1971 road test, *Motor Trend* listed the good points of the Volkswagen van as: 1) Good mileage for

a van, over 17 miles per gallon;
2) Size seems just right for city travel;
3) Good road feel and easy steering;
4) Sliding door on side works perfectly, is solid; 5) Finish on interior and exterior is best of lot; 6) Sunroof availability adds sportiness to van concept and, more important, improves already excellent ventilation; 7) Disc brakes provide best stopping of all vans though more anti-dive is needed up front; 8) Air-cooled engine doesn't overheat; 9) Best visibility; 10) Lowest initial investment; and 11) Highest resale value. The station wagon had 176 cubic feet of space and carried a 1,764-pound load.

In the April 1971 issue, *Motor Trend* writer Wally Wyss summarized, "On balance, the VW van [bus] has a severe power shortage and if you have two snowmobiles, it may not carry them; but at nearly $2,000 less ($50 a month for 36 months), it has to be the best value, never mind the fact that on any snowy or ice-slick surface, the front-bias American vans will not move." VW sales success in 1970, more than 65,000 units, was ahead of Dodge, but behind Ford and Chevy.

NEXT PAGE: In 1971, Volkswagen continued to promote the Station Wagon as a "big, roomy box." While the split-window buses caught the eyes of collectors first, the bay window models are being hunted down and restored today.

BELOW: The 1971 Volkswagen Station Wagon was the passenger-carrying bus. In a comparison with Ford, Dodge, and Chevy vans, the VW was rated best in size, finish, quality, and ease of handling. It did not have the power of the others. *Archives/TEN: The Enthusiast Network Magazines, LLC*

The Wagon is finished with 3 coats of paint
to protect the body against rust and corrosion for years.

Electric
defogger
defogs
rear
window.

Vent window.

48.4" x 28.7" door lifts up,
gives separate access to 35.0 cu. ft.
carpeted luggage compartment.

Separate engine compartment door lets you
get to the engine without having to unload luggage.

253 lb. engine is mounted above rear wheels to provide extra
traction in snow, sand and slush, and eliminate need for a
drive shaft.

3½' x 4' side door slides close to body.
Doesn't open into anyone's way,
or into a car parked beside you.

Double-jointed axle makes
each drive wheel more secure.
Improves stability and handling
on curves and turns.

Nearly 16,000 spot welds join the Wagon's body into one unitized
piece of steel (even the sunroof is steel) strong enough to carry almost a ton.

and the big roomy box it comes in.

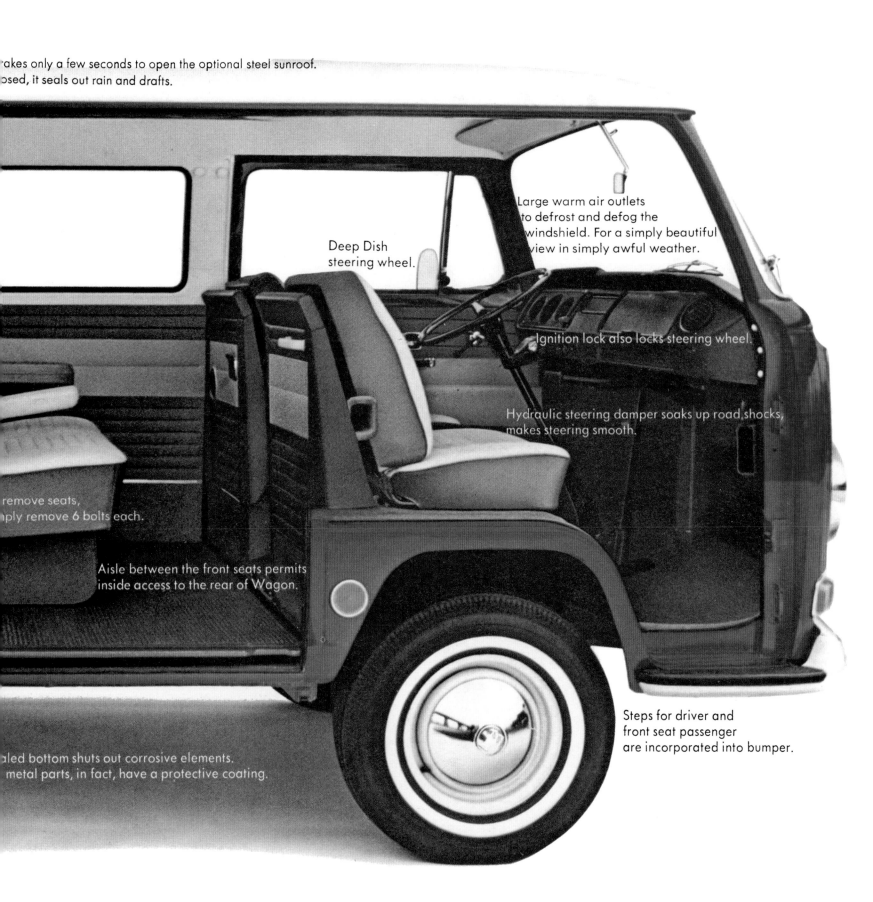

...akes only a few seconds to open the optional steel sunroof. ...osed, it seals out rain and drafts.

Deep Dish steering wheel.

Large warm air outlets to defrost and defog the windshield. For a simply beautiful view in simply awful weather.

Ignition lock also locks steering wheel.

Hydraulic steering damper soaks up road shocks, makes steering smooth.

...remove seats, ...ply remove 6 bolts each.

Aisle between the front seats permits inside access to the rear of Wagon.

Steps for driver and front seat passenger are incorporated into bumper.

...led bottom shuts out corrosive elements. ...metal parts, in fact, have a protective coating.

1972

In 1972, the 1,679cc Type 4 engine developed for the company's 411 and 412 models became an option for the Type 2 Transporters sold in Europe. The 1700 Type 4 engine was standard in Transporters headed for the US market. That market was becoming a good place to sell Volkswagen buses as *Ward's 1973*

Automotive Yearbook reported sales of 49,235 Type 2 models there and most were the Station Wagons commonly referred to as buses. *Ward's* also indicated that Volkswagen sold only 485 trucks in the USA, other than vans. In all, 66,400 Transporters were produced, so it's clear that most went to the United States.

Enlarging the Transporter's rear engine bay required the elimination of the removable rear apron and also led to the use of larger taillights. The engine air intakes were also enlarged to provide more cooling air for the larger 1700 engine.

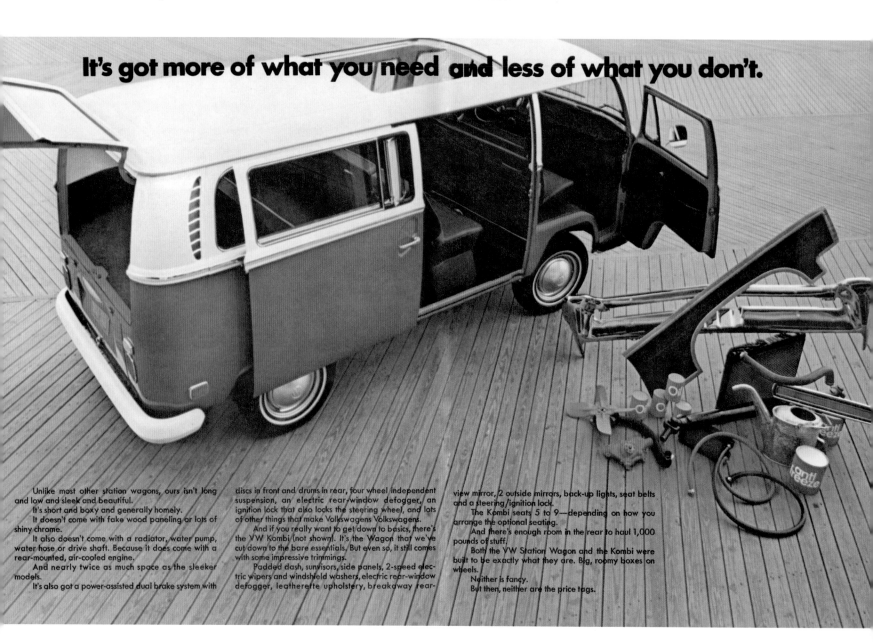

It's got more of what you need and less of what you don't.

Unlike most other station wagons, ours isn't long and low and sleek and beautiful.

It's short and boxy and generally homely.

It doesn't come with fake wood paneling or lots of shiny chrome.

It also doesn't come with a radiator, water pump, water hose or drive shaft. Because it does come with a rear-mounted, air-cooled engine.

And nearly twice as much space as the sleeker models.

It's also got a power-assisted dual brake system with

discs in front and drums in rear, four wheel independent suspension, an electric rear-window defogger, an ignition lock that also locks the steering wheel, and lots of other things that make Volkswagens Volkswagens.

And if you really want to get down to basics, there's the VW Kombi (not shown). It's the Wagon that we've cut down to the bare essentials. But even so, it still comes with some impressive trimmings.

Padded dash, sunvisors, side panels, 2-speed electric wipers and windshield washers, electric rear-window defogger, leatherette upholstery, breakaway rear-

view mirror, 2 outside mirrors, back-up lights, seat belts and a steering/ignition lock.

The Kombi seats 5 to 9—depending on how you arrange the optional seating.

And there's enough room in the rear to haul 1,000 pounds of stuff.

Both the VW Station Wagon and the Kombi were built to be exactly what they are. Big, roomy boxes on wheels.

Neither is fancy.

But then, neither are the price tags.

Enlarging the 1972 Transporter's rear engine bay required elimination of the removable rear apron and led to the use of larger taillights. The engine air intakes were also enlarged to provide more cooling air for a new 1,700cc engine.

It goes more places more easily.

One of the most surprising things about our Station Wagon is that it's the smallest as well as the biggest. Not only can you put more into it than in two ordinary wagons, but you can also put it into parking spots two feet shorter than an ordinary station wagon.

The fact is, our Wagon is only about one foot longer than our Bug. So it can fit into almost all the same places the Bug fits. Which is almost anywhere.

And, because it's higher, it gives the driver a clearer view of the road, as well as a clearer view of parking spots.

But tight parking spots aren't the only places where a VW makes the best of it.

It was built to keep going when the going gets rough. The body is welded and unitized with the chassis. And because it's more than 7 inches above the road,

it's also well above most rocks.

But whether or not the road is bumpy, you won't really care.

The Wagon has a 4-wheel independent torsion bar suspension system. Which means that the wheels take the bumps, not the passengers.

It's also got a 4-speed synchromesh transmission that helps to smooth out hills.

Snow, sand or dirt won't hold you back either because of the added traction you get with a rear-mounted engine. And because the engine is air-cooled, you don't have to worry about boiling over in summer. Or freezing up in winter.

In fact, you won't have to worry at all. With everything our Wagon has going for it, you'll be in good shape on just about any road, any time of year.

Volkswagen said the 1972 Station Wagon was built to keep going when driving conditions got rough. Maybe that's why most of the 49,235 Type 2 models sold in the US that year were Station Wagons. Only 485 were commercial trucks.

1973

Ward's said that 58,442 Transporters were produced in 1973 and 42,656 Type 2 models (trucks and buses) were sold in the United States. However, only 247 of them were trucks, which never caught on big there.

Up front, the amber safety lights were mounted further up, on either side of the grille work for the fresh air system. Enthusiasts call these post-1972 Transporters high light models and the earlier ones built before late 1971 are low light models. The VW bus also gained a 5-mile-per-hour crash bumper, more crash-worthy front-end sheet metal, and an engine access hatch in the trunk. The VW emblem just below the front-end air intake louvers was also a bit smaller.

On the bus, engine torque was improved to accept a new optional automatic transmission that was essentially the same as the ZF three-speed unit used in the Fastback and Squareback. The 102.5-cubic-inch engine was now rated at 63 SAE net horsepower when used in the Transporter with manual transmission and 66 horsepower when attached to the new automatic transmission.

VW BUS and TRUCK FACTS

▥ A chart in the 1959 Volkswagen Truck sales catalog listed production at the Volkswagen Hanover, Germany, factory as 30 units a day in 1950, 47 units a day in 1951, 84 units a day in 1952, 106 units a day in 1953, 153 units a day in 1954, 189 units a day in 1955, 247 units a day in 1956 after a new plant opened there, 383 units a day in 1957, and 420 units a day in 1958.

The popularity of the Bay Window Transporters began to wane rather quickly in the mid-1970s. Only 38,700 were produced in 1974 and most of them were intended for the US market, where 29,919 were sold.

The 1974 Type 4 engine used in the Transporter models was enlarged to 1.8 liters and the output increased to 65 horsepower in 1974 (67 horsepower with automatic). This engine had a 3.66 x 2.59-inch bore and stroke and 1,795cc displacement.

Design-wise, the second-generation Type 2s would not change again until the Vanagon replaced them. So, the 1974 versions retained the higher, squarer front safety lights introduced in the 1973 model year, as well as the 5-mile-per-hour compressible crash bumpers that satisfied US safety standards for passenger cars of the time, even though van-type vehicles did not have to meet these.

And if you want a little more you can get a lot more.

The VW Station Wagon has just about everything you need but the kitchen sink.

The VW Campmobile even has the sink.

Along with an icebox. A dining table. Work tables. Closets (including a full-length closet with a mirrored door). Bins and cabinets for groceries and utensils. And a 110-volt outlet that connects to an outside power source and can handle anything from can openers to TVs.

For sleeping, the back seat becomes a double bed. With a mattress. A bench seat becomes a child's bed. There's even a hammock for the littlest member of the family.

What's more, all of these are standard equipment.

There are lots of other homey, built-in touches, too. Like curtains on all windows. A 3-way ceiling lamp. Vinyl flooring. And insulated wood paneling.

Two side windows are louvered and screened. And there's a snap-on screen for the door in the rear.

But if you still need more room, there are a few optional extras that might interest you. Like a pop-up top and tent for extra headroom. And extra sleeping room.

The tent can be an extra bedroom, a screened-in living room or a playroom. It's got its own floor and is completely free standing. So you can drive away for

the day and le
And whe
and tables fol
And then
basic advanta
Same roc
Same ec
Same 4-
the same smoc
And the s
And ever
nets left in, yo
station wagon
Of cours
beaches and
room in the wo

1975

Electronic fuel injection was now standard in the boxy Station Wagon's rear engine. Prices climbed roughly $500 on most models, but a little more on the Campmobile, which was priced with camping equipment. Very few other changes were made. Even the color choices remained the same for the third year in a row. A total of 29,082 Transporters left the Hanover plant during the model year and calendar-year sales in the United States amounted to 21,547 vehicles.

ABOVE: The 1974 Volkswagen Bus retained the higher, squarer front safety lights introduced in the 1973 model year, as well as the 5-mile-per-hour compressible crash bumpers that satisfied US safety standards for passenger cars of the time.

LEFT: For 1973, the price of a Volkswagen Campmobile was up to $3,499, but that included the wooden cabinets, folding bed, folding table, and closet (shown in the inset photos). The side tent was still optional.

1976-1978

The 1976–1978 Volkswagen Transporter received a larger new 2.0-liter engine. Also starting in 1976, an exposed fuel filler cap was used. Prices climbed again and were nearly $800 higher on most models. New colors were introduced this year. Total production went up slightly to 31,390 and US sales were 19,464.

Volkswagen's new Transporter engine was again a horizontally opposed, overhead-valve, air-cooled four-cylinder with a 3.70 x 2.80-inch (94 x 71mm) bore and stroke. It displaced 120.2 cubic inches (1,970cc). The engine had a 7.3:1 compression ratio and made 67 horsepower at 4,200 rpm and 101 pounds-feet of torque at 3,000 rpm. It had four main bearings, solid valve lifters, and electronic fuel injection.

All through these Bay Window years, Volkswagen continued to provide special order versions of Panels, Pick-Ups, and Kombis for commercial buyers, mostly for sales in Europe. More than fifty models were offered by the Pon family dealerships that were still selling Volkswagens in Holland. The lineup included fire trucks, refrigerated vans, snowplows, a glazer's truck, a street cleaner, dump (tipper) trucks, boom trucks, ice cream trucks, and produce delivery trucks.

Production totals for Transporters were 31,390 in 1976, 38,068 in 1977, and 34,331 in 1978. In the United States, Volkswagen dealers sold 19,464 of these vehicles in 1976, a bit more in 1977 when 26,108 were sold, and 23,322 in 1978. It's possible that tourist deliveries added a few sales, but not many.

LEFT: This beautifully preserved 1976 Camper owned by Jerry Hartley has a pop-up roof that adds more height and light in the interior. A covered spare tire is carried up front.

BELOW: The interior of Jerry Hartley's 1976 Volkswagen Type 2 Camper includes cabinetry, a sofa bed, a sink, an icebox, and other camping necessities. Note how neatly and efficiently everything is set up and packaged.

1979

This was the last year that the Model T2 or Bay Window Transporter was produced. The Transporter again was little changed. Only 22,384 were built and just 15,901 were sold in the United States. By this time, Volkswagen had experimented with prototype four-wheel-drive vans.

This Volkswagen Bus dates from 1978, the next-to-last year for the "high lights." The color combination is Pastel White over Sage Green. It is one of 34,331 built for the model year.

1980-1982
Air-Cooled Vanagon

The new-for-1980 Volkswagen Bus was still a Type 2 (van or bus), but had a T3 series designation that could fool people. To make things even more confusing, it is also called the T25. Instead of calling it a Transporter, Volkswagen dubbed it the Vanagon. It was one of the final new models to use an air-cooled engine and that was true only in the first few years it was offered.

Compared to Bay Window models, the Vanagon was larger, with an accompanying increase in weight. The body was longer and cleaner looking. It had more of a square or wedge shape than any of Volkswagen's previous boxcars. The windshield glass was larger. It had something no other Transporter ever had—a grille. A small VW emblem was in the center of the grille.

The Vanagon had single round headlights at the outboard edges of the narrow grille, low-mounted front amber safety lights, low-mounted brake lights, and a sliding door on the right side of the body. It had vent windows and four windows on each side and a one-piece rear glass. The D-pillar had seven-slot air vents. Vanagons came in the same passenger-carrying models: Kombi, Seven-Passenger Station Wagon and Nine-Passenger Station Wagon, and Campmobile. Commercial versions with special order work bodies were also available.

Though still rear-engined, the Volkswagen Microbus series was restyled for 1980. The new version was a longer, wider, and cleaner-looking vehicle than its predecessor. Rather than Transporter, the new series adopted the Vanagon designation. In 1983, the Vanagon received a water-cooled engine.

Vanagon production came to 28,673 units in 1980, 25,083 in 1981, and 24,203 in 1982. Sales in the United States for the same three years in order were 13,167, 10,881, and 12,848. Out of the 13,167 sold in the United States in 1980, the following equipment installations were made: Four-speed manual transmission (90.2 percent), automatic transmission (9.8 percent), power disc brakes (100 percent), radial tires (100 percent), reclining bucket seats (92 percent), tinted glass (100 percent), rear defogger (100 percent), clock (100 percent), and sunroof (6.6 percent).

The new-for-1980 "Volkswagen Bus" was dubbed the Vanagon (a combination of "van" and "wagon"). It was one of the final new VW models to use an air-cooled engine, and that was true only in the first few years it was offered.

1983

Although the early air-cooled Vanagons were replaced by the water-cooled version in 1983, production of air-cooled models continued in some countries, such as Mexico and Brazil.

Transporter manufacturing had actually begun in Mexico during 1970, when the nine-passenger Kombi went into production at the Puebla plant. Panel truck versions started coming off the assembly line three years later. At one point in 1975, production of Pick-Up trucks was considered, but this concept was never followed through on after the evaluation period.

The Mexican-built vehicles used the air-cooled 1500 engine originally and switched to the air-cooled 1600 in 1974. Only the four-speed manual gearbox was installed. Production continued until sometime in 1987, when a water-cooled 1800 engine was adopted instead. The water-cooled models required a grille.

The air-cooled Transporter (called by the Kombi designation) was also a popular vehicle in Brazil, where it was introduced in 1950 and marketed all the way through late December of 2005. Bus versions and Panel trucks were made there, including a 12-passenger metro bus and school bus model.

Brazilian emission laws were being tightened for 2006 and the only way

Volkswagens could meet them were to change to water-cooled engines. The last air-cooled Volkswagen engine ever built was used in a specially trimmed Kombi van made in Brazil toward the end of production in 2005. It had special silver paint and limited-edition badges and two hundred copies were made as 2006 models.

Vanagons came in the same passenger-carrying models including this Camper. Commercial versions with special order "work bodies" were available. P22 Standard and P27 Deluxe (with a three-way refrigerator) models were offered.

Vanagon Camper.
Two new ones to keep you "at home" on the go.

What's happened to most other leisure vehicles is quite obvious. They've become much too heavy to keep up with today's travel style. Vanagon Campers carry on a long tradition of careful craftsmanship and flawless interior design. There's room for four people in the deluxe version (P27), even more — five people — in the standard model (P22). Vanagon Campers provide double beds — one upper, one lower. There's storage virtually everywhere. No nook is wasted. Part of your enjoyment comes from the combination of the swivel front bucket seats and swivel store away tables. The driver's seat swivels 90° to the right, and the passenger seat can be swung 180° to face the rear. Swivel tables have no "legs" to

New aerodynamic styling provides greater directional control.

get in your way. The biggest difference between our two new Vanagon Campers centers around cooling and cooking. The more-deluxe version (P27) comes with a 3-way refrigerator and a two-burner propane cookstove. The **big difference** in Vanagon Campers over others is, of course, the tremendous amount of headroom provided by the pop-up roof. You enjoy maximum ceiling height where you need it most — over the food preparation area and the access to the upper double bed. Ask for the EPA Mileage Guide and compare Vanagon fuel economy with similar vehicles. A closer look at Vanagon Camper should be your next stop, before heading for the great outdoors.

Deluxe (P27) interior, has 2-burner cookstove and 3-way refrigerator. Seating: Gazelle background "Boogie Woogie" cloth.

1950

VOLKSWAGEN TRANSPORTER

FACTORY PAINT COLORS

Not Available

MODEL AVAILABILITY	4-door Standard ($2,058)
	4-door Deluxe ($2,195)
WHEELBASE	94.5 inches
LENGTH	(Standard) 159.3 inches
WIDTH	67.0 inches
HEIGHT	(Standard) 74.5 inches
WEIGHT	(all) 2,100 lbs.
TREAD	(front/rear) 53.4/53.5 inches
TIRES	(Standard) 5.50 x 16
BRAKES	Hydraulic, front/rear drum
CONSTRUCTION	Steel unibody on stamped-steel floorpan
FUEL TANK	10.5 gallons
FRONT SUSPENSION	Independent: two square section torsion bars
REAR SUSPENSION	Independent: circular torsion bars each side
ENGINE	1,131cc 24.5-hp horizontally opposed four-cylinder, overhead valve, air cooled, light alloy block and head, finned cylinders with cast-iron liners
TRANSMISSION	four-speed manual
FINAL DRIVE RATIO	6.2:1

1951

VOLKSWAGEN TRANSPORTER

FACTORY PAINT COLORS

Not Available

MODEL AVAILABILITY	4-door Standard ($2,058)
	4-door Deluxe ($2,195)
WHEELBASE	94.5 inches
LENGTH	(Standard) 155 inches; (Deluxe) 156.1 inches
WIDTH	67.0 inches
HEIGHT	74.5 inches
WEIGHT	(all) 2,100 lbs.
TREAD	(front/rear) 53.4/53.5 inches
TIRES	5.50 x 16
BRAKES	Hydraulic, front/rear drum
CONSTRUCTION	Steel unibody on stamped-steel floorpan
FUEL TANK	10.5 gallons
FRONT SUSPENSION	Independent: two square section torsion bars
REAR SUSPENSION	Independent: circular torsion bars each side
ENGINE	1,131cc 24.5-hp horizontally opposed four-cylinder, overhead valve, air cooled, light alloy block and head, finned cylinders with cast-iron liners
TRANSMISSION	four-speed manual
FINAL DRIVE RATIO	6.2:1

1952

VOLKSWAGEN TRANSPORTER

FACTORY PAINT COLORS

L31 Dove Blue
L62 Ivory (Ambulance)
L28 Grey (Ambulance)
L73/L53 Chestnut Brown/
Sealing Wax Red

L76/L75 Brownish Beige/
Light Beige
L23 Silver Grey

MODEL AVAILABILITY	4-door Standard ($1,905)
	4-door Deluxe ($2,169)
WHEELBASE	94.5 inches
LENGTH	(Standard) 161.5 inches
WIDTH	67.0 inches
HEIGHT	74.8 inches
WEIGHT	(Standard) 2,200 lbs.
TREAD	(front/rear) 53.4/53.5 inches
TIRES	5.50 x 16
BRAKES	Hydraulic, front/rear drum
CONSTRUCTION	Steel unibody on stamped-steel floorpan
FUEL TANK	10.5 gallons
FRONT SUSPENSION	Independent: two square section torsion bars
REAR SUSPENSION	Independent: circular torsion bars each side
ENGINE	1,131cc 24.5-hp horizontally opposed four-cylinder, overhead valve, air cooled, light alloy block and head, finned cylinders with cast-iron liners
TRANSMISSION	four-speed manual
FINAL DRIVE RATIO	6.2:1

1953

VOLKSWAGEN TRANSPORTER

FACTORY PAINT COLORS

L31 Dove Blue
L62 Ivory (Ambulance)
L21 Pearl Grey
L73/L53 Chestnut Brown/
Sealing Wax Red

L76/L75 Brownish Beige/
Light Beige
L23 Silver Grey

MODEL AVAILABILITY	4-door Standard (n/a)
	4-door Deluxe (n/a)
WHEELBASE	94.5 inches
LENGTH	(Standard) 161.5 inches
WIDTH	67.0 inches
HEIGHT	74.8 inches
WEIGHT	(Standard) 2,200 lbs.
TREAD	(front/rear) 53.4/53.5 inches
TIRES	5.50 x 16
BRAKES	Hydraulic, front/rear drum
CONSTRUCTION	Steel unibody on stamped-steel floorpan
FUEL TANK	10.5 gallons
FRONT SUSPENSION	Independent: two square section torsion bars
REAR SUSPENSION	Independent: circular torsion bars each side
ENGINE	1,131cc 24.5-hp horizontally opposed four-cylinder, overhead valve, air cooled, light alloy block and head, finned cylinders with cast-iron liners
TRANSMISSION	four-speed manual
FINAL DRIVE RATIO	6.2:1

1954

VOLKSWAGEN TRANSPORTER

FACTORY PAINT COLORS

L31 Dove Blue
L62 Ivory (Ambulance)
L29 Grey (Ambulance)
L73/L53 Chestnut Brown/
Sealing Wax Red

L76/L75 Brownish Beige/
Light Beige
L21 Pearl Grey

MODEL AVAILABILITY	4-door Standard (n/a)
	4-door Deluxe (n/a)
	Kombi (n/a)
WHEELBASE	94.5 inches
LENGTH	(Standard) 161.5 inches
WIDTH	67.0 inches
HEIGHT	74.8 inches
WEIGHT	(Standard) 2,200 lbs.
TREAD	(front/rear) 53.4/53.5 inches
TIRES	5.50 x 16
BRAKES	Hydraulic, front/rear drum
CONSTRUCTION	Steel unibody on stamped-steel floorpan
FUEL TANK	10.5 gallons
FRONT SUSPENSION	Independent: two square section torsion bars
REAR SUSPENSION	Independent: circular torsion bars each side
ENGINE	1,192cc 30-hp horizontally opposed four-cylinder, overhead valve, air cooled, light alloy block and head, finned cylinders with cast-iron liners
TRANSMISSION	four-speed manual
FINAL DRIVE RATIO	6.2:1

1955

VOLKSWAGEN TRANSPORTER

FACTORY PAINT COLORS

L31 Dove Blue
(to Feb. 28, 1955)
L31 Dove Blue
(from March 1, 1955)
L62 Ivory (Ambulance)
L28 Grey (Ambulance)
L73/L53 Chestnut Brown/
Sealing Wax Red
(to Feb. 28, 1955)

L73/L53 Chestnut Brown/
Sealing Wax Red
(from March 1, 1955)
L76/L75 Brownish Beige/
Light Beige
L312/L311 Palm Green/
Sand Green

MODEL AVAILABILITY	4-door Standard (n/a)
	4-door Deluxe (n/a)
	Kombi (n/a)
WHEELBASE	94.5 inches
LENGTH	(Standard) 165 inches
WIDTH	67.0 inches
HEIGHT	74.8 inches
WEIGHT	(Standard) 2,127 lbs.
TREAD	(front/rear) 53.4/53.5 inches
TIRES	5.50 x 16
BRAKES	Hydraulic, front/rear drum
CONSTRUCTION	Steel unibody on stamped-steel floorpan
FUEL TANK	10.5 gallons
FRONT SUSPENSION	Independent: two square section torsion bars
REAR SUSPENSION	Independent: circular torsion bars each side
ENGINE	1,192cc 30-hp horizontally opposed four-cylinder, overhead valve, air cooled, light alloy block and head, finned cylinders with cast-iron liners
TRANSMISSION	four-speed manual
FINAL DRIVE RATIO	6.2:1

1956

VOLKSWAGEN TRANSPORTER

PAINT COLORS

211 DELUXE VAN, 231–235 KOMBI, 261–264 PICK-UP

L2 Pearl Grey

L28 Grey

L31 Dove Blue

L62 Ivory

MODEL AVAILABILITY	4-door Standard ($2,095)
	4-door Deluxe ($2,545)
	Kombi ($1,995)
WHEELBASE	94.5 inches
LENGTH	(Standard) 165 inches
WIDTH	67.0 inches
HEIGHT	76.5 inches
WEIGHT	(Standard) 2,100 lbs.
TREAD	(front/rear) 53.9/53.5 inches
TIRES	5.40 x 16
BRAKES	Hydraulic, front/rear drum
CONSTRUCTION	Steel unibody on stamped-steel floorpan
FUEL TANK	10.5 gallons
FRONT SUSPENSION	Independent: two square section torsion bars
REAR SUSPENSION	Independent: circular torsion bars each side
ENGINE	1,192cc 36-hp horizontally opposed four-cylinder, overhead valve, air cooled, light alloy block and head, finned cylinders with cast-iron liners
TRANSMISSION	four-speed manual
FINAL DRIVE RATIO	6.2:1

1957

VOLKSWAGEN TRANSPORTER

FACTORY PAINT COLORS

L11 Pastel Green

L14 Mignonette

L31 Dove Blue

L53 Sealing Wax Red

L73 Chestnut Brown

L271 Texas Brown

L315 Jungle Green Metallic

MODEL AVAILABILITY	4-door Kombi ($1,995)
	4-door Standard Microbus ($2,095)
	4-door Deluxe ($2,235)
	Camper ($2,712)
WHEELBASE	94.5 inches
LENGTH	(Standard) 165 inches
WIDTH	68.0 inches
HEIGHT	76.5 inches
WEIGHT	(Standard) 2,072 lbs.
TREAD	(front/rear) 53.9/53.5 inches
TIRES	5.40 x 16
BRAKES	Hydraulic, front/rear drum
CONSTRUCTION	Steel unibody on stamped-steel floorpan
FUEL TANK	10.5 gallons
FRONT SUSPENSION	Independent: two square section torsion bars
REAR SUSPENSION	Independent: circular torsion bars each side
ENGINE	1,192cc 36-hp horizontally opposed four-cylinder, overhead valve, air cooled, light alloy block and head, finned cylinders with cast-iron liners
TRANSMISSION	four-speed manual
FINAL DRIVE RATIO	6.2:1

1958

VOLKSWAGEN TRANSPORTER

FACTORY PAINT COLORS

L14 Mignonette	**L87** Pearl White
L31 Dove Blue	**L345** Pate Grey
L53 Sealing Wax Red	**L346** Mango Green
L73 Chestnut Brown	**L472** Beige Grey
L82 Silver White	

MODEL AVAILABILITY	4-door Kombi ($2,020)
	4-door Standard Microbus ($2,120)
	4-door Deluxe ($2,576)
	Camper ($2,888)
WHEELBASE	94.5 inches
LENGTH	(Standard) 165 inches
WIDTH	68.0 inches
HEIGHT	76.5 inches
WEIGHT	(Standard) 2,072 lbs.
TREAD	(front/rear) 53.9/53.5 inches
TIRES	5.40 x 16
BRAKES	Hydraulic, front/rear drum
CONSTRUCTION	Steel unibody on stamped-steel floorpan
FUEL TANK	10.5 gallons
FRONT SUSPENSION	Independent: two square section torsion bars
REAR SUSPENSION	Independent: circular torsion bars each side
ENGINE	1,192cc 36-hp horizontally opposed four-cylinder, overhead valve, air cooled, light alloy block and head, finned cylinders with cast-iron liners
TRANSMISSION	four-speed manual
FINAL DRIVE RATIO	6.2:1

1959

VOLKSWAGEN TRANSPORTER

FACTORY PAINT COLORS

211 DELUXE VAN, 231–235 KOMBI, 261–264 PICK-UP (DOUBLE CAB)

L31 Dove Blue	**L345L** Light Grey
L53 Sealing Wax Red	

221–228 MICROBUS, 281–295 MICROBUS (SPLIT BUCKET SEATS)

L346/L347 Mango Green/ Sea Gull Grey	**L21** Pearl Grey

241–251 MICROBUS DELUXE

L21 Pearl Grey	Red/Beige Grey
L53/L472 Sealing Wax	

AMBULANCE

L62 Ivory

MODEL AVAILABILITY	4-door Kombi ($2,045)
	4-door Standard Microbus ($2,120)
	4-door Deluxe ($2,576)
	Camper ($2,886)
WHEELBASE	94.5 inches
LENGTH	(Station Wagon/Panel/Kombi) 168.9 inches (Pick-Up and Double Cab) 169.3 inches
WIDTH	(Deluxe Station Wagon) 70.9 inches (Other Models) 68.9 inches
HEIGHT	(Except Pick-Up) 76.4 inches (Pick-Up) 75.6 inches (with bows & tarp) 87.0 inches
WEIGHT	(Panel Delivery) 2,249 lbs. (Station Wagon) 2,447 lbs.
TREAD	(front/rear) 53.9/53.5 inches
TIRES	6.40 x 15
BRAKES	Hydraulic, front/rear drum
CONSTRUCTION	Steel unibody on stamped-steel floorpan
FUEL TANK	10.6 gallons
FRONT SUSPENSION	Independent: two laminated torsion bars
REAR SUSPENSION	Independent: one round torsion bar each side
ENGINE	1,192cc 36-hp horizontally opposed four-cylinder, overhead valve, air cooled, light alloy block and head, finned cylinders with cast-iron liners
TRANSMISSION	four-speed manual
FINAL DRIVE RATIO	6.2:1

1960

VOLKSWAGEN TRANSPORTER

FACTORY PAINT COLORS

211 DELIVERY VAN, 231–235 KOMBI, 261–264 PICK-UP/DOUBLE CAB

L31 Dove Blue   **L345** Light Grey

L53 Sealing Wax Red

221–228 MICROBUS, MICROBUS (SPLIT, BUCKET SEATS)

L346/347 Mango Green/Sea   **L21** Pearl Grey
Gull Grey

241–251 MICROBUS DELUXE

L21 Pearl Grey   **L53/L472** Sealing Wax Red/
Beige Grey

AMBULANCE

L62 Ivory

MODEL AVAILABILITY	4-door Kombi ($2,095)
	4-door Standard Microbus ($2,245)
	4-door Deluxe ($2,620)
	Camper ($2,886)
WHEELBASE	94.5 inches
LENGTH	(Station Wagon/Panel/Kombi) 168.9 inches
	(Pick-Up and Double Cab) 169.3

WIDTH	(Deluxe Station Wagon) 70.9 inches
	(Other Models) 68.9 inches
HEIGHT	(Except Pick-Up) 76.4 inches
	(Pick-Up) 75.6 inches (with bows & tarp)
	87.0 inches
WEIGHT	(Panel Delivery) 2,249 lbs.
	(Station Wagon) 2,447 lbs.
TREAD	(front/rear) 53.9/53.5 inches
TIRES	6.40 x 15
BRAKES	Hydraulic, front/rear drum
CONSTRUCTION	Steel unibody on stamped-steel floorpan
FUEL TANK	10.6 gallons
FRONT SUSPENSION	Independent: two laminated torsion bars
REAR SUSPENSION	Independent: one round torsion bar each side
ENGINE	1,192cc 36-hp horizontally opposed four-cylinder, overhead valve, air cooled, light alloy block and head, finned cylinders with cast-iron liners
TRANSMISSION	four-speed manual
FINAL DRIVE RATIO	6.2:1

VOLKSWAGEN TRANSPORTER

FACTORY PAINT COLORS

211 DELIVERY VAN, 231–235 KOMBI, 261–268 PICK-UP/DOUBLE CAB

L31 Dove Blue   **L345** Light Grey
L53 Sealing Wax Red

221–228 MICROBUS, 281–285 MICROBUS (SPLIT, BUCKET SEATS)

L346/L347 Mango Green/ Sea Gull Grey (to 3/31/61)

L21 Pearl Grey (to 3/31/61)

L380/L289 Turquoise/ Blue White (from 4/1/61)

L53/L472 Sealing Wax Red/Beige Grey (from 4/1/61)

L325/L87 Mouse Grey/ Pearl White (from 4/1/61)

L1009 Yukon Yellow

L325/L87 Mouse Grey/ Pearl White (from 4/1/61)

241–251 MICROBUS DELUXE

L21 Pearl Grey (to 3/31/61)

L53/L472 Sealing Wax Red/Beige Grey (to 3/31/61)

L380/L289 Turquoise/ Blue White (from 4/1/61)

L53/L472 Sealing Wax Red/Beige Grey (from 4/1/61)

L325/L87 Mouse Grey/ Pearl White (from 4/1/61)

AMBULANCE

L62 Ivory

MODEL AVAILABILITY	4-door Kombi ($1,995)
	4-door Standard Microbus ($2,245)
	4-door Deluxe ($2,620)
	Camper ($2,973)
SERIAL NUMBERS	623734–802426
WHEELBASE	94.5 inches
LENGTH	(Station Wagon/Panel/Kombi) 168.9 inches
	(Pick-Up and Double Cab) 169.3 inches
WIDTH	(Deluxe Station Wagon) 70.9 inches
	(Other Models) 68.9 inches
HEIGHT	(Except Pick-Up) 76.4 inches
	(Pick-Up) 75.6 inches (with bows & tarp) 87.0 inches
WEIGHT	(Panel Delivery) 2,249 lbs.
	(Station Wagon) 2,447 lbs.
TREAD	(front/rear) 53.9/53.5 inches
TIRES	6.40 x 15
BRAKES	Hydraulic, front/rear drum
CONSTRUCTION	Steel unibody on stamped-steel floorpan
FUEL TANK	10.6 gallons
FRONT SUSPENSION	Independent: two laminated torsion bars
REAR SUSPENSION	Independent: one round torsion bar each side
ENGINE	1,192cc 40-hp horizontally opposed four-cylinder, overhead valve, air cooled, light alloy block and head, finned cylinders with cast-iron liners
TRANSMISSION	four-speed manual
FINAL DRIVE RATIO	6.2:1

1962

VOLKSWAGEN TRANSPORTER

FACTORY PAINT COLORS

211 DELIVERY VAN, 231–235 KOMBI, 261–268 PICK-UP/DOUBLE CAB

L31 Dove Blue   **L345** Light Grey

L53 Sealing Wax Red   **L380** Turquoise

L87 Pearl White   **L456** Ruby Red

221–228 MICROBUS, 281–285 MICROBUS

L380/L289 Turquoise/ Blue White   **L325/L87** Mouse Grey/ Pearl White

L53/L472 Sealing Wax Red/Beige Grey

241–251 MICROBUS DELUXE

L380/L289 Turquoise/ Blue White   **L325/L87** Mouse Grey/ Pearl White

L53/L472 Sealing Wax Red/Beige Grey

AMBULANCE

L62 Ivory

MODEL AVAILABILITY	4-door Kombi ($1,995)
	4-door Standard Microbus ($2,275)
	4-door Deluxe ($2,655)
	Camper ($2,982)
SERIAL NUMBERS	802427–971550
WHEELBASE	94.5 inches

LENGTH	(Station Wagon/Panel/Kombi) 168.9 inches
	(Pick-Up and Double Cab) 169.3 inches
WIDTH	(Deluxe Station Wagon) 70.9 inches
	(Other Models) 68.9 inches
HEIGHT	(Except Pick-Up) 76.4 inches
	(Pick-Up) 75.6 inches (with bows & tarp)
	87.0 inches
WEIGHT	(Panel Delivery) 2,249 lbs.
	(Station Wagon) 2,447 lbs.
TREAD	(front/rear) 53.9/53.5 inches
TIRES	6.40 x 15
BRAKES	Hydraulic, front/rear drum
CONSTRUCTION	Steel unibody on stamped-steel floorpan
FUEL TANK	10.6 gallons
FRONT SUSPENSION	Independent: two laminated torsion bars
REAR SUSPENSION	Independent: one round torsion bar each side
ENGINE	1,192cc 40-hp horizontally opposed four-cylinder, overhead valve, air cooled, light alloy block and head, finned cylinders with cast-iron liners
TRANSMISSION	four-speed manual
FINAL DRIVE RATIO	6.2:1

1963

VOLKSWAGEN TRANSPORTER

FACTORY PAINT COLORS

211 DELIVERY VAN, 231–235 KOMBI, 261–268 PICK-UP/DOUBLE CAB

L31	Dove Blue	**L345**	Light Grey
L53	Sealing Wax Red	**L380**	Turquoise
L87	Pearl White	**L456**	Ruby Red

221–228 MICROBUS, 241–251 MICROBUS DELUXE, 281–285 MICROBUS

L380/L289 Turquoise/
Blue White

L53 Sealing Wax Red/L472
Beige Grey

L325/L87 Mouse Grey/
Pearl White

241–251 MICROBUS DELUXE

L380/L289 Turquoise/
Blue White

L53/L472 Sealing Wax
Red/Beige Grey

L325/L87 Mouse Grey/
Pearl White

AMBULANCE

L62 Ivory

MODEL AVAILABILITY	4-door Kombi ($1,995)
	4-door Standard Microbus ($2,275)
	4-door Deluxe ($2,655)
	Camper ($2,982)
SERIAL NUMBERS	802427–971550
WHEELBASE	94.5 inches

LENGTH	(Station Wagon/Panel/Kombi) 168.9 inches
	(Pick-Up and Double Cab) 169.3 inches
WIDTH	(Models) 68.9 inches
HEIGHT	(Except Pick-Up) 76.4 inches
WEIGHT	(Kombi) 2,095 lbs.
	(Station Wagon) 2,447 lbs.
TREAD	(front/rear) 54.1/53.5 inches
TIRES	6.40 x 15
BRAKES	Hydraulic, front/rear drum
CONSTRUCTION	Steel unibody on stamped-steel floorpan
FUEL TANK	10.6 gallons
FRONT SUSPENSION	Independent: two laminated torsion bars
REAR SUSPENSION	Independent: one round torsion bar each side
STANDARD ENGINE	1,192cc 40-hp horizontally opposed four-cylinder, overhead valve, air cooled, light alloy block and head, finned cylinders with cast-iron liners
ENGINE	1,493cc 50-hp horizontally opposed four-cylinder, overhead valve, air cooled, light alloy block and head, finned cylinders with cast-iron liners
TRANSMISSION	four-speed manual
FINAL DRIVE RATIO	6.2:1

1964

VOLKSWAGEN TRANSPORTER

FACTORY PAINT COLORS

211 DELIVERY VAN, 231–235 KOMBI, 261–268 PICK-UP/DOUBLE CAB

L31 Dove Blue
L87 Pearl White
L345 Light Grey

L380 Turquoise
L456 Ruby Red

221–228 MICROBUS, 241–251 MICROBUS DELUXE, 281–285 MICROBUS

L380/L289 Turquoise/
Blue White
L53/L472 Sealing Wax
Red/Beige Grey

L325/L87 Mouse Grey/
Pearl White

AMBULANCE

L62 Ivory

MODEL AVAILABILITY	4-door Kombi ($2,140)
	4-door Standard Station Wagon ($2,385)
	4-door Deluxe Station Wagon ($2,605)
	4-door Panel ($2,197)
	4-door Pick-Up ($2,197)
	4-door Double Cab Pick-Up ($2,499)
SERIAL NUMBERS	1144303-up
WHEELBASE	94.5 inches

LENGTH	(Station Wagon/Panel/Kombi) 168.9 inches (Pick-Up and Double Cab) 169.3 inches
WIDTH	68.9 inches
HEIGHT	(Except Pick-Up) 76.4 inches
WEIGHT	(Kombi) 2,095 lbs.; (Station Wagon) 2,447 lbs.
TREAD	(front/rear) 54.1/53.5 inches
TIRES	7.00 x 14
BRAKES	Hydraulic, front/rear drum
CONSTRUCTION	Steel unibody on stamped-steel floorpan
FUEL TANK	10.6 gallons
FRONT SUSPENSION	Independent: two laminated torsion bars
REAR SUSPENSION	Independent: one round torsion bar each side
STANDARD ENGINE	1,192cc 40-hp horizontally opposed four-cylinder, overhead valve, air cooled, light alloy block and head, finned cylinders with cast-iron liners
ENGINE:	1,493cc 50-hp horizontally opposed four-cylinder, overhead valve, air cooled, light alloy block and head, finned cylinders with cast-iron liners
TRANSMISSION	four-speed manual
FINAL DRIVE RATIO	6.2:1

1965

VOLKSWAGEN TRANSPORTER

PAINT COLORS

211 DELIVERY VAN, 231–235 KOMBI, 261–268 PICK-UP/DOUBLE CAB

L31 Dove Blue   **L345** Light Grey
L87 Pearl White   **L512** Velvet Green

221–228 MICROBUS, 241–251 MICROBUS DELUXE, 281–285 MICROBUS

L360/L289 Sea Blue/ Blue White
L512/L289 Velvet Green/ Blue White
L53/L472 Sealing Wax Red/Beige Grey

AMBULANCE

L567 Ivory

MODEL AVAILABILITY	4-door Kombi ($2,195)
	4-door Standard Station Wagon ($2,385)
	4-door Deluxe Station Wagon ($2,765)
	4-door Panel ($2,197)
	2-door Pick-Up ($2,197)
	4-door Double Cab Pick-Up ($2,499)
SERIAL NUMBERS	20-5000001-up
WHEELBASE	94.5 inches
LENGTH	(Station Wagon/Panel/Kombi) 168.9 inches (Pick-Up and Double Cab) 169.3 inches
WIDTH	68.9 inches
HEIGHT	(Except Pick-Up) 76.4 inches
WEIGHT	(Kombi) 2,095 lbs. (Station Wagon) 2,447 lbs.
TREAD	(front/rear) 54.1/53.5 inches
TIRES	7.00 x 14
BRAKES	Hydraulic, front/rear drum
CONSTRUCTION	Steel unibody on stamped-steel floorpan
FUEL TANK	10.6 gallons
FRONT SUSPENSION	Independent: two laminated torsion bars
REAR SUSPENSION	Independent: one round torsion bar each side
ENGINE	1,493cc 50-hp horizontally opposed four-cylinder, overhead valve, air cooled, light alloy block and head, finned cylinders with cast-iron liners
TRANSMISSION	four-speed manual
FINAL DRIVE RATIO	5.53:1

1966

VOLKSWAGEN TRANSPORTER

FACTORY PAINT COLORS

211 DELIVERY VAN, 231–235 KOMBI, 261–268 PICK-UP/DOUBLE CAB

L31 Dove Blue   **L345** Light Grey
L87 Pearl White   **L512** Velvet Green

221–228 MICROBUS, 281–285 MICROBUS

L360/L680 Sea Blue/ Cumulus White
L512/L87 Velvet Green/ Pearl White
L555/L472 Titan/Beige Grey
L282 Lotus White

241–251 MICROBUS DELUXE

L360/L680 Sea Blue/ Cumulus White
L512/L87 Velvet Green/Pearl White
L555/L472 Titan/ Beige Grey
L282 Lotus White

AMBULANCE

L567 Ivory

MODEL AVAILABILITY	4-door Kombi ($2,150)
	4-door Standard Station Wagon ($2,337)
	4-door Deluxe Station Wagon ($2,595)
	4-door Panel ($2,197)
	2-door Pick-Up ($2,197)
	4-door Double Cab Pick-Up ($2,499)
SERIAL NUMBERS	206-000001-up
WHEELBASE	94.5 inches
LENGTH	(Station Wagon/Panel/Kombi) 168.9 inches (Pick-Up and Double Cab) 169.3 inches
WIDTH	68.9 inches
HEIGHT	(Except Pick-Up) 76.4 inches (Pick-Up) 75.6 inches
WEIGHT	(Kombi) 2,095 lbs.; (Station Wagon) 2,447 lbs.
TREAD	(front/rear) 54.1/53.5 inches
TIRES	7.00 x 14
BRAKES	Hydraulic, front/rear drum
CONSTRUCTION	Steel unibody on stamped-steel floorpan
FUEL TANK	10.6 gallons
FRONT SUSPENSION	Independent: two laminated torsion bars
REAR SUSPENSION	Independent: one round torsion bar each side
ENGINE	1,493cc 53-hp horizontally opposed four-cylinder, overhead valve, air cooled, light alloy block and head, finned cylinders with cast-iron liners
TRANSMISSION	four-speed manual
FINAL DRIVE RATIO	5.53:1

1967

VOLKSWAGEN TRANSPORTER

FACTORY PAINT COLORS
211 DELIVERY VAN, 231–235 KOMBI, 261–268 PICK-UP/ DOUBLE CAB

L31 Dove Blue **L345** Light Grey
L87 Pearl White **L512** Velvet Green

221–228 MICROBUS, 281–285 MICROBUS

L360/L680 Sea Blue/ Cumulus White **L512/L87** Velvet Green/ Pearl White
L555/L472 Titan/Beige Grey **L282** Lotus White

241–251 MICROBUS DELUXE

L360/L680 Sea Blue/ Cumulus White **L512/L87** Velvet Green/ Pearl White
L555/L472 Titan/Beige Grey **L282** Lotus White

AMBULANCE

L567 Ivory

MODEL AVAILABILITY	4-door Kombi ($2,150)
	4-door Standard Station Wagon ($2,337)
	4-door Deluxe Station Wagon ($2,595)
	4-door Campmobile ($2,667)
	4-door Panel ($2,197)
	2-door Pick-Up ($2,197)
	4-door Double Cab Pick-Up ($2,595)
STARTING SERIAL NUMBER	217-000001
WHEELBASE	94.5 inches
LENGTH	(Station Wagon/Panel/Kombi) 168.9 inches
	(Pick-Up and Double Cab) 169.3 inches
WIDTH	68.9 inches
HEIGHT	(Except Pick-Up) 76.4 inches; (Pick-Up) 75.6 inches
WEIGHT	(Kombi) 2,095 lbs.; (Station Wagon) 2,447 lbs.
TREAD	(front/rear) 54.1/53.5 inches
TIRES	7.00 x 14
BRAKES	Hydraulic, front/rear drum
CONSTRUCTION	Steel unibody on stamped-steel floorpan
FUEL TANK	10.6 gallons
FRONT SUSPENSION	Independent: two laminated torsion bars
REAR SUSPENSION	Independent: one round torsion bar each side
ENGINE	1,493cc 54-hp horizontally opposed four-cylinder, overhead valve, air cooled, light alloy block and head, finned cylinders with cast-iron liners
TRANSMISSION	four-speed manual
FINAL DRIVE RATIO	5.53:1

1968

VOLKSWAGEN TRANSPORTER

FACTORY PAINT COLORS
TYPE 22, TYPE 24 STATION WAGON

L61/L68 Cloud White/ Montana Red **L61/L620** Cloud White/ Bahama Beige
L61/L22 Cloud White/ Delta Green **L61/L67** Cloud White/ Brilliant Blue

MODEL AVAILABILITY	4-door Kombi ($2,269)
	4-door Standard Station Wagon ($2,499)
	4-door Campmobile ($2,765)
	4-door Panel ($2,299)
	2-door Pick-Up ($2,299)
	4-door Double Cab Pick-Up ($2,389)
SERIAL NUMBER	238-000001
WHEELBASE	94.5 inches
LENGTH	174.0 inches
WIDTH	69.5 inches
HEIGHT	76.4 inches
WEIGHT	(Kombi) 2,535 lbs.
	(Station Wagon) 2,634 lbs.
TREAD	(front/rear) 54.4/56.1 inches
TIRES	7.00 x 14
BRAKES	Dual hydraulic, front/rear drum
CONSTRUCTION	Steel unibody on stamped-steel floorpan
FUEL TANK	16 gallons
FRONT SUSPENSION	Independent: two laminated torsion bars
REAR SUSPENSION	Independent: one round torsion bar each side
ENGINE	1,684cc 57-hp horizontally opposed four-cylinder, overhead valve, air cooled, light alloy block and head, finned cylinders with cast-iron liners
TRANSMISSION	four-speed manual
FINAL DRIVE RATIO	5.375:1

1969

VOLKSWAGEN TRANSPORTER

FACTORY PAINT COLORS
TYPE 22, TYPE 24 STATION WAGON

L61/L68 Cloud White/
Montana Red

L61/L22 Cloud White/
Delta Green

L61/L620 Cloud White/
Bahama Beige

L61/L67 Cloud White/
Brilliant Blue

MODEL AVAILABILITY	4-door Kombi ($2,414)
	4-door 7-Passenger Station Wagon ($2,650)
	4-door 8-Passenger Station Wagon ($2,672)
	4-door Campmobile ($2,850)
	4-door Panel ($2,428)
	2-door Pick-Up ($2,428)
	4-door Double Cab Pick-Up ($2,870)
STARTING SERIAL NUMBER	(Kombi) 2302000001
	(Transporter) 2202000001
WHEELBASE	94.5 inches
LENGTH	174.0 inches
WIDTH	69.5 inches
HEIGHT	76.4 inches
WEIGHT	(Kombi) 2,535 lbs.; (Station Wagon) 2,634 lbs.
TREAD	(front/rear) 54.4/56.1 inches
TIRES	7.00 x 14
BRAKES	Dual hydraulic, front/rear drum
CONSTRUCTION	Steel unibody on stamped-steel floorpan
FUEL TANK	16 gallons
FRONT SUSPENSION	Independent: two laminated torsion bars
REAR SUSPENSION	Independent: one round torsion bar each side
ENGINE	1,684cc 57-hp horizontally opposed four-cylinder, overhead valve, air cooled, light alloy block and head, finned cylinders with cast-iron liners
TRANSMISSION	four-speed manual
FINAL DRIVE RATIO	5.375:1

1970

VOLKSWAGEN TRANSPORTER

FACTORY PAINT COLORS
TYPE 22, TYPE 24 STATION WAGON

90D/31H Pastel White/
Chianti Red

90D/11H Pastel White/
Sierra Yellow

90D/91D Pastel White/
Kansas Beige

90D/60D Pastel White/
Elm Green

90D/53D Pastel White/
Niagra Blue

MODEL AVAILABILITY	4-door Kombi ($2,495)
	4-door 7-Passenger Station Wagon ($2,750)
	4-door 8-Passenger Station Wagon ($2,772)
	4-door Campmobile ($3,077)
	4-door Panel ($2,495)
	2-door Pick-Up ($2,498)
	4-door Double Cab Pick-Up ($2,940)
STARTING SERIAL NUMBERS	(Kombi) 2302000001
	(Transporter) 2202000001
WHEELBASE	94.5 inches
LENGTH	174.0 inches
WIDTH	69.5 inches
HEIGHT	77.0 inches
WEIGHT	(7-Passenger Station Wagon) 2,811 lbs.
TREAD	(front/rear) 54.6/56.6 inches
TIRES	7.00 x 14 radials
BRAKES	Dual hydraulic, front/rear drum
CONSTRUCTION	Steel unibody on stamped-steel floorpan
FUEL TANK	16 gallons
FRONT SUSPENSION	Independent: two laminated torsion bars
REAR SUSPENSION	Independent: one round torsion bar each side
ENGINE	1,584cc 57-hp horizontally opposed four-cylinder, overhead valve, air cooled, light alloy block and head, finned cylinders with cast-iron liners
TRANSMISSION	four-speed manual
FINAL DRIVE RATIO	5.375:1

1971

VOLKSWAGEN TRANSPORTER

FACTORY PAINT COLORS

11H Sierra Yellow   **90D** Pastel White
31H Chianti Red   **91D** Kansas Beige
50K Neptune Blue   **567** Ivory
53D Niagara Green   **345** Light Gray
60D Elm Green
ROOF: Pastel White 06 and Black 10 for
L 11H, L 31H, L 53D, L 60D, L 90D, and L 91D

MODEL AVAILABILITY	4-door Kombi ($2,720)
	4-door 7-Passenger Station Wagon ($2,795)
	4-door 8-Passenger Station Wagon ($3,100)
	4-door Campmobile ($2,645)
	4-door Panel ($2,720)
	2-door Pick-Up ($2,723)
	4d Double Cab Pick-Up ($3,165)
STARTING SERIAL NUMBERS	(Kombi/Campmobile) 2312000001
	(Transporter) 2212000001
WHEELBASE	94.5 inches
LENGTH	174.0 inches
WIDTH	69.5 inches
HEIGHT	76.4 inches
WEIGHT	(Kombi) 2,535 lbs.
	(Station Wagon) 2,634 lbs.
TREAD	(front/rear) 54.4/56.1 inches
TIRES	185R14 radials
BRAKES	Dual hydraulic, front/rear drum
CONSTRUCTION	Steel unibody on stamped-steel floorpan
FUEL TANK	16 gallons
FRONT SUSPENSION	Independent: two laminated torsion bars
REAR SUSPENSION	Independent: one round torsion bar each side
ENGINE	1,584cc 60-hp horizontally opposed four-cylinder, overhead valve, air cooled, light alloy block and head, finned cylinders with cast-iron liners
TRANSMISSION	four-speed manual
FINAL DRIVE RATIO	5.375:1

1972

VOLKSWAGEN TRANSPORTER

FACTORY PAINT COLORS

Same as 1971

MODEL AVAILABILITY	4-door Kombi ($2,989)
	4-door 7-Passenger Station Wagon ($3,299)
	4-door 8-Passenger Station Wagon ($3,329)
	4-door Campmobile ($3,848)
	4-door Panel ($3,290)
STARTING SERIAL NUMBERS	(Kombi/Campmobile) 2312000001
	(Transporter) 2212000001
WHEELBASE	94.5 inches
LENGTH	175.0 inches
WIDTH	71.5 inches
HEIGHT	76.4 inches
WEIGHT	(Kombi) 2,623 lbs.
	(Station Wagon) 2,778 lbs.
TREAD	(front/rear) 54.5/56.1 inches
TIRES	185R14 radials
BRAKES	Dual hydraulic, front/rear drum
CONSTRUCTION	Steel unibody on stamped-steel floorpan
FUEL TANK	16 gallons
FRONT SUSPENSION	Independent: two laminated torsion bars
REAR SUSPENSION	Independent: one round torsion bar each side
ENGINE	1,679cc 60-hp horizontally opposed four-cylinder, overhead valve, air cooled, light alloy block and head, finned cylinders with cast-iron liners
TRANSMISSION	four-speed manual
FINAL DRIVE RATIO	5.375:1

1973-1975

VOLKSWAGEN TRANSPORTER

FACTORY PAINT COLORS

13H Ceylon Beige	**90D** Pastel White
20B Brilliant Orange	**345** Light Gray
30B Kasan Red	**567** Ivory
50K Neptune Blue	**62H** Bali Yellow
53H Orient Blue	**50A** Chrome Yellow
61B Sumatra Green	**63H** Sage Green

ROOF: Ivory for Model 211–228, 241, 244; Pastel White for L 13H, L 53D, L 20B, L 53H, L61B, and L 90D

MODEL AVAILABILITY	4-door Kombi ($3,500) 4-door 7-Passenger Station Wagon ($3,799) 4-door 8-Passenger Station Wagon ($3,850) 4-door Campmobile ($3,499) 4-door Panel ($3,825)
S TARTING SERIAL NUMBERS	(Kombi/Campmobile) 2332000001 (Transporter) 2232000001
WHEELBASE	94.5 inches
LENGTH	175.0 inches
WIDTH	71.5 inches
HEIGHT	76.4 inches
WEIGHT (LOW/HIGH)	(Kombi) 2,759 lbs.; (Station Wagon) 3,096 lbs.
TREAD	(front/rear) 54.5/56.1 inches
TIRES	185R14 radials
BRAKES	Dual hydraulic, front/rear drum
CONSTRUCTION	Steel unibody on stamped-steel floorpan
FUEL TANK	16 gallons
FRONT SUSPENSION	Independent: two laminated torsion bars
REAR SUSPENSION	Independent: one round torsion bar each side
OPTIONAL ENGINE	1,684cc 63-hp (with manual transmission); 66 hp (with automatic transmission) horizontally opposed four-cylinder, overhead valve, air cooled, light alloy block and head, finned cylinders with cast-iron liners
TRANSMISSION	four-speed manual
FINAL DRIVE RATIO	5.375:1

1974

VOLKSWAGEN TRANSPORTER

FACTORY PAINT COLORS

Same as 1973

MODEL AVAILABILITY	4-door Kombi ($4,000) 4-door 7-Passenger Station Wagon ($4,350) 4-door 9-Passenger Station Wagon ($4,400) 4-door Campmobile ($5,274) 4-door Panel Delivery ($4,380)
STARTING SERIAL NUMBERS	(Panel) 2132000001 (Station Wagons) 2232000001 (Kombi & Campmobile) 2332000001
WHEELBASE	94.5 inches
LENGTH	175.0 inches
WIDTH	71.5 inches
HEIGHT	76.4 inches
WEIGHT	(Panel) 2,649 lbs. (Campmobile w/equipment) 3,105 lbs.
TREAD	(front/rear) 54.5/56.1 inches
TIRES	185R14 radials
BRAKES	Dual hydraulic, front/rear drum
CONSTRUCTION	Steel unibody on stamped-steel floorpan
FUEL TANK	16 gallons
FRONT SUSPENSION	Independent: two laminated torsion bars
REAR SUSPENSION	Independent: one round torsion bar each side
ENGINE	1,795cc 65-hp (with manual transmission); 67 hp (with automatic transmission) horizontally opposed four-cylinder, overhead valve, air cooled, light alloy block and head, finned cylinders with cast-iron liners
TRANSMISSION	four-speed manual
FINAL DRIVE RATIO	5.375:1

1975

VOLKSWAGEN TRANSPORTER

FACTORY PAINT COLORS

Same as 1973

MODEL AVAILABILITY	4-door Kombi ($4,750)
	4-door 7-Passenger Station Wagon ($5,100)
	4-door 9-Passenger Station Wagon ($5,150)
	4-door Campmobile ($6,174 with camp equipment)
	4-door Panel Delivery ($5,150)
STARTING SERIAL NUMBERS	(Panel) 2142000001
	(Station Wagons) 2242000001
	(Kombi) 2342000001
WHEELBASE	94.5 inches
LENGTH	175.0 inches
WIDTH	71.5 inches
HEIGHT	76.4 inches
WEIGHT	(Panel) 2,649 lbs.
	(Campmobile w/equipment) 3,105 lbs.
TREAD	(front/rear) 54.5/56.1 inches
TIRES	185R14 radials
BRAKES	Dual hydraulic, front/rear drum
CONSTRUCTION	Steel unibody on stamped-steel floorpan
FUEL TANK	16 gallons
FRONT SUSPENSION	Independent: two laminated torsion bars
REAR SUSPENSION	Independent: one round torsion bar each side
ENGINE	1,795cc 65-hp (with manual transmission); 67 hp (with automatic transmission) horizontally opposed four-cylinder, overhead valve, air cooled, light alloy block and head, finned cylinders with cast-iron liners
TRANSMISSION	four-speed manual
FINAL DRIVE RATIO	5.375:1

1976-1978

VOLKSWAGEN TRANSPORTER

FACTORY PAINT COLORS

20A Chrome Yellow (871)	**567** Ivory
21H Chrome Yellow (872)	**20B** Brilliant Orange
31A Senegal Red	**86Z** Agata Brown
50K Neptune Blue	**12A** Panama Brown
57H Reef Blue	**13A** Dakota Beige
63H Sage Green	**H8A** Date Brown
90D Pastel White	**EM1** Mexican Beige
345 Light Grey	

MODEL AVAILABILITY	4-door Kombi ($5,235, $5,249, $6,185)
	4-door 7-Passenger Station Wagon ($5,495, $5,725, $6,445)
	4-door 9-Passenger Station Wagon ($5,545, $5,775, $6,495)
	4-door Campmobile ($5,194, $5,299, $6,145)
STARTING SERIAL NUMBER	The third symbol was 6 in 1976, 7 in 1977, and 8 in 1988
WHEELBASE	94.5 inches
LENGTH	175.0 inches
WIDTH	71.5 inches
HEIGHT	76.4 inches
WEIGHT (1978)	(Campmobile) 2,754 lbs.
	(Station Wagon) 2,952 lbs.
TREAD	(front/rear) 54.5/56.1 inches
TIRES	185R14 radials
BRAKES	Dual hydraulic, front/rear drum
CONSTRUCTION	Steel unibody on stamped-steel floorpan
FUEL TANK	16 gallons
FRONT SUSPENSION	Independent: two laminated torsion bars
REAR SUSPENSION	Independent: one round torsion bar each side
ENGINE	1,970cc, 67 hp, horizontally opposed four-cylinder, overhead valve, air cooled, light alloy block and head, finned cylinders with cast-iron liners
TRANSMISSION	four-speed manual
FINAL DRIVE RATIO	5.375:1

1979

VOLKSWAGEN TRANSPORTER

FACTORY PAINT COLORS

20B Brilliant Orange
57H Reef Blue
63H Sage Green
86Z Agata Brown
90D Pastel White
EM1 Mexican Beige

MODEL AVAILABILITY	4-door Kombi ($7,285) 4-door 7-Passenger Station Wagon ($7,937) 4-door 9-Passenger Station Wagon ($7,987) 4-door Campmobile ($7,295)
STARTING SERIAL NUMBERS	292000001-up or 2392000001-up
WHEELBASE	94.5 inches
LENGTH	175.0 inches
WIDTH	71.5 inches
HEIGHT	76.4 inches
WEIGHT	(Campmobile) 2,724 lbs. (Station Wagon) 2,952 lbs.
TREAD	(front/rear) 54.5/56.1 inches
TIRES	185R14 radials
BRAKES	Dual hydraulic, front/rear drum
CONSTRUCTION	Steel unibody on stamped-steel floorpan
FUEL TANK	16 gallons
FRONT SUSPENSION	Independent: two laminated torsion bars
REAR SUSPENSION	Independent: one round torsion bar each side
ENGINE	1,970cc, 67 hp, horizontally opposed four-cylinder, overhead valve, air cooled, light alloy block and head, finned cylinders with cast-iron liners
TRANSMISSION	four-speed manual
FINAL DRIVE RATIO	5.375:1

1980

VOLKSWAGEN VANAGON

FACTORY PAINT COLORS

B9/20B Ivory/Bright Orange
J9/J8 Guinea Blue/ Cornat Blue
D8/T6 Samos Beige/Assuan Brown
B9/B5 Ivory/Bambo Yellow

VOLKSWAGEN VANAGON CAMPMOBILE

FACTORY PAINT COLORS

H5G Medium Blue   **T6** Assuan Brown   **B9** Ivory

MODEL AVAILABILITY	4-door Kombi ($9,540, $10,380, n/a) 1980/1981/1932 4-door 7-Passenger Station Wagon ($9,900, $10,690, $10,860) 4-door 9-Passenger Station Wagon ($9,950, $10,740, $10,915) 4-door Campmobile ($9,540, $10,330, $14,900)
STARTING SERIAL NUMBERS	('80) 25A0000001; ('81) 25B0000001; ('82) 25C0000001
WHEELBASE	96.8 inches
LENGTH	179.9 inches
WIDTH	72.6 inches
HEIGHT	77.2 inches
WEIGHT	3,087 lbs.
TREAD	(front/rear) 61.8/61.8 inches
TIRES	185SR14 radials
BRAKES	Dual hydraulic, power-assisted, inertia-controlled brake pressure regulator (rear), self-adjusting disc/drum brakes, 9-inch brake booster
CONSTRUCTION	Unitized construction: box-shaped side/crossmembers
FUEL TANK	15.9 gallons
FRONT SUSPENSION	Independent with upper and lower control arms, coil springs, and telescopic shock absorbers
REAR SUSPENSION	Independent with semi trailing arms, integrated axle supports, coil springs, and telescopic shock absorbers
ENGINE	1,970cc, 67 hp, horizontally opposed four-cylinder, overhead valve, air cooled, light alloy block and head, finned cylinders with cast-iron liners
TRANSMISSION	four-speed manual (three-speed automatic optional)
FINAL DRIVE RATIO	(manual transmission) 4.57:1; (automatic) 4.09:1

CHAPTER 9

Coupé

KARMANN GHIA TYPE 14

The Karmann Ghia Type 14 is more or less the Beetle with a sporty body. Ghia designer Luigi Segre styled the car in Italy. The car has much of the look of some early 1950s dream cars that Ghia did for Chrysler Corporation. Karmann of Osnabrück hand-built the Karmann Ghia body. There were no performance upgrades, but the lighter sports car was faster. In 1961, Volkswagen introduced the Type 34 Karmann Ghia, which was a Type 3 Volkswagen with a different look.

The Type 14 took its bow at the 1953 Paris Auto Show and turned out to be a popular car. On July 14, 1955, Karmann held a press review and exactly two months later the now-named Karmann Ghia was shown at the Frankfurt auto show. The Karmann-built coupe had changes from Ghia's prototype, including a twin nostril nose, curved window glass, wider window trim, full-width bumpers, repositioned front blinkers, and restyled air intake louvers on the deck. The Ghia fender badges were also repositioned.

More than 10,000 units were sold during its first twelve months on the market, spanning two model years. In total, 445,000 were built between 1956 and 1973. Karmann of Brazil also produced 41,600 of the cars between 1962 and 1975.

The 1958 Karmann Ghia was a very luxurious sports car for its day. It included lots of upscale features and appointments. There was special paint and a fancy, new bright metal horn ring designed just for the Ghia.

1956

This was the first year for the stylish Karmann Ghia coupe that blended the mechanical components and structure of the Beetle with a handsome Italian-designed coupe body with 2+2 seating. Karmann of Osnabrück, the firm that also turned out Volkswagen convertibles, manufactured the body.

The Karmann Ghia driving position was lower than that of a Beetle sedan. *Motor Trend* described it as being "more like Porsche." The shapely body had a sculpted line leading from the lower door, upward, and along the rear quarter panel. There was more of a hood up front than in the Beetle. The roofline was low. It looked great, but a tall person's head would touch the roof. Rear quarter windows were installed, along with curved door windows.

Motor Trend said, "The interior finish is flawless and chastely classic."

There were upholstered, individually adjustable bucket seats in front and a foam rubber-cushioned bench seat in the rear. A storage compartment and full-width parcel tray were behind the seat backrest. The wide doors had large storage pockets. The back of the upholstered rear seat folded down to provide a platform that doubled the storage space for luggage and personal belongings.

The 1956 Karmann Ghia coupe was a dressy looking sports car when buyers added whitewall tires and chrome wheel trim rings. Underneath that sexy Italian-styled body was a VW Beetle platform and drive train. *Archives/TEN: The Enthusiast Network Magazines, LLC*

LEFT: Like the Beetle, the Ghia Volkswagen had a rear-mounted flat four, while the luggage compartment was at the front of the car. As you can see, the spare tire also resided in that location. *Archives/TEN: The Enthusiast Network Magazines, LLC*

RIGHT: The 1956 Karmann Ghia interior featured front bucket seats and four-on-the-floor shifting. The dashboard was a simple affair. *Archives/TEN: The Enthusiast Network Magazines, LLC*

Either cloth or leatherette upholstery was available. Driving controls were like those of the Beetle, but not identical. The small grilles on each side of the nose admitted floor-level fresh air. The rear end was less skitterish than that of the Beetle, thanks to the Karmann Ghia's front-end roll bar and wider frame rails.

The sports car had better low-end acceleration than other Volkswagens. "On a lonely stretch," declared *Motor Trend* of their test coupe, the "Ghia's high-speed behavior proved impeccable." According to the magazine, this was a result of the car's lighter weight, better front-to-rear weight distribution, and streamlining.

Nevertheless, the Karmann Ghia's 0-to-60 time was a slow 34.2 seconds.

The horizontally opposed, overhead-valve four-cylinder air-cooled engine was shared with the Beetle. It used a light alloy block, heads, and finned cylinders with cast-iron cylinder liners. Bore and stroke was 3.03 x 2.52 inches (77 x 64mm) for 72.7 cubic inches (1,192cc). It had 6.6:1 compression and 36 horsepower at 3,700 rpm. It used four main bearings, solid lifters, and a Solex 28 PCI downdraft carburetor. A top speed of over 70 miles per hour was claimed. It had 6-volt electrics.

"Analyzing the growing Volkswagen Family," said the tag line on the cover of the May 1956 issue of *Motor Trend*. The cover photo showed the new Karmann Ghia coupe, a Volkswagen Microbus, and thirteen Beetle sedans. Inside was a comparison road test of the Karmann Ghia coupe.

Production of Karmann Ghias was 2,452 units this year, but it would quickly double. At the Frankfurt International Automobile Show in mid-1956, Volkswagen introduced a Karmann Ghia Cabriolet. The open car would be put into production on August 1, 1957, when changeover to 1958 models occurred.

In the rear, bench-type jump seat cushioned with foam rubber; storage compartment and deep, full-width parcel tray behind backrest.

Wide doors—fitted with big pockets—provide easy entry and exit. The two upholstered "bucket-type" front seats are independently adjustable.

The back of the upholstered rear seat folds down. It thereby provides a platform which more than doubles the capacity of the storage compartment.

K A R M A N N
Ghia

– 1957 –

Volkswagen was proud of its new sports car and put out a classy tri-fold brochure heralding the 1957 coupe model. "Every flowing, graceful line . . . every breathtaking detail . . . every magic touch of luxury and comfort of the beautiful Karmann Ghia Coupe has a truly 'Continental' accent," said the copyrighters. It pointed out that Ghia, of Turin, Italy, was a renowned European car designer.

"Even at sustained cruising speeds you get a king-size 32 miles per gallon," the sales catalog claimed. "Maintenance costs are phenomenally low, too . . . 75,000 miles without any major repairs is common!" Again upholstered, adjustable bucket seats were up front and a small, bench-type jump seat in the rear could be used for occasional accommodation for two passengers.

"Beauty is definitely not just 'skin deep,'" read the sales folder. "You'll find that top-notch engineering skills and careful consideration have been lavished on each detail." There was a fancy new bright metal horn ring designed for just the Ghia. Special paint, deeply upholstered front bucket seats that adjusted fore and aft and up and down, a bench-type rear jump seat, a spacious front storage compartment, and new east-to-care-for vinyl door panels were among the fine details. The original roller-type accelerator was replaced with a pedal type.

The 1957 Karmann Ghia was a very luxurious sports car for its day. It included lots of upscale features and appointments. There was special paint and a fancy, new bright metal horn ring designed just for the Ghia.

The small grilles on each side of the Karmann Ghia's nose admitted floor-level fresh air. Over the years, these were first widened a bit and then changed to a thinner shape with a more pointed inner end.

1958

The Karmann Ghia line continued to offer the coupe introduced in 1956 and added the Cabriolet that entered production in the summer of 1957 as a 1958 model. Volkswagen literature pointed out that the Karmann Ghia was "styled and engineered by Europe's finest master craftsmen." Part of the engineering effort for the Cabriolet went into beefing up the body structure for topless driving.

The coupe's form-fitting front bucket seats again had large, expandable storage pockets. The gearshift and hand brake were conveniently arranged between the seats. The upholstery materials were fabric and imitation leather for durability and ease of cleaning. Squarer new bumper guards were seen.

The large velour-trimmed area in the rear added to the coupe's practicality. The seat back again folded down for additional storage. The interior side panels were made of durable, washable, and fade-proof plastic in matching colors. Extra sound absorption was achieved by a perforated plastic roof lining.

The new Karmann Ghia Cabriolet (also called a Sports Cabriolet) was virtually a two-in-one-car according to Volkswagen. On sunny days, the owner could put the top down to have a low-slung, racy sports car. In bad weather, the owner could remove the matching tonneau cover and put the fabric top up.

The Karmann Ghia's instrument panel had a new fuel gauge between

Cabriolet

The new Karmann Ghia Cabriolet is virtually two-cars-in-one. On sunny days with the top down, it is a low and racy sports car (right). In bad weather the matching cover is removed — up goes the top, and behold! — all the comfort, quiet and protection of a closed automobile is yours (above).

K A R M A N N
Ghia

Even with the top up, the new Karmann Ghia Cabriolet provides all'round visibility. This important safety factor is achieved by the use of an unusually large and low rear window; large, curved side windows; narrow corner posts; and a high, wide and handsome one-piece windshield. And how easily the fitted top goes up and down! It is a one-person, one-minute operation that can practically be done blindfolded. Just as in the Coupé, there is ample luggage space behind the front seats and under the front hood. The Cabriolet has been designed and built with the same loving care that has made the famous Karmann Ghia Coupé a standard of beauty and quality throughout the world.

TOP: The Karmann Ghia convertible that entered production in the summer of 1957 as a 1958 model was an attractive Sports Cabriolet model that retailed for just $2,725 in the United States.

BOTTOM: This cutaway illustration of a 1958 Karmann Ghia Coupe depicts the drive train layout, seating and storage spaces, and the spare tire storage near the front of the car. The fuel tank was between the front wheels and tires.

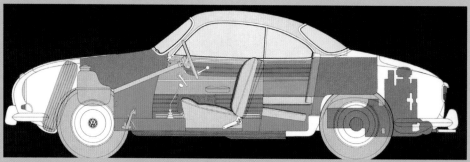

the electric clock and the speedometer. Other features included a two-spoke steering wheel with horn ring and opaque sun visors that were contoured to the lines of the roof and the windows. Karmann Ghias produced for the American market had reinforced front and rear bumpers. New multiposition

door check straps were another minor convenience change. Starting January 7, 1958, Karmann Ghia Pearl White wheel finish was used on coupes and cabriolets in ten colors.

It seems like Volkswagens were already becoming collectibles. The August 1958 issue of *Motor Trend*

had a classified ad from Charles Pasco of Seattle offering to trade his '55 Morgan Drophead Coupe for a Beetle or Karmann Ghia. Possibly he contacted D. E. Salmeier of Clovis, New Mexico, who had an ad on the same page offering a 1958 Karmann Ghia with 3,000 miles for $2,625.

1959

The 1959 Karmann Ghia also had a number of running changes. In the coupe, new padded sun visors replaced the transparent plastic type on January 20, 1959. On January 26,1959, the Sport Cabriolet got this change too. Also, the studded trim on the front of the Sport Cabriolet's folding top was eliminated on January 26, 1958. At the same time, the top covering and the method

of weather sealing were improved and the passenger grab handle was redesigned. In April, the window riser mechanisms and windows were revised.

On July 6, 1959, the dashboard cover was modified to include new shutters for the heating outlets and a lower retaining strip. On August 6, 1959, new colors were introduced for both Karmann Ghia body styles. The side windows were

modified to pivot at the rear. Also, the right armrest had a recess for better gripping. A new two-spoke steering wheel with a deep-set hub and a bright horn ring was used and the steering column was changed. The majority of mechanical changes on 1959 Beetles were also done to the Karmann Ghias.

Coupé

Now step back. Gaze upon her ... this Volkswagen Karmann Ghia. Every line says quality ... quietly. The easy curvature of the body, the large contoured windows tell a story of great skill in design, in engineering. And a promise of roominess that comes true the minute you step inside ... of comfort that delights you ... on your very first ride. And what a ride! Sure and steady, she handles with consummate ease ... sharp turns notwithstanding. You see, both Coupé and Cabriolet have independent torsion-bar suspension of all four wheels, plus a stabilizer bar. And inside this luxuriously-fabric-trimmed master-piece, you find cushioned contour seats ... sporty seats with a personality all their own. They adjust easily, individually, to suit your leg length, your most comfortable back angle. Just relax and enjoy complete driving pleasure ... for brief errands, for hours-long trips.

Do you like a car that's easy to enter? With nice wide doors ... and "stops" that hold the door open at convenient angles? Volkswagen's Karmann Ghia is for you, then!

Volkswagen used the same Karmann Ghia Coupe art-work in its 1959 literature as it did in 1958. The left-hand outside rearview mirror was an option. The car was roomy for a sports car, though it was only 163 inches long.

1960

In August 1959, with changeover to 1960 models, the front fender contour was resculpted and the headlights were set a few inches higher. These changes also required revisions to the front wheelwell shape. The nostrils on the nose were made wider and dressed up with little finned horizontal bar grilles. Larger, more rounded taillights arrived. Most of these changes came from the drawing board of Sergio Sartorelli, who also designed the Type 34 Karmann Ghia.

In January 1960, a resistor-type ignition system was introduced. In March 1960, the plastic frame was removed from the Karmann Ghia's outside rearview mirror. Door window sealing and convertible top sealing were also improved. In October 1960, *Motor Trend* said, "On Ghia models, windshield washers are standard, directionals are self-canceling and there is more soundproofing."

Other interior changes for Karmann Ghias included a new safety padded dashboard, a sports car-like dashboard grab bar for the front seat passenger, an armrest on the driver's side door, and a new deep-dished steering wheel with a less exclusive Beetle horn ring. The exterior side trim was also slightly revised.

When the top was lowered on the 1960 Karmann Ghia Sport Cabriolet, a top boot that sat high on the deck could be fitted for a neater look. Raising the roof in essence gave the Volkswagen owner a weather-tight coupe.

The Volkswagen Karmann Ghia Cabriolet. Top up. Top down. Nobly styled. Mechanically delightful. For instance: the problem of how to open, push back and close the top quickly has been solved by a centrally-located handle. It can be turned easily with one hand while you remain seated. Half the top folds into the body. And, in spite of its soundproof padding, the top lies flat and blends in with the striking lines of the body.

*The Volkswagen Karmann Ghia. Beauty plus Sense.
Surely it's sensible to treat yourself to economy.
And economy you get—whether your desire runs to either
Coupé or Cabriolet. The spirited Volkswagen engine is capable of
turning up a cruising speed of 70 m.p.h.—yet it can be run
at full throttle for miles and miles and still deliver
unparalleled gas economy. It's fun to drive a VW Karmann
Ghia. It's fun to get 32 miles to a gallon, too!*

*The large, velour-trimmed area in the rear is another
feature of the VW Karmann Ghia.
And most practical, too. The foam-rubber upholstered
bench serves as storage space or
seats two additional passengers, if desired!*

*Very neat! A flick of the wrist and the rear
storage space is doubled in size! And
there's more room for additional packages under th
front hood. Coupé or Cabriolet,
every bit of space is sensibly put to good use.*

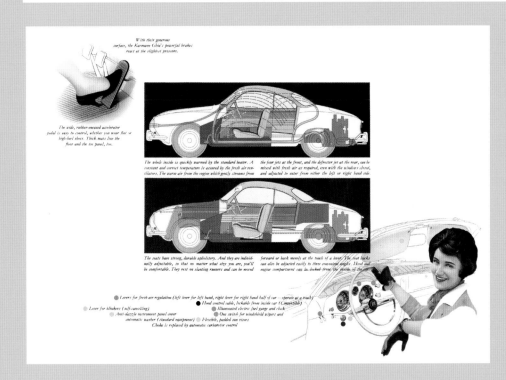

ABOVE: The front fender contour was resculpted in 1960 and the headlights sat a few inches higher. These changes required revisions to the front wheel well. The nostrils were made wider and dressed up with little finned horizontal-bar grilles.

LEFT: This top drawing of a 1961 Karmann Ghia Coupe shows how the car's standard heater completely warmed the interior in cold weather. The bottom illustration shows the individually adjusted front bucket seats and other features.

KARMANN GHIA TYPE 14

1961

Although the smartly styled Karmann Ghia was a Volkswagen Beetle underneath, its completely different coachwork gave it a new function and put it in its own class. One variation was a wider platform than the Beetle had. Due to its improved streamlining, it was about 3 miles per hour faster than a Beetle.

Handling, braking, and ride quality were about the same for both models, and both were highly rated. The Karmann Ghia was almost 7 inches lower and 3 inches longer than the Beetle and held two people in semi-bucket front seats. There was a padded platform in the rear where children could sit or luggage could be stored. The seat backs folded to increase luggage space.

On the Sports Cabriolet model, the outside of the convertible top was padded to hide the top bows. The inside was also padded, giving the open car a hardtop look when the roof was raised.

New-for-1961 features included a 40-horsepower version of the carryover 1,200cc engine, the use of a new four-speed manual transmission with synchromesh on all forward gears, and a new Solex carburetor with an automatic electric choke. The 1961 gas tank had a flatter shape to provide more storage space in the front "trunk." This was also the last appearance of a lever for a reserve fuel tank.

Production of Volkswagen's Karmann Ghia Sport Coupe and Karmann Ghia models had a run of 9,300 units in 1961. A new Karmann Ghia 1500 Type 3 was depicted in the "European Report" in the December 1961 issue of *Motor Trend*. That car was introduced first in Europe. It was unpopular, but eventually made it to the United States for a short time.

BELOW: The Volkswagen 1200 Karmann Ghia of 1961 showcased Italian car design at its finest. This sailor found a sports car that could "float his boat," so his mate may want to stop leaning on it before she scratches the Sea Blue finish.

OPPOSITE: A sales theme for 1962 focused on what kind of people bought Karmann Ghias. In this case, the woman driver has attracted attention from three men who are obviously well-dressed car buffs.

What kind of people buy the Karmann Ghia?

Production of Volkswagen's Sport Coupe and convertible continued without major change. Several modifications for 1962 models went into effect with chassis number 3933247, built on June 30, 1961. At that point, a worm-and-roller steering system was adopted and a combination ignition/starter switch was used in home market cars. A nonrepeat starter was optional on these units. The Volkswagen badge on the front of the car was redesigned and seat belt anchors were installed to meet new safety regulations taking effect in the United States.

In its sales catalog, Volkswagen asked, "What kind of people buy the Karmann Ghia?" (Note that they did not hyphenate the name this year, either). The catalog went on to show photos of the car with different types of people. It said that conventional people buy the car because it was conservative on its surface and because it was designed by Turin of Italy. It also pointed out that it took 185 men working by hand to build the body alone.

Next came convertible people, who liked top-down driving. The copywriters pointed out that the canvas convertible top was made by hand and that it was very water-tight. City people were said to like the Karmann Ghia because it could slink through traffic and slip into tight parking spaces. Country people were said to like it because of its traction and air cooling system.

LEFT: This typical American couple went for the conservative-looking 1962 Karmann Ghia Coupe in monotone L41 Black with a red interior. Volkswagen hinted that its sports car was "non-conformist underneath" despite its clean look.

RIGHT: This golfer and his lady friend were depicted in this 1962 promotional piece as "Convertible people." Their choice was a Karmann Ghia ragtop with whitewall tires and a chrome towel-rack–style front bumper guard.

Traveling people, it said, liked the car's adjustable seats, good acoustics, fresh air ventilation, heater, and luggage space. And stay-at-home folks liked the behind-the-seat storage and two-kid rear seat, plus its easy-to-clean upholstery. Thrifty people liked the 38-mile-per-gallon fuel economy and 40,000-mile tire life, while spend-thrifty people liked the upscale image. Then came the do-it-yourselfer who appreciated the now-all-synchromesh transmission and four coats of paint. The final category was called Volkswagen people, who appreciated the practicality.

In January 1962, *Road and Track* magazine stated, "You'll see a lot more Ghias simply because more are being made and the car will receive a greater share of VW's advertising budget." The magazine's forecast proved correct.

1963

Production of Volkswagen's Karmann Ghia Sport Coupe and Convertible continued without major change, except that most of the minor changes made to 1963 Beetles were also carried out on the Karmann Ghia. In 1963, you could pick out a new model by the Volkswagen script added to the rear deck lid. Also, if you were very observant, you might notice a smaller Ghia emblem. It was pirated from the Type 3 model.

Upholstery in different shades of blue was used when the 1963 Karmann Ghia coupe was ordered in this blue-and-white two-tone color combination. At $2,295, this model offered particularly good value for the money.

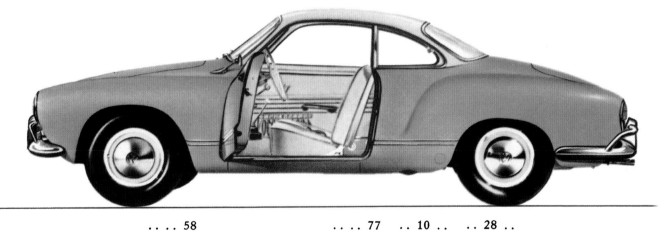

.. .. 58 .. .. 77 .. 10 .. .. 28 ..

pacific blue, blue white
bleu pacific,
blanc bleuté

26 17 ..

TOP: Volkswagen claimed that the Karmann Ghia cornered like a sports car because of its low center of gravity. Notice how the white tire sidewalls got a lot thinner in 1964. A full-synchromesh transmission was standard.

BOTTOM: The 1964 Karmann Ghia Convertible was open to the sun and the sky. The smooth-fitting convertible top was vinyl on the outside and leatherette on the inside. It included a rear fold-down jump seat with storage space behind it.

OPPOSITE: A total of ten different colors were offered for the 1963 Volkswagen Karmann Ghia: Black, Pearl White, Sea Blue, Pacific, Ruby Red, Anthracite, Emerald, Polar Blue, Manila Yellow, and Terra Brown.

1964

Production of Volkswagen's Karmann Ghia Sport Coupe and convertible continued. At the start of the model year, a new fresh air heating system was introduced, the semicircular horn blow ring disappeared, and Karmann Ghia 1500 Type 3 door locks were used. Later, the license plate holder grew larger.

The body side trim was revised again and a new interior light was used.

A number of changes took place in April 1964 when Volkswagen revised the convertible top on the Cabriolet model. The goal was the make the top less bulky, so some cast-metal bits were replaced with sheet-metal stampings. On the inside of both Karmann Ghia models, the heater controls were revised from one knob to two levers and the sun visors were redesigned so they could be pulled down and swiveled to shade the side windows. A new basket-weave vinyl seat trim was made available in six colors: Numbers 57, 58, 59, 60, 61, and 62.

1965

Production of Volkswagen's Karmann Ghia Sport Coupe and convertible continued without major change.

Karmann Ghias got most of the same refinements given the 1965 Beetles. Exterior color and interior trim options changed and the price of both models was lowered a bit. This was the final year for the 1200 engine in the Karmann Ghias.

VOLKSWAGEN 1200
KARMANN-GHIA

1966

The 1966 coupe and Cabriolet models that went into production in August 1965 (as 1966 models) featured a larger, more powerful 1,300cc engine. A Solex 30 PICT carburetor helped the Karmann Ghia accelerate better than before.

The 1300 was of the same type as previous Volkswagen powerplants, but had a 3.03 x 2.72-inch (77 x 69mm) bore and stroke and was displaced 78.42 cubic inches (1,285cc). The compression ratio was 7.3:1. Volkswagen rated it for 50 horsepower

at 4,600 rpm and 69 pounds-feet of torque at 2,600 rpm. It continued with four main bearings, solid valve lifters, a Solex one-barrel sidedraft carburetor, and a 6-volt electrical system.

A new ball-joint front suspension contributed to more precise steering. A blast from the past was the return of the neat-looking semi-circular steering wheel horn ring. Also added were new hubcaps with a flatter look and new vented wheel rims. The battery was relocated to the driver's

side of the car inside the engine compartment. The air cleaner was then moved to the opposite side.

Inside the Karmann Ghia, the ashtray had a new hiding spot underneath the dashboard, which was also dressed up with new chrome-finish plastic trim. The delicate swan's neck outside rearview mirrors of past years were gone, with door-mounted breakaway types used instead. Drain tubes were added to the luggage compartment lid.

1967

The 1967 Karmann Ghia Type 14 had a new 1,493cc 1500 engine and is considered one of the best Ghias, since after this year tighter US emissions standards would start robbing engines' power. So, the 1967 models wound up with more power, plus a new front disc/rear drum brake system with a dual master cylinder. Rear tread width was also wider and new rear springs

gave a softer ride. The wheels had a new four-bolt attaching pattern. And Volkswagen really moved into the modern age (about a decade late) with 12-volt electricals. A new numerically lower final drive ratio lowered the new engine's revs per minute.

Exterior changes in 1967 were few, except for a rear Z-bar, but the interior was revamped with a simulated wood

dashboard insert, kneepads under the dash, a new instrument panel with a large speedometer in its center, new fresh-air controls, and a tiny Ghia script. The lock buttons were moved to the tops of the doors. Surprisingly, the window sticker prices did not go up.

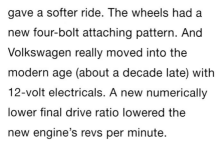

New-for-1967 Karmann Ghia features included kneepads under the dash, a new instrument panel with a large central speedometer, new fresh-air controls, and a tiny Ghia script. The lock buttons were moved to the tops of the doors.

VW Karmann Ghia Convertible

A kid riding a bicycle stops to look over a 1967 Karmann Ghia Coupe. There weren't many exterior changes in 1967, except for a rear Z-bar, but the interior was revamped with a simulated wood dashboard insert.

1968

Ever more stringent US safety regulations required Volkswagen to add rear side marker reflectors to all of its vehicles, including the Karmann Ghia Coupe and Cabriolet, for model-year 1968. Another change related to safety was relocating the gas filler to the passenger side front fender. A

wide rubber gasket was provided to protect the paint from spilled fuel.

On the inside, Volkswagen used new seats with taller back sections and the ignition switch was now found on the steering column. A front trunk release was inside the glovebox. Front shoulder belts were standard and air

conditioning was optional. An Automatic Stick-Shift transmission was available.

The outside door handles were of a new trigger-action design. A number of new colors and interior trims were offered. Prices rose, but only by a few dollars.

1969

This was the last year for the 1500 engine. A new independent rear suspension was used in cars with the four-speed manual transmission. Separate seat headrests were used. A new feature was an electric rear

window defroster and the Cabriolet had a glass window in the fabric top. The gas filler now had a remote control release to unlatch the filler door. There was also a locking steering column. A new suspension setup that

Volkswagen described as Independent Rear Suspension (IRS) combined double-jointed constant-velocity joints with semi trailing arms to improve the ride and handling characteristics.

1970

This year the Karmann Ghia models received a 1600 engine. The 1600s were the fastest Karmann Ghias ever made. They could knock off a 0-to-60 run in twenty-one seconds and a top speed of around 82 miles per hour was claimed.

Also in 1970, the front and rear blinkers were made larger and the

taillights and back-up lights were integrated together. The rear side reflectors were redesigned too. As a running change, vacuum-type or dashpot-type throttle positioners were adopted to reduce emissions. The cooling system thermostat controlled the new air intake preheating system.

An evaporative emissions system was installed on California cars and eventually became standard on all US models. Also new was a removable rear deck lid drain tray.

Volkswagen is an Italian designed sports car with a bug in it.

Take away this beautiful Italian designed body and what have you got? A Volkswagen. A Volkswagen Karmann Ghia that is—the Italian-designed sports car with a bug in it.

How is the Karmann Ghia like an Italian sports car?

Well for one thing, it looks like one— with sleek, racy lines. And it was designed by the Ghia studios of Turin, Italy.

The Karmann Ghia is built like a sports car. With hand-welded, hand-filled, and hand-sanded seams. All done by the Karmann coach works of Osnabrück.

And, it has more than its fair share of sports-car-like features. Like adjustable bucket seats with padded headrests. A 4-speed stick shift. (Or, if you prefer, an optional automatic stick shift.) Torsion bar suspension on all 4 wheels. And self-adjusting front disc brakes.

And the engine? Well, that's where the bug comes in. It's a Volkswagen engine. Which means it'll give you things other sports cars won't.

Like gasoline mileage.

About 27 miles to the gallon's worth.

And service. The Karmann Ghia is full of VW parts, and can be serviced quickly and inexpensively.

The price? You can almost get two Karmann Ghias for the price of one racy Italian sports car.

Another nice thing about the Karmann Ghia is that you can cruise at its top speed indefinitely. And though you may never enter it in the Grand Prix, you'd never know to look at it.

The Karmann Ghia.

1971

The 1971 Karmann Ghia upgraded to a dual-port 1600 engine. A new device mounted on the air cleaner was a thermostat that controlled the engine air preheating system. Bigger defroster outlets and felt-type carpets were also new.

PREVIOUS PAGES: Volkswagen's ad agency never gave up being cute, and so the 1971 Karmann Ghia was described as "an Italian sports car with a bug in it." A Volkswagen Bug, of course.

BELOW: Leather-like vinyl seat upholstery was optional in the 1970 Karmann-Ghia, as was a very '70s-style fake woodgrain insert for the instrument panel. The vinyl door panels included large map pockets, and carpeting was standard equipment.

The Karmann Ghia. Our Idea Of A Sports Car.

From the outside, Karmann Ghia buyers saw a new bumper design and larger Type 3 taillights in 1972. Of course, the reason behind the larger, easier-to-see taillights was to try to keep the "safety police" happy.

KARMANN GHIA TYPE 14

1972

From the outside, Karmann Ghia buyers saw a new bumper design and larger Type 3 taillights in 1972. Of course the reason behind the single-blade bumper was to make them sturdier and try to keep the car "safety police" happy.

Inside changes included a pebble-grain plastic covering on the dashboard and top edge of the window openings. The instrument panel was also restyled to group the fuel gauge, and clock into two round instruments. The safety police also liked the year's new four-spoke safety steering wheel (with wiper switch on the right-hand stalk) that was designed to collapse upon driver impact and the new inertia reel-type safety belts with just one latching tab.

Additional alterations were made to the vacuum-operated system that preheated incoming air. The controls for the fresh-air system were relocated and changes were made to the door-and-window seals. One color was changed, the seat upholstery was revised, and the engine's compression ratio was lowered; the horsepower rating began to be expressed in net SAE horsepower numbers. Stick-shift cars had a new final drive ratio that boosted top speed to about 90 miles per hour.

LEFT: In 1972, the Karmann Ghia engine's compression ratio was lowered and horsepower rating began to be expressed in net SAE horsepower numbers. Stick-shift cars got a new final drive ratio that boosted top speed to about 90 miles per hour.

RIGHT: This 1972 Karmann Ghia catalog photo has the same theme as the 1971 catalog photo, although it's not the same art. These cars wear the new bumpers and the positions of the Coupe and Cabriolet are reversed.

1973

The Karmann Ghia was heading toward the end of the line and Volkswagen resisted degrading a beautiful design just to meet new US federal safety standards like some other imported cars had done.

The 1973 Karmann Ghia also had wider front and rear track measurements and a computer-analysis function. During the year, Volkswagen again came out of the Stone Age by changing the 12-volt electrical system from a generator to an alternator. Changes were also made to the fuel pump casting and rod, the brake calipers (new Girlings), and the mounts for the engine and transaxle. The rear jump seat was legislated out of existence with new seat safety regulations that also required a seat belt warning system. Cars sold in California and high-altitude counties received an exhaust gas recirculating system.

The 1973 Karmann Ghia had a computer-analysis function. The 12-volt electrical system finally got an alternator. Changes were made to the fuel pump and the mounts for the engine and transaxle. Girling brake calipers were new.

Sports cars can have a lot of expensive extras.

On the Karmann Ghia they're just a little extra.

By now you probably realize that you can spend a lot of money on a fancy sports car. And if you want to make it even fancier, you can spend even more.

Compared to other sports cars, the Karmann Ghia doesn't cost as much to begin with. And compared to most other sports cars, neither do our extras.

In addition to the ones in the picture, we also have Rubber Floor Mats. Whitewall Tires. Formula Vee Racing Stripe Kits. And Tissue Dispensers.

Ask your dealer to show any or all of them to you.

You may not really need any of our extras. But some people like to take a good thing, and make it even better.

Walnut Shift Knob.
It may not help you shift any better. But you'll look a lot better shifting.

Radios.
AM or AM/FM models, with antenna. Transistorized. Push-button tuning.

Cigarette Lighter.
Nice to have around, just in case you're ever caught matchless.

Automatic Stick Shift.
Does shifting leave you caught in a clutch? Not with our automatic stick shift. It comes with 3 forward gears—and no clutching, because there isn't any clutch pedal.

Air Conditioner.
Now you can keep your cool no matter how hot it is, without loss of legroom. Completely automatic temperature control.

1974

This was the final year for the stylish Karmann Ghia Sport Coupe and Sport Cabriolet. It wasn't really a lack of buyers that brought a close to Karmann Ghia history. Demand was still fairly strong, but Karmann was ramping up to crank out water-cooled Sciroccos and didn't have the factory capacity to keep making the old air-cooled Type 1s, which also struggled with pollution laws.

At the same time, Karmann Ghia prices were constantly rising to cover the cost of meeting safety and pollution regulations. Volkswagen realized rising costs would soon drive down demand. In

PREVIOUS PAGE: In its next-to-last year, the 1973 Karmann Ghia could be ordered with an AM or AM/FM transistorized radio incorporating push-button tuning. An automatic stick-shift and air conditioning were available. A walnut shifter knob was extra.

BELOW: *Road Test* wrote up the 1974 Karmann Ghia in its February 1974 issue. It noted the 1974 model had a few improvements for quieter running and greater durability. The sporty VW was now covered by a "security blanket" warranty.

In its last year, Volkswagen reverted to calling the Karmann Ghia ragtop a "convertible." The extended rear bumper met federal standards. All cars got an EGR valve and California cars got Solex carbs and a twin-tube intake preheater.

August 1973, production of 1974 models began. The company stopped building Karmann Ghias for the European market on December 21, 1973. Production for the US market continued until the same date in June 1974. Production since 1956 totaled 283,501 Karmann Ghia Coupes and 80,897 Cabriolets in Germany, and 23,577 Coupes in Brazil.

Road Test magazine tried to give the stylish Karmann Ghia's sales a shot in the arm with a write-up of the 1974 model in its February 1974 issue. It noted the Karmann Ghia had a few improvements for quieter running and greater durability. A "Security Blanket" warranty now covered the sporty VW.

Karmann Ghias offered 14 cubic feet of storage space behind its front bucket seats. New for 1973 were space-saving front disc brakes with floating calipers and larger brake pads, as well as self-restoring energy-absorbing bumpers that added ½-inch to vehicle length. A new alloy cylinder head was used in the Karmann Ghia engine and a new muffler system reduced noise.

The rear bumper was extended to meet new federal standards. This increased the cars' length a little bit. All engines were fitted with exhaust gas recirculation valves and California cars got Solex 34 PICT-4 carburetors and a twin-tube intake manifold preheating system.

Karmann Ghia Type 34, 1962-1969

Also available outside the United States in 1962 was the Karmann Ghia Type 3 with a 1500 engine. With looks something like a cross between a Karmann Ghia and a mutant Corvair, it debuted at the Frankfurt Auto Show.

The 1500's (AKA T34) completely fresh body design bore no resemblance to its successful older brother. It shared the chassis and drivetrain with the Volkswagen 1500 Notchback and Fastback models. Karmann planned a 1500 convertible that was scheduled for production and even designed a sales catalog for it, but technical problems with body flexing killed it. At least three were made. Karmann displayed one and another is in the hands of the Karmann family. Volkswagen in Germany retained the third one.

The coupe had a rectangular front emblem and small Karmann nameplates on the lower front of each rear quarter panel. Mass production of the Type 34 Coupe began in March 1962 at the Karmann factory.

The Type 34 was not a great seller, largely due to the fact that it cost as much as the 356 Porsche. The unusual styling kept customer demand low. Some 30,000 cars of the 42,510 built stayed in Germany. About 12,500 were exported to England, Canada, Australia, New Zealand, and other countries, but the fact that the Type 34 was not brought into the American market hurt its chances.

The Type 34 KG Registry believes that about two thousand of the rust-prone cars survive worldwide. Production ceased in July 1969. The cars are rare

and have been for a long time. Just after I started working for *Old Cars Weekly* in the late 1970s, we spotted one on a used car lot in Minneapolis and put a photo of it in the newspaper.

ABOVE: The Karmann Ghia 1500 was a sport coupe, but not a true sports car. It could accommodate four people and hold fourteen pieces of luggage. The front-end styling was a bit contrived and hard to get used to, but these cars are rare today.

RIGHT: The 1500 Karmann Ghia (a.k.a. T34) also had a fresh new body design that bore no resemblance to its successful older brother. It shared its chassis and drive train with the Beetle-based Volkswagen 1500 Notchback and Fastback models.

The phone calls from interested collectors continued for months.

Very few design or engineering changes were made between 1962 and 1969, but Type 34s can be still sorted into different generations according to their design or engineering changes: (early 1962) rare and have some characteristics of the 1961 prototype; (late 1962–1963) 1500 engine and single side-draft carburetor; (1964–1965/1500S) dual carburetors, domed pistons, and locking backrest seats; (1966) 6-volt electrical system and dual-carburetor 1600 engine; and (1967–1969) 12-volt electrical system and dual-carbureted 1,600cc engine.

1956

VOLKSWAGEN Karmann Ghia
TYPE 14

FACTORY PAINT COLORS

L41 Black   **L259** Pelican Red
L317 Lizard Green   **L330** Trout Blue
L375 Antelope Brown   **L376** Gazelle Beige

MODEL AVAILABILITY	2-door 2+2 Coupe ($2,395)
SERIAL NUMBERS	Same range as 1956 Type 1 Beetle
WHEELBASE	94.5 inches
LENGTH	163.0 inches
WIDTH	64.2 inches
HEIGHT	52.2 inches
WEIGHT	1,786 lbs.
TREAD	(front/rear) 50.8/49.2 inches
TIRES	5.60 x 15
BRAKES	Hydraulic, front/rear drum
LAYOUT	Rear-engine, rear-drive
CONSTRUCTION	Tubular center section, forked at rear, welded-on platform
FUEL TANK	10.6 gallons
FRONT SUSPENSION	Independent: upper and lower trailing arms with square torsion bars
REAR SUSPENSION	Independent: swinging half-axle shafts with torsion bars
ENGINE	1,192cc 36-hp horizontally opposed four-cylinder, overhead valve, air cooled, light alloy block and head, finned cylinders with cast-iron liners
TRANSMISSION	four-speed manual, nonsynchromesh first
FINAL DRIVE RATIO	spiral bevel 4.40:1

1957

VOLKSWAGEN Karmann Ghia
TYPE 14

All specs are the same as 1956, including price.

1958

VOLKSWAGEN Karmann Ghia
TYPE 14

FACTORY PAINT COLORS

L41 Black   **L417** Amazon Green
L97 Pearl White   **L428** Graphite Silver
L243 Diamond Gray   **L431** Bernina Blue
L354 Cardinal Red

MODEL AVAILABILITY	2-door 2+2 Coupe ($2,445) 2-door Sport Cabriolet ($2,725)
SERIAL NUMBERS	Same range as 1958 Type 1 Beetle
WHEELBASE	94.5 inches
LENGTH	163.0 inches
WIDTH	64.2 inches
HEIGHT	(Coupe) 52.2 inches; (Sport Cabriolet) 52.4 inches
WEIGHT	(Coupe) 1,720 lbs. (Sport Cabriolet) 1,786 lbs.
TREAD	(front/rear) 50.8/49.2 inches
TIRES	5.60 x 15
BRAKES	Hydraulic, front/rear drum
LAYOUT	Rear-engine, rear-drive
CONSTRUCTION	Tubular center section, forked at rear, welded-on platform
FUEL TANK	10.6 gallons
FRONT SUSPENSION	Independent: upper and lower trailing arms with square torsion bars
REAR SUSPENSION	Independent: swinging half-axle shafts with torsion bars
ENGINE	1,192cc 36-hp horizontally opposed four-cylinder, overhead valve, air cooled, light alloy block and head, finned cylinders with cast-iron liners
TRANSMISSION	four-speed manual, nonsynchromesh first
FINAL DRIVE RATIO	spiral bevel 4.40:1

1959

VOLKSWAGEN Karmann Ghia
TYPE 14 FACTORY

PAINT COLORS

1969 models made from January 1959 to July 1959 offered the 1958 options.

MODEL AVAILABILITY	2-door 2+2 Coupe ($2,445) 2-door Sport Cabriolet ($2,725)
SERIAL NUMBERS	Same range as 1959 Type 1 Beetle
WHEELBASE	94.5 inches
LENGTH	163.0 inches
WIDTH	64.2 inches
HEIGHT	(Coupe) 52.2 inches; (Sport Cabriolet) 52.4 inches
WEIGHT	(Coupe) 1,720 lbs.; (Sport Cabriolet) 1,786 lbs.
TREAD	(front/rear) 50.8/49.2 inches
TIRES	5.60 x 15
BRAKES	Hydraulic, front/rear drum
LAYOUT	Rear-engine, rear-drive
CONSTRUCTION	Tubular center section, forked at rear, welded-on platform
FUEL TANK	10.6 gallons
FRONT SUSPENSION	Independent suspension of wheels through upper and lower trailing arms; two laminated square torsion bars protected by tubes
REAR SUSPENSION	Independent suspension of wheels through swing-axle shafts, trailing arms, one torsion bar on each side, mounted and protected in transverse tubes
ENGINE	1,192cc 36-hp horizontally opposed four-cylinder, overhead valve, air cooled, light alloy block and head, finned cylinders with cast-iron liners
TRANSMISSION	four-speed manual, nonsynchromesh first
FINAL DRIVE RATIO	spiral bevel 4.40:1

1960

VOLKSWAGEN Karmann Ghia
TYPE 14

FACTORY PAINT COLORS

Chassis number 2 528 666–3 192 506

L41 Black	**L444** Malachite Green
L87 Pearl White	**L452** Paprika
L265 Platinum Gray	**L433** Ferrite Brown
L360 Sea Blue	

Chassis number 2 528 668–3 192 506

L41 Black	**L364** Strato Blue
L346 Mango Green	**L432** Malachite Green
L347 Seagull Gray	**L452** Paprika
L362 Midnight Blue	

MODEL AVAILABILITY	2-door 2+2 Coupe ($2,430) 2-door Sport Cabriolet ($2,695)
SERIAL NUMBERS	Same range as 1960 Type 1 Beetle
WHEELBASE	94.5 inches
LENGTH	163.0 inches
WIDTH	64.2 inches
HEIGHT	(Coupe) 52.2 inches; (Sport Cabriolet) 52.4 inches
WEIGHT	(Coupe) 1,720 lbs.; (Sport Cabriolet) 1,786 lbs.
TREAD	(front/rear) 50.8/49.2 inches
TIRES	5.60 x 15
BRAKES	Hydraulic, front/rear drum
LAYOUT	Rear-engine, rear-drive
CONSTRUCTION	Tubular center section, forked at rear, welded-on platform
FUEL TANK	10.6 gallons
FRONT SUSPENSION	Independent suspension of wheels through upper and lower trailing arms; two laminated square torsion bars protected by tubes
REAR SUSPENSION	Independent suspension of wheels through swing-axle shafts, trailing arms, one torsion bar on each side, mounted and protected in transverse tubes
ENGINE	1,192cc 36-hp horizontally opposed four-cylinder, overhead valve, air cooled, light alloy block and head, finned cylinders with cast-iron liners
TRANSMISSION	four-speed manual, nonsynchromesh first
FINAL DRIVE RATIO	spiral bevel 4.43:1

1961-1962

VOLKSWAGEN Karmann Ghia TYPE 14

FACTORY PAINT COLORS

L41 Black	**L398** Pacific
L87 Pearl White	**L452** Paprika
L360 Sea Blue	**L456** Red
L384 Pampas Green	**L459** Anthracite
L397 Lavender	**L490** Sierra Beige

Same specifications and prices as 1960 except all-synchromesh four-speed manual transmission and 1,192cc engine is up-rated to 40 horsepower. The final drive ratio also became 4.37:1 in order to slow down the engine speed somewhat.

The voluptuous Ghia Volkswagen stood out like the queen of the harem on the cover of *Motor Trend*'s May 1956 issue, but it was her plainer sisters the Beetle and the Camper that caught the fancy of the car-buying public.
Archives/TEN: The Enthusiast Network Magazines, LLC

1962

VOLKSWAGEN Karmann Ghia TYPE 14

FACTORY PAINT COLORS

Same as 1961

MODEL AVAILABILITY	2-door 2+2 Coupe ($2,295) 2-door Sport Cabriolet ($2,495)
SERIAL NUMBERS	Same range as 1962 Type 1 Beetle
WHEELBASE	94.5 inches
LENGTH	163.0 inches
WIDTH	64.3 inches
HEIGHT	(Coupe) 52.2 inches; (Sport Cabriolet) 52.4 inches
WEIGHT	(Coupe) 1,742 lbs.; (Sport Cabriolet) 1,808 lbs.
TREAD	(front/rear) 51.4/50.7 inches
TIRES	5.60 x 15
BRAKES	Hydraulic, front/rear drum
LAYOUT	Rear-engine, rear-drive
CONSTRUCTION	Tubular center section, forked at rear, welded-on platform
FUEL TANK	10.6 gallons
FRONT SUSPENSION	Independent suspension of wheels through upper and lower trailing arms; two laminated square torsion bars protected by tubes
REAR SUSPENSION	Independent suspension of wheels through swing-axle shafts, trailing arms, one torsion bar on each side, mounted and protected in transverse tubes
ENGINE	1,192cc 40-hp horizontally opposed four-cylinder, overhead valve, air cooled, light alloy block and head, finned cylinders with cast-iron liners
TRANSMISSION	four-speed manual, all-synchromesh
FINAL DRIVE RATIO	spiral bevel 4.37:1

1963

VOLKSWAGEN
Karmann Ghia TYPE 14

FACTORY PAINT COLORS

L41 Black	**L489** Anthracite
L87 Pearl White	**L514** Emerald
L360 Sea Blue	**L532** Polar Blue
L398 Pacific	**L560** Manila Yellow
L456 Ruby Red	**L571** Terra Brown

MODEL AVAILABILITY	2-door 2+2 Coupe ($2,295)
	2-door Sport Cabriolet ($2,495)
SERIAL NUMBERS	Same range as 1963–1965 Type 1 Beetles
WHEELBASE	94.5 inches
LENGTH	163.0 inches
WIDTH	64.3 inches
HEIGHT	(Coupe) 52.2 inches; (Sport Cabriolet) 52.4 inches
WEIGHT	(Coupe) 1,742 lbs.; (Sport Cabriolet) 1,808 lbs.
TREAD	(front/rear) 51.4/50.7 inches
TIRES	5.60 x 15
BRAKES	Hydraulic, front/rear drum
LAYOUT	Rear-engine, rear-drive
CONSTRUCTION	Tubular center section, forked at rear, welded-on platform
FUEL TANK	10.6 gallons
FRONT SUSPENSION	Independent suspension of wheels through upper and lower trailing arms; two laminated square torsion bars protected by tubes
REAR SUSPENSION	Independent suspension of wheels through swing-axle shafts, trailing arms, one torsion bar on each side, mounted and protected in transverse tubes
ENGINE	1,192cc 40-hp horizontally opposed four-cylinder, overhead valve, air cooled, light alloy block and head, finned cylinders with cast-iron liners
TRANSMISSION	four-speed manual, all-synchromesh
FINAL DRIVE RATIO	spiral bevel 4.37:1

1964

VOLKSWAGEN
Karmann Ghia TYPE 14

Same prices and specifications as 1963

1965

VOLKSWAGEN Karmann Ghia
TYPE 14

FACTORY PAINT COLORS

L285 Bermuda	**L568** Sea Sand
L360 Sea Blue	**L582** Arcona White
L544 Roulette Green	**L594** Smoke Grey
L553 Henna Red	**L595** Fontana Grey
L554 Cherry Red	**L41** Black
L560 Manila Yellow	

Same specifications as 1963–1964. Prices were lowered to $2,295 for the Coupe and $2,495 for the Sport Cabriolet.

1966

VOLKSWAGEN Karmann Ghia
TYPE 14

FACTORY PAINT COLORS

L41 Black	**L554** Cherry Red
L288 Bermuda Blue	**L560** Manila Yellow
L360 Sea Blue	**L568** Sea Sand
L398 Pacific	**L582** Arcona White
L544 Roulette Green	**L282** Lotus White

MODEL AVAILABILITY	2-door 2+2 Coupe ($2,250)
	2-door Sport Cabriolet ($2,445)
SERIAL NUMBERS	Same range as 1966 Type 1 Beetle
WHEELBASE	94.5 inches
LENGTH	163.0 inches
WIDTH	64.3 inches
HEIGHT	(Coupe) 52.2 inches; (Sport Cabriolet) 52.4 inches
WEIGHT	1,764 lbs.
TREAD	(front/rear) 51.4/50.7 inches
TIRES	5.60 x 15
BRAKES	Hydraulic, front/rear drum
LAYOUT	Rear-engine, rear-drive
CONSTRUCTION	Tubular center section, forked at rear, welded-on platform
FUEL TANK	10.6 gallons
FRONT SUSPENSION	Independent suspension of wheels through upper and lower trailing arms; two laminated square torsion bars protected by tubes
REAR SUSPENSION	Independent suspension of wheels through swing-axle shafts, trailing arms, one torsion bar on each side, mounted and protected in transverse tubes
ENGINE	1,285cc 50-hp horizontally opposed four-cylinder, overhead valve, air cooled, light alloy block and head, finned cylinders with cast-iron liners
TRANSMISSION	four-speed manual, all-synchromesh
FINAL DRIVE RATIO	spiral bevel 4.37:1

1967

VOLKSWAGEN Karmann Ghia
TYPE 14

FACTORY PAINT COLORS

L41 Black	**L10K** Castillian Yellow
L282 Lotus White	**L544** Roulette Green
L620 Savannah Beige	**L50K** Neptune Blue
L288 Bermuda Blue	**L554** Cherry Red
L70K Vulcan Grey	

MODEL AVAILABILITY	2-door 2+2 Coupe ($2,250)
	2-door Sport Cabriolet ($2,445)
SERIAL NUMBERS	Same range as 1967 Type 1 Beetle
WHEELBASE	94.5 inches
LENGTH	163.0 inches
WIDTH	64.3 inches
HEIGHT	(Coupe) 52.2 inches; (Sport Cabriolet) 52.54 inches
WEIGHT	1,786 lbs.
TREAD	(front/rear) 51.4/51.2 inches
TIRES	5.60 x 15
BRAKES	Hydraulic, front disc/rear drum
LAYOUT	Rear-engine, rear-drive
CONSTRUCTION	Tubular center section, forked at rear, welded-on platform
FUEL TANK	10.6 gallons
FRONT SUSPENSION	Independent suspension of wheels through upper and lower trailing arms; two laminated square torsion bars protected by tubes
REAR SUSPENSION	Independent suspension of wheels through swing-axle shafts, trailing arms, one torsion bar on each side, mounted and protected in transverse tubes
ENGINE	1,493cc (01.10 cubic-inch) 53 hp at 4,200 rpm, 78 lb-ft of torque at 2,600 rpm, horizontally opposed four-cylinder, overhead valve, air cooled, light alloy block and head, finned cylinders with cast-iron liners, single downdraft carburetor
TRANSMISSION	four-speed manual, all-synchromesh
FINAL DRIVE RATIO	7.5:1 compression ratio, spiral bevel

1968

VOLKSWAGEN Karmann Ghia
TYPE 14

FACTORY PAINT COLORS

L41 Black
L30K Velour Red
L50F Regatta Blue
L61K Pine Green
L70F Chinchilla

L80K Gobi Beige
L282 Lotus White
L288 Bermuda Blue
L554 Cherry Red

MODEL AVAILABILITY	2-door 2+2 Coupe ($2,254) 2-door Sport Cabriolet ($2,449)
SERIAL NUMBERS	148-000001-up
WHEELBASE	94.5 inches
LENGTH	163.0 inches
WIDTH	64.3 inches
HEIGHT	(Coupe) 52.2 inches; (Sport Cabriolet) 52.4 inches
WEIGHT	1,852 lbs.
TREAD	(front/rear) 51.4/53.1 inches
TIRES	5.60 x 15
BRAKES	Hydraulic, front disc/rear drum
LAYOUT	Rear-engine, rear-drive
CONSTRUCTION	Tubular center section, forked at rear, welded-on platform
FUEL TANK	10.6 gallons
FRONT SUSPENSION	Independent suspension of wheels through upper and lower trailing arms; two laminated square torsion bars protected by tubes
REAR SUSPENSION	Independent suspension of wheels through swing-axle shafts, trailing arms, one torsion bar on each side, mounted and protected in transverse tubes
ENGINE	1,493cc (01.10 cubic inches) 53 horsepower at 4,200 rpm, 78 lb-ft of torque at 2,600 rpm, horizontally opposed four-cylinder, overhead valve, air cooled, light alloy block and head, finned cylinders with cast-iron liners, single downdraft carburetor
TRANSMISSION	four-speed manual, all-synchromesh
FINAL DRIVE RATIO	7.5:1 compression ratio, spiral bevel

1969

VOLKSWAGEN Karmann Ghia
TYPE 14

FACTORY PAINT COLORS

L11K Oriole Yellow
L31K Sunset Red
L51K Chrome Blue

L62K Cypress Green
L90C Toga White
L554 Cherry Red

Same as 1968, except

MODELS AND PRICES	2-door 2+2 Coupe ($2,365) 2-door Sport Cabriolet ($2,575)
SERIAL NUMBERS	149-000001-up
REAR SUSPENSION	Independent suspension with double-jointed constant-velocity joints with semi-trailing arms

1970

VOLKSWAGEN Karmann Ghia
TYPE 14

FACTORY PAINT COLORS

L10E Pampas Yellow
L20E Amber
L30E Bahia Red
L41 Black

L51E Albert Blue
L52E Pastel Blue
L60# Irish Green
L80E Light Ivory

Same as 1969 except:

MODEL AVAILABILITY	2-door 2+2 Coupe ($2,399) 2-door Sport Cabriolet ($2,609)
STARTING SERIAL NUMBER	1402000001
LENGTH	163.0–165.0 inches
WEIGHT	1,918 lbs.
TREAD	(front/rear) 51.4/52.7 inches
TIRES	6.00 x 15L
ENGINE	1,585cc (96.7 cubic inches) 65 horsepower at 4,600 rpm, 87 lb-ft of torque at 2,800 rpm, horizontally opposed four-cylinder, overhead valve, air cooled, light alloy block and head, finned cylinders with cast-iron liners, 7.7:1 compression ratio, single downdraft carburetor

1971

VOLKSWAGEN Karmann Ghia
TYPE 14

FACTORY PAINT COLORS

L13 Bahia Red	**L20E** Amber
L41 Black	**L21E** Blood Orange
L50E Adriatic Blue	**L96D** Silver Metallic
L60F Irish Green	**L96E** Gemini Metallic
L63K Willow Green	**L97G** Gold Metallic
L80E Light Ivory	**L11E** Lemon Yellow

Same as 1970, except:

MODELS AND PRICING	2-door 2+2 Coupe ($2,575)
	2-door Sport Cabriolet ($2,750)
STARTING SERIAL NUMBER	1412000001
ENGINE	1,600cc dual-port with Solex 34 PICT-3 carburetor and 60 hp at 4,400 rpm

1972

VOLKSWAGEN
Karmann Ghia TYPE 14

FACTORY PAINT COLORS

Same as 1971, except **L13M** Saturn Yellow replaced **L11E** Lemon Yellow

Same as 1971, except:

MODEL AVAILABILITY	2-door 2+2 Coupe ($2,750)
	2-door Sport Cabriolet ($3,099)
WEIGHT	(Coupe) 1,874 lbs.; (Sport Cabriolet) 1,896 lbs.
ENGINE	Compression ratio 7.3:1, 46 hp (SAE net) at 4,000 rpm, 72 lb-ft of torque at 3,000 rpm

1973

VOLKSWAGEN Karmann Ghia
TYPE 14

FACTORY PAINT COLORS

L13 Bahia Red	**L32K** Phoenix Red
L41 Black	**L13K** Sunshine Yellow
L51P Olympic Blue	**L96B** Alaska Metallic
L65K Zambesi Green	**L96M** Marathon Metallic
L80E Light Ivory	**L13M** Saturn Yellow
L20E Amber	**L99A** Saturn Yellow Metallic

Same as 1972, except:

MODEL AVAILABILITY	2-door 2+2 Coupe ($3,050)
	2-door Sport Cabriolet ($3,450)
WEIGHT	1,853 lbs.

1974

VOLKSWAGEN Karmann Ghia
TYPE 14

FACTORY PAINT COLORS

Same as 1973.

Same as 1973, except:

MODEL AVAILABILITY	2-door 2+2 Coupe ($3,475)
	2-door Sport Cabriolet ($3,935)
LENGTH	166 inches
WEIGHT	1,919 lbs.

1962–1969

VOLKSWAGEN Karmann Ghia
TYPE 34

MODEL AVAILABILITY (1966)	2-door 2+2 Coupe ($2,850 West Coast P.O.E.)
WHEELBASE	94.5 inches
LENGTH	168.5 inches
WIDTH	64.28 inches
HEIGHT	52.54 inches
WEIGHT	1,852–2,006 lbs. (over eight years)
BRAKES	Hydraulic, front/rear drum (front disc from 1965 on)
LAYOUT	Rear-engine, rear-drive
FUEL TANK	10.52 gallons
ENGINE (1500)	1,492cc 53 hp at 4,400 rpm, horizontally opposed four-cylinder, overhead valve, air cooled, light alloy block and head, finned cylinders with cast-iron liners
ENGINE (1600)	1,584cc 66-hp at 4,600 rpm, horizontally opposed four-cylinder, overhead valve, air cooled, light alloy block and head, finned cylinders with cast-iron liners
TRANSMISSION	four-speed manual

CHAPTER 10

Type 3, Type 4, and The Thing

As the 1950s wound down and Volkswagen sales ramped up, the company decided that the introduction of a larger, more upscale car would build on the success of the Beetle, Transporter, and Karmann Ghia. By 1960 the company was testing prototypes and in early 1961 Volkswagan officially unveiled the Type 3 1500 sedan. The new car looked completely different from anything Volkswagen had ever built, but in reality the new car retained the Beetle's 94.5-inch wheelbase and in most aspects was really just an inventive take on the basic Beetle theme.

In 1962 Volkswagen followed up with a station wagon variant called the "Variant" in Germany, but renamed the "Squareback Sedan" when it was introduced to the US market in late 1965. Volkswagen never officially imported the 1500 Sedan to the US, though the company had imported the 1500 series to Canada earlier. A 1.5-liter air-cooled flat-four engine powered all versions of the original Type 3. The long block remained the same as that used on the Type 1, but Volkswagen redesigned the engine cooling to reduce the height of the engine profile, thus allowing greater cargo volume, and earning the nicknames of "Pancake" or "Suitcase" engine. Engine displacement would later increase to 1.6 liters.

The Volkswagen Squareback sedan was exhibited at the Frankfurt Auto Show in the fall of 1961. Some called it a "Beetle in disguise," but the Type 3 (or 1500) had a completely different appearance and a slightly larger engine. This is the original 1962 production model. *Archives/TEN: The Enthusiast Network Magazines, LLC*

Type 3 1500

The idea of a new Volkswagen always excited auto writers. In May 1961, *Motor Trend* ran a two-page story entitled "The New VW" on the Type 3 notchback and wagon. It noted that the 1500s would be "exported from Germany to every country in the world except the United States" and explained that this was because sales of the Beetle were still increasing at the time. A month later, *Motor Trend* ran, "The first complete picture report on the new Volkswagen."

The Squareback sedan was exhibited at the Frankfurt Auto Show in the fall of 1961. Some called it a "Beetle in disguise," but the Type 3 (or 1500) had a completely different appearance and a slightly larger engine. In October, *Motor Trend* ran a third story called "Official Debut of the VW-1500." It estimated that the cost of a 1500 with the equipment required in the US market would be "in excess of $2,000." The Karmann Ghia 1500 Type 3 was also shown again in the "European Report" section of *Motor Trend* in December 1961.

The 1500 was a conventional notchback sedan with squarish lines. A wagon was added during 1962. A convertible was planned and a prototype was made, but it was not put into production. However photos of the pilot model exist.

In April 1963, *Motor Trend* printed a comparison test of the Volkswagen Beetle 1200 and the Volkswagen Type 3 1500. "It's rare that we devote a road test to a European car not currently being imported to the US, but in the case of the VW 1500, there seems good reason to make an exception," Wayne Thomas wrote. "The fact is that the car's now available in Canada and Mexico and significant numbers have been brought in from Europe by servicemen and tourists, so you're likely to see the 1500 with fair regularity in larger cities."

The magazine found both to be "top-quality" small cars, but rated the 1500 the best choice because it was bigger, faster, and had fancier features. It had a fully padded dashboard that hooded three circular instruments. The steering wheel was a locking type and a button

OPPOSITE: The 91.5-cid flat four in the Volkswagen 1500 was mounted at the rear of the car under a platform similar to that of the Chevrolet Corvairs. The fan for the air-cooled engine was mounted above the engine and was also Corvair-like. *Archives/TEN: The Enthusiast Network Magazines, LLC*

BELOW: The most distinctive styling points of the Volkswagen 1500 were the front and rear ends. An independent front suspension was used and swing arms were attached at the rear. Drum brakes were used at all four corners. *Archives/TEN: The Enthusiast Network Magazines, LLC*

on back of the turn signal stalk operated the headlight dimmer. The 1500 was about 12 miles per hour faster than the Beetle. A seven-position front seat was standard equipment. Recessed interior door handles were featured. The engine was similar in design to the flat-four used in the Beetle, but it included a cooling fan driven off the front of the crankshaft.

The 1500 engine was quieter and flatter than the 1200. The 1500 had a front luggage compartment, plus a rear one above the engine. An external dipstick was provided in the rear of the car for checking the oil level without opening the engine cover. Volkswagen delayed US introductions until 1965. It wasn't until model year 1966 that these cars came to the United States with a 1600 engine powering both Fastback and Squareback models. They were sold through 1973.

ABOVE: The engine for the Volkswagen 1500 was similar in design to the Beetle engine, but had the cooling fan driven by the crank nose so it was much quieter and formed a flatter engine package. *Archives/TEN: The Enthusiast Network Magazines, LLC*

BELOW: Here's the 1961 Volkswagen Type 3 in its Notchback format. The concept behind this car was very practical, but it never caught on with the car-buying public the way that Beetles and Buses did.

ABOVE: A convertible version of the Volkswagen 1500 was planned and a prototype was made in 1961, but this body style did not make it to the assembly line. A photo of the 1961 pilot model was shown in the sales catalog, however.

BELOW: The Type 3 Notchback had a wider floorpan than a Beetle and more luggage capacity. Its disc brakes, flat hubcaps, and 1,500cc engine eventually made their way into the Volkswagen Beetle.

NEXT PAGE: When *Motor Trend* wrote up the Volkswagen Squareback sedan, it said it was really a station wagon. Its fit and finish were excellent and it had plenty of cargo room. The basic car sold for $2,621. Leatherette upholstery was $37 and an AM radio was $64.95. *Archives/TEN: The Enthusiast Network Magazines, LLC*

TYPE 3, TYPE 4, AND THE THING

1966–1967

The 1600 evolved from the European Type 3 and came in two-door Fastback or Squareback models. It used a 1,585cc horizontally opposed engine that developed 65 horsepower. The 1600's appearance was similar to the 1500 that had been marketed elsewhere in the world since 1962. These cars used a different type of horizontally opposed air-cooled engine than the Beetle. This powerplant was sometimes referred to as a suitcase engine because of its overall shape.

The Fastback's body had long rear quarter windows, a sharply slanted back window, and vertical taillights at the rear fender tips. The Squareback's rear window was almost vertical, similar to that of a station wagon.

Options for these more deluxe Volkswagens included an AM radio for $69.95 or AM/FM radio for $120, a rear speaker for $8.67, a cigarette lighter for $2.95, an outside mirror for $3.95, a parcel shelf for $12.25, a roof luggage rack for $24.95, vent shades for $6.50, front armrests for $4.95, whitewall tires for $35, cocoa mats for $16.95, wheel trim rings for $5.95, a set of rubber bumper guards for $8.95, fender protectors for $4.50, and, starting in 1967, a sunroof for $90.

Production of the Fastback and Squareback sedans continued in 1968 in much the same format, except that the fuel filler door went on the right front fender and the engine gained

The family-oriented Volkswagen Squareback sedan bowed at the Frankfurt Auto Show in the fall of 1961. Some called it a "Beetle in disguise," but this Type 3 (1500) had a much different appearance and slightly larger engine.

The Volkswagen 411 was considered a failure in the marketplace by 1971, even though improvements had been made to the original version. Sales remained slow and showed no signs of changing. *Archives/TEN: The Enthusiast Network Magazines, LLC*

electronic fuel injection during the year (though many specifications sheets show twin carburetors used on early 1968 models). An automatic transmission also became available during the model year.

1968

In June 1968, *Motor Trend* did a comparison test of the Volkswagen 1600 Squareback and the Chevy II in snowy conditions in the California mountains not far from Reno, Nevada. The test crew logged 406.4 miles in its Volkswagen, which was equipped

with the base four-speed manual transmission. The car, a late-year model with electronic fuel injection, averaged 39.07 miles per gallon for the entire trip and reached as high as 45.21 miles per gallon. Comparable numbers for the Chevy II were 28.92 miles per gallon and 33.10 miles per gallon. Performance figures were not reported for either car.

1969

The 1969 sales catalog for the Fastback emphasized the car's fastback styling, swing-out rear windows,

louvered air intakes on the tops of the rear fenders, and its slotted wheel discs. Technical highlights included electronic fuel injection, a magnesium-aluminum alloy engine, front wheel disc brakes, and a choice of a four-speed synchromesh gearbox or fully automatic transmission. Inside the Fastback featured bucket seats that adjusted to forty-nine positions, door-to-door carpeting, and color-matched padded interiors and upholstery.

The Squareback sedan looked like a station wagon and was often called that. Its features included adjustable

Fastback styling.
Swing-out rear windows.
Louvred air intakes.
Slotted wheel discs.

front bucket seats and push-down rear seats with a fold-flat seatback, a 42.7 x 25.4-inch cargo area, an oil cap with dipstick attached under the back door, recessed door handles, a pull-out dashboard ashtray with a pop-up metal ash guard, and a spare tire that sat upright in the forward part of the front trunk. It also had louvers on the upper rear fenders.

In a *Motor Trend* test (February 1969), the 1600 Station Wagon with automatic transmission required 21.1 seconds to move from 0 to 60 miles per hour. The station wagon covered the standing-start quarter-mile in 21.1 seconds at 60.5 miles per hour. It reached 25–35 miles per gallon full economy over the entire test and averaged 32 miles per gallon. During the 1969 model year, air conditioning was available as a dealer option.

1970–1971

In 1971, *Ward's Automotive Yearbook* began reporting US sales breakouts for the Type 3 Volkswagen and the total for 1970 was 99,012 Type 3 models, including both Fastback and Squareback Sedans.

Production of the Squareback and the Fastback continued in 1971 without major change. Options this year included whitewalls for $29.50, leatherette upholstery for $37, and air conditioning for $320. Volkswagen sold 80,186 Type 3 Fastbacks and Squarebacks in the United States during the calendar year.

1972–1973

Production of the Squareback sedan and the Fastback sedan (or Type 3)

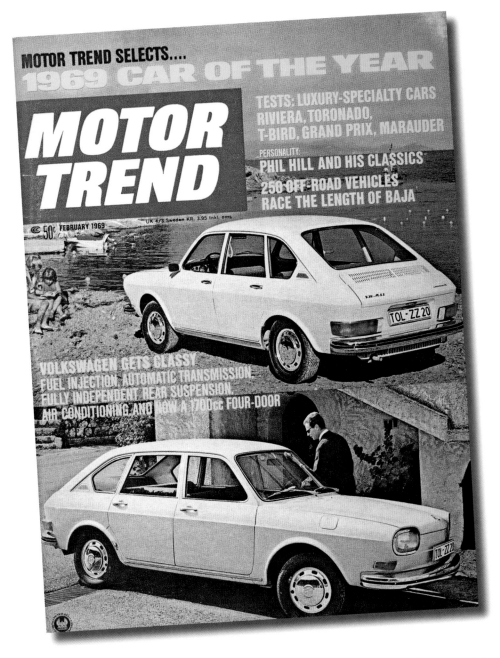

continued with no major changes in 1972. A road test of the Squareback included the following performance figures: 0–30 miles per hour: 5.1 seconds, 0–45 miles per hour: 10.3 seconds, 0–60 miles per hour: 17.7 seconds, 0–75 miles per hour: 31.5 seconds. It completed the quarter-mile in 20.9 seconds at 65 miles per hour and its passing speeds were 40–60 miles per hour: 10.0 seconds and 50–70 miles per hour: 13.9 seconds. Its gas mileage was 19–24 miles per gallon. The car was losing oomph and economy.

TOP: Volkswagen dominated the cover of the February 1969 issue of *Motor Trend* magazine. *Archives/TEN: The Enthusiast Network Magazines, LLC*

OPPOSITE: The 1600 evolved from the European Type 3 and came as the two-door Fastback, shown here, or as the Squareback model. This 1969 Fastback featured swing-out rear windows, louvered rear-fender air intakes, and slotted wheel discs.

The Volkswagen Squareback Sedan looks the way it looks because we wanted to fit a lot of space inside a family car.

So instead of curving or sloping the back, we extended the roof line, squared off the rear end and enclosed all the space that sits outside a conventional sedan above the trunk.

But don't let its less-than-rakish appearance fool you. The Squareback is as advanced a car as any of the 9 million Volkswagens we ever built.

Take the engine . . . if you can find it.

It's an air-cooled, 1,584 cc., 65-horsepower engine. Our most powerful passenger car engine yet. Top speed is 84 mph with this new engine.

But you won't find it under the front hood. We put those 6.5 cubic feet of space to work as a luggage compartment. You won't find the engine when you swing up the back door either. What you will find is a second luggage area, this one 24.7-cubic-feet big. Larger than the trunks in most conventional sedans.

Where's the engine? It's tucked under the floor at the back of the car, pressing down its weight on the drive wheels for extra traction in mud and snow. It's the most compact engine we ever built. Just 16 inches high.

So if somebody tells you there's nothing unusual about the Squareback, you can put him in his place. Just ask him to find the engine.

but it's sure built like one

You'll find many technical features in our newest Volkswagen that were proven in our older VW models. (In this respect, the Squareback is a throwback.)

You'll find that the flat new engine is air-cooled, not water-cooled. Since air won't freeze or boil, your Squareback will always perform reliably. Winter and summer.

The transmission is synchromesh. All four forward gears are synchronized to make shifting easy and quiet in every gear. You can even shift down to first without stopping or clashing gears.

The wheels are independently suspended by torsion bar springs. Each wheel travels its own road and takes its lumps and bumps without passing them on to the other wheels. You'll ride smoother for it.

The Squareback seats five adults, two up front in individual bucket seats and three in back on the bench seat.

But for all its interior space, outside the Squareback is only six inches longer than the bug, our standard VW Sedan. So a parking space that's snug as a bug should fit the Squareback, too.

Another comforting thought: while the Squareback may be new to you, it isn't a new car. It's been in production since 1962. We've had four years to test and prove its new features.

For a look at some of those features, open the fold.

Type 4: 411/412

The Type 4 was Heinrich Nordhoff's idea. Volkswagen aimed the new series at the midsize car market and produced Type 4 models from 1968 to 1974. They were packaged as a two-door sedan, a four-door sedan, and a two-door station wagon. The 411 versions were manufactured from 1968 to 1972 and the 412 versions were made from 1972 to 1974. The Type 4 was sold in the United States only from 1971 to 1974. Throughout the rest of the world, 367,728 Type 4s were sold, and in the United States, total sales were 117,110, most being 412s.

The Italian design firm Carrozzeria Pininfarina is credited with the original 411 design. An air-cooled, rear-mounted flat-four was used for power.

1971

The Volkswagen Type 4 became available in the United States in 1971. Two body styles were offered: a three-door hatchback and four-door sedan. The rear-mounted 1,679cc (102.5 cubic-inch) horizontally opposed four-cylinder developed 85 horsepower. It used a 3.54 x 2.60-inch (90mm x 66mm) bore and stroke and an 8.2:1 compression ratio. The horsepower rating was 85 at 5,000 rpm and it made 99.4 pounds-feet of torque at 3,500 rpm. Automatic transmission was an extra-cost item.

Volkswagen is a big new sedan full of extras at nothing extra.

How many extras can you get in a Volkswagen? Quite a few.
And if the Volkswagen is one of our new 411s, you'll be getting a lot of the extras at no extra cost.
Volkswagen feels that if you're going to spend extra money for a bigger car, you should get more than extra metal and chrome. So here are a few of the things that come with the 4-Door and 3-Door Sedans:
A fully automatic transmission.
Adjustable front bucket seats.
Door-to-door carpeting and metallic paint.
Radial ply tires.
A thermostatically controlled auxiliary heater, as well as a regular heater.
Then there's an extra big engine. The 411s have the most powerful engines ever built by Volkswagen. But that doesn't mean they're not economical. Both the 4-Door and the 3-Door Sedan give you about 22 miles to the gallon. Both need pints of oil instead of quarts. And because Volkswagen engines are air-cooled, they won't boil over in the summer. Or need antifreeze in the winter.
Extra comfort. Both Sedans are equipped with coil spring/shock absorber suspension struts to give you smoother riding, easier handling and better road-holding and cornering.
And they come with an undercoated bottom, which means there's extra protection of the car's vital parts. And an extra quiet ride.
And each has a dual brake system with self-adjusting disc brakes in front and drums in the rear.
Now that you've seen what the 411s have to offer, don't you think it would be silly to pay a lot of money for a big car that's full of nothing?
Come in and size up a 4-Door or a 3-Door Sedan.
You'll find we're really on to something.

The 411 4-Door and the 411 3-Door Sedan.

ABOVE: The Type 4 aimed the new series at the midsize car market. Volkswagen produced Type 4 models from 1968 to 1974 (1970 shown). They came as a two-door Sedan, a four-door Sedan, and a two-door Station Wagon.

OPPOSITE: The Squareback looked like a station wagon and was often called that. Production of Squarebacks and Fastbacks continued in 1971 without major change. Whitewalls were optional for $29.50 and leatherette upholstery for $37. A total of 80,186 Type 3 Fastbacks and Squarebacks sold in the US that year.

ABOVE: The 412 model replaced the 411 in 1973. Its horizontally opposed engine was rated 76 horsepower (SAE net) instead of 85 horsepower. *Motor Trend* (in January of 1973) described the new 412 dashboard as "almost Detroit-like in execution." It had integrated air-conditioner registers and a woodgrain dashboard inlay. *Archives/TEN: The Enthusiast Network Magazines, LLC*

OPPOSITE: The Type 4 was Heinrich Nordhoff's idea. VW aimed the new series at the midsize car market and produced Type 4 models from 1968 to 1974. They were packaged as a two-door Sedan, a four-door Sedan, and this two-door Station Wagon. *Archives/TEN: The Enthusiast Network Magazines, LLC*

1972–1973

A two-door sedan was added to the 411 lineup early in the 1972 model year. The 412 model replaced the 411 in 1973. It was offered in two- and four-door sedan styles, as well as a station wagon. The horizontally opposed engine was rated 76 horsepower (SAE net) instead of 85 horsepower. *Motor Trend* (January 1973) described the new 412 dashboard as "almost Detroit-like in execution." It had integrated air-conditioner registers and a woodgrain dashboard inlay.

1974

The final season for the Type 4 series was 1974. A larger engine went into the four-door sedan and station wagon, but it had a lower compression ratio and less SAE net horsepower and less torque.

TOP LEFT: In 1972, the term "station wagon" was already being used by Volkswagen to describe its passenger-carrying bus. So, the correct name for this model was "Squareback Sedan," even though it technically was a wagon. *Archives/TEN: The Enthusiast Network Magazines, LLC*

TOP RIGHT: Cargo access in the Squareback Sedan was good, but operating the rear seat was a little tough. The car had a pronounced rear weight bias that hurt its handling and hurt it in comparison to other station wagons in its class. *Archives/TEN: The Enthusiast Network Magazines, LLC*

BOTTOM LEFT: The 1972 Squareback had high-quality soft trim, but it was Spartan-looking inside and the interior arrangement was awkwardly laid out. Getting in an out was no problem, but the seating was upright and the pedals went straight up. *Archives/TEN: The Enthusiast Network Magazines, LLC*

BOTTOM RIGHT: The 1972 Squareback had unitized body/frame construction with independent torsion bar suspensions front and rear. Its base price was $2,749, and it placed last in a *Motor Trend* comparison report against other small wagons. *Archives/TEN: The Enthusiast Network Magazines, LLC*

—Volkswagen Type 181 Thing—

Pictured in the April 1969 issue of *Motor Trend* was a vehicle that was photographed at the Australian Embassy in Jakarta, Indonesia. It appeared to be a World War II German Jeep or Kübelwagen, but was actually something that Volkswagen was working on for the military. The vehicle was a predecessor of the Type 181 introduced at the Frankfort Auto Show for just over $2,200.

The Type 181 was a two-wheel-drive, four-door knockoff of the Kübelwagen ("bucket car") that had originally been developed for military use in Europe. This model would end up being sold to civilians as the Kurierwagen in Germany, the Trekker in England (where it was coded Type 182 with right-hand drive), the Safari in Mexico and South America, and the Pescaccia in Italy. It was only marketed as "The Thing" in the United States and only in 1973 and 1974.

In *Motor Trend* (July 1971), Wally Wyss wrote about the Volkswagen Type 181. Wyss said at the time, "VW of America has no plans to market the car in the States, probably because it hasn't been tested for compliance to various federal regulations and possibly, too, because they aren't convinced there's a market."

That thinking changed a little while later and the Type 181 came to the United States. The basic vehicle was built in three different Volkswagen plants, including Hanover, Germany (1968–1974); Puebla, Mexico (1970–1980); and Jakarta, Indonesia (1973–1980). It used the wider Type 14 Karmann Ghia floorpan and mechanical parts from the Type 1 Beetle. The split window Transporter's double-reduction axle was originally used, but in 1973 that setup was replaced by a Porsche design with double-jointed axles used on US-market Beetles.

Tightening US safety regulations chased The Thing away and halted German production, but in Mexico and Indonesia The Thing stuck around for six more years. More than fifty thousand Type 181s were

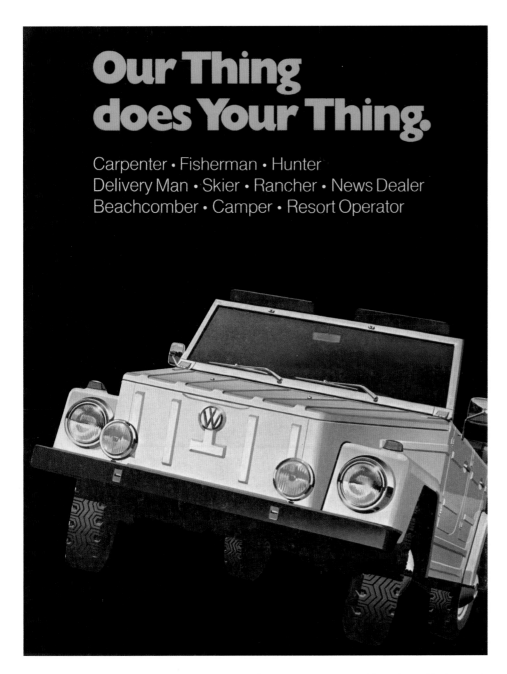

Our Thing does Your Thing.

Carpenter • Fisherman • Hunter
Delivery Man • Skier • Rancher • News Dealer
Beachcomber • Camper • Resort Operator

In the late 1970s, my boss bought two VW Things and I thought he was nuts. Today, I wish I had a couple dozen of them to bring to a classic car auction. They appealed to people from many walks of life.

Whatever your thing may be.

Say, for example, you're a carpenter who likes to fish and hunt. And you're looking for a vehicle that can take your tools to the job, and your gear to the woods.

A vehicle that's rugged enough to take you where you want to go—even if that means leaving the road behind.

Well, we've got just the thing.

The Thing.

With back seats that fold down for extra storage space. Removable top and doors, and a windshield that snaps down for dune buggy fun. A double-jointed rear axle to keep the wheels in contact with the ground, even over the roughest terrain. Four wheel independent suspension to smooth out the bumps. High ground clearance and special protection for rough terrain use. And of course, an air-cooled, rear-mounted engine for extra traction.

The Thing offers all this, plus gas economy: 21 miles per gallon.*

And that is some thing.

*DIN 700

actually delivered to NATO soldiers. The military versions have different specifications than the civilian versions.

1973–1974

Introduced elsewhere in the world during 1969, The Thing became available in the United States in 1973, after production moved to a Volkswagen factory in Mexico. Power came from the same rear-mounted 46-horsepower engine used in the Beetle. The car's spare tire was under the tall front hood. The doors were removable and the windshield folded flat. Three colors were offered: Pumpkin Orange, Sunshine Yellow, and Blizzard White. All came with a black convertible top and black leatherette interior. Also available was the Acapulco Thing with a striped surrey top, striped seats, and blue and white body paint.

Volkswagen claimed a 71-mile-per-hour top speed. John Lamm reported on The Thing in *Motor Trend* (December 1973), covering all aspects of the car—from its appeal to Chevelle SS-396 owners to its driving characteristics. "Regardless of what [Ralph] Nader thinks, The Thing is a kick to drive," Lamm said.

"You start by suffering, just trying to get into it without getting the back of your pant leg dirty on the doorsill," Lamm continued. "Once in, the interior has all the warmth and style of a military scout car . . . there are knobs or levers for headlights, heater/fan, hazard flashers, ventilation and a brake-failure warning light. One handy

PREVIOUS PAGE: Volkswagen had a lot of fun with The Thing name in its ads and promotional materials. Derived from the World War II Kübelwagen design, The Thing could be a Phaeton, a Convertible, or a door-less, Surrey-type resorter.

OPPOSITE: Writer Jon Lamm thought that the 1973 Volkswagen Thing looked like "a good thing five years too late." He felt that the Volkswagen Jeep would have done even better if it had been brought to the US during the dune buggy craze. *Archives/TEN: The Enthusiast Network Magazines, LLC*

BELOW: This see-through illustration highlighted twenty features of The Thing. In reality, the Type 181 Thing was a very simple vehicle. Despite its popularity, the car challenged the safety cops and was sold in the US only in 1973 and 1974.

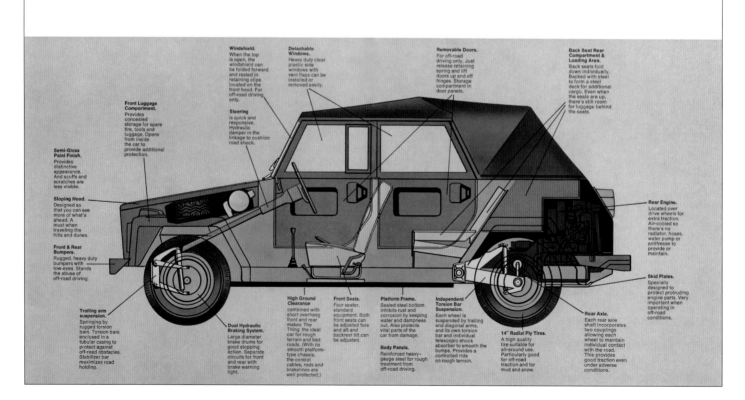

Your own special Thing.

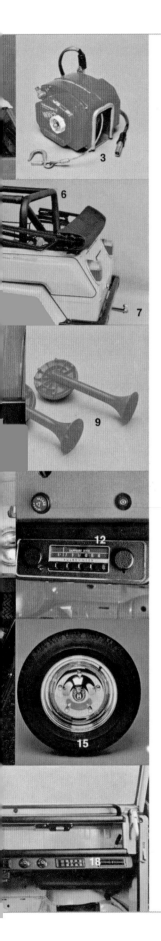

Here's how to make the most of a good thing. With accessories.

Say you like to go fishing. You'll want to bring a boat, right? So we designed a trailer hitch especially for The Thing. And even when you're getting away from it all, you'll want to hear some music and news. So choose from our wide selection of radios and tapeplayers. Then, you might want your Thing to gleam a little. Chrome wheel covers ought to do it.

And there's more. Look through this list, and ask a salesman to help you plan your own special Thing.

The Thing.

We make it special. You make it your own.

1. The Top.
2. Luggage Rack.
3. Electric Winch.
4. Spare Tire Carrier.
5. Chrome Wheel Covers.
6. Roll Cage.
7. Trailer Hitch.
8. Bumper Overriders.
9. Sport Horn Set.
10. Fog Lamps.
11. Front Push Bar.
12. Radios.
13. Sports Gearshift Lever.
14. Tunnel Console.
15. Chrome Wheels.
16. Sports Shifter.
17. Steering Wheel Cover.
18. Air Conditioner.

ABOVE: The Volkswagen Thing's interior and dash had minimal frills. A fuel indicator was located on the speedometer and was the only dashboard gauge. There were four front-hinged doors. *Archives/TEN: The Enthusiast Network Magazines, LLC*

OPPOSITE: A total of eighteen accessories aimed at the recreational market were available for the 1973–1974 Volkswagen Thing. They ranged from a hardtop to an electric winch to, believe it or not, air conditioning.

feature is a 12-volt electrical tap on the dash. The overall effect should warm the heart of any reconstructed Army driver. The seats go along with the theme: stark, but practical. In back, the seats can be folded down and, unlike most utility vehicles, firmly held down . . . the top and side curtains are less Army than Austin-Healey. Whether putting it up or bringing it down, the top is simple and two people can get the trick down to about 30 seconds."

Motor Trend (March 1973) carried a cover photo of a Kübelwagen and a VW Type 181. "Volkswagen's 'Jeep' 1943–1973" was the headline and Steve Smith's feature story inside was entitled "Volkswagen's 'Jeep' Is Alive and Well in Mexico, Literally." Smith explained that the Jeep-like vehicle had been available in Europe since the fall of 1969 and that production had been moved to Mexico in August 1972. The Type 181 sold for roughly $2,700 south of the border.

1966

TYPE 3 VOLKSWAGEN 1600

GENERAL SPECIFICATIONS

MODEL AVAILABILITY	2-door Fastback Sedan ($2,140) 2-door Squareback Sedan ($2,295)
STARTING SERIAL NUMBER	(1600 Fastback) 316-000001 (1600 Squareback) 366-000001
WHEELBASE	94.5 inches
LENGTH	(Fastback) 170.8 inches (Squareback) 166.3 inches
WIDTH	63.2 inches
HEIGHT	(Fastback) 57.9 inches (Squareback) 58.1 inches
WEIGHT	(Fastback) 1,962 lbs.; (Squareback) 2,029 lbs.
TREAD	(front/rear) 51.6/53.0 inches
TIRES	6.00 x 15
BRAKES	Hydraulic, front/rear drum
CONSTRUCTION	semiunitized body with platform frame
STEERING	worm and sector
FRONT SUSPENSION	Rubber-mounted independent suspension by two torsion arms on each side; horizontally crossed torsion bars; four large rubber stops to prevent excessive wheel movement, double-acting telescopic hydraulic shock absorbers
REAR SUSPENSION	Rear-axle rubber-mounted in subframe. Independent suspension by trailing arms and diagonal links and rear axles, each with two constant velocity joints. Rubber stops and shock absorbers as in front axle.
FUEL TANK	10.6 gallons
ENGINE	Horizontally opposed, overhead-valve four-cylinder (air cooled). Light alloy block and heads and finned cylinders with cast-iron cylinder liners. Displacement: 96.7 cubic inches (1,584cc); bore and stroke: 3.36 x 2.72 inches (85 x 69 mm); compression ratio: 7.7:1; brake horsepower: 65 at 4,600 rpm; torque: 87 lb-ft at 3,000 rpm. Four main bearings, solid valve lifters, twin Solex single-barrel sidedraft carburetors. 6-volt electrical system.
TRANSMISSION	four-speed manual
FINAL DRIVE RATIO	spiral bevel; gear ratio (1969 manual) 4.125:1

1967

TYPE 3 VOLKSWAGEN 1600

GENERAL SPECIFICATIONS

Same as 1966, except:

MODEL AVAILABILITY	2-door Fastback Sedan ($2,148); with sunroof ($2,273) 2-door Squareback Sedan ($2,295); with sunroof ($2,420)
STARTING SERIAL NUMBER	(1600 Fastback) 317-000001 (1600 Squareback) 367-000001

1968

TYPE 3 VOLKSWAGEN 1600

GENERAL SPECIFICATIONS

Same as 1967, except:

MODEL AVAILABILITY	2-door Fastback Sedan ($2,179); with sunroof ($2,349) 2-door Squareback Sedan ($2,299); with sunroof ($2,469)
SERIAL NUMBERS	(1600 Fastback) 318-000001-up (1600 Squareback) 368-000001-up
ENGINE	Horizontally opposed, overhead-valve four-cylinder (air cooled). Light alloy block and heads and finned cylinder with cast-iron cylinder liners. Displacement: 96.7 cubic inches (1,585cc); bore and stroke: 3.36 x 2.72 inches (85 x 69 mm). Compression ratio: 7.7:1. Brake horsepower: 65 at 4600 rpm. Torque: 87 lb.-ft. at 2800 rpm. Four main bearings. Solid valve lifters. (Early 1968) Two single-barrel carburetors. (Late 1968) Electronic fuel injection. 12-volt electrical system.

1969

TYPE 3 VOLKSWAGEN 1600

GENERAL SPECIFICATIONS

Same as 1968, except:

MODEL AVAILABILITY	2-door Fastback Sedan ($2,295); with sunroof ($2,415) 2-door Squareback Sedan ($2,470); with sunroof ($2,590)
SERIAL NUMBERS	(1600 Fastback) 319-0000010-up (1600 Squareback) 369-000001-up
WEIGHT	(Fastback Sedan) 2,226 lbs. (Squareback Sedan) 2,095 lbs.
TIRES	6.00 x 15L (low profile)
BRAKES	Front disc/rear drum

1970

TYPE 3 VOLKSWAGEN 1600

GENERAL SPECIFICATIONS

Same as 1969, except:

MODEL AVAILABILITY	2-door Fastback Sedan ($2,339); with sunroof ($2,459) 2-door Squareback Sedan ($2,499); with sunroof ($2,619)
SERIAL NUMBERS	(1600 Fastback) 310-2000001-up (1600 Squareback) 360-2000001-up

1971

TYPE 3 VOLKSWAGEN 1600

GENERAL SPECIFICATIONS

Same as 1970, except:

MODEL AVAILABILITY	2-door Fastback Sedan ($2,339); with sunroof ($2,459) 2-door Squareback Sedan ($2,499); with sunroof ($2,619)
SERIAL NUMBERS	(1600 Fastback) 310-2000001-up (1600 Squareback) 360-2000001-up
LENGTH	172 inches
TIRES	6.00 x 15L
HORSEPOWER	52–60 hp

1972

TYPE 3 VOLKSWAGEN 1600

GENERAL SPECIFICATIONS

Same as 1971, except:

MODEL AVAILABILITY	2-door Fastback Sedan ($2,549); with sunroof ($2,675) 2-door Squareback Sedan ($2,749); with sunroof ($2,875)
SERIAL NUMBERS	(1600 Fastback) 31120000001-up (1600 Squareback) 3612000001-up
LENGTH	172 inches
WEIGHT	(Fastback) 2,117 lbs. (Squareback) 2,161 lbs.

1973

TYPE 3 VOLKSWAGEN 1600

GENERAL SPECIFICATIONS

Same as 1972, except:

MODEL AVAILABILITY	2-door Fastback Sedan ($2,650); with sunroof ($2,795) 2-door Squareback Sedan ($2,995)
SERIAL NUMBERS	(1600 Fastback) 31120000001-up (1600 Squareback) 3612000001-up

1971

TYPE 4/411 VOLKSWAGEN 1600

GENERAL SPECIFICATIONS

MODEL AVAILABILITY 4-door Sedan ($2,999)
3-door Hatchback ($2,999)

SERIAL NUMBERS 4212-0000001-up
4613-0000001-up

WHEELBASE 98.4 inches

LENGTH 181 inches

WIDTH 65.0 inches

HEIGHT 58.5 inches

WEIGHT (Sedan) 2,315 lbs.; (Hatchback) 2,381 lbs.

TREAD (front/rear) 52.4/53.1 inches

TIRES 155SR15

BRAKES Hydraulic, front/rear drum

CONSTRUCTION semiunitized body with platform frame

STEERING recirculating ball

FRONT SUSPENSION transverse torsion bars with upper/lower trailing arms

REAR SUSPENSION semitrailing arms with coil springs

FUEL TANK 10.6 gallons

ENGINE Horizontally opposed, overhead-valve four-cylinder (air cooled); displacement: 102.5 cubic inches (1,679cc); bore & stroke: 3.54 x 2.60 inches (90 x 66 mm). Compression ratio: 8.2:1; brake horsepower: 85 at 5,000 rpm; torque: 99.4 lb-ft 3,500 rpm. Four main bearings, solid valve lifters, Bosch fuel injection.

TRANSMISSION four-speed manual

FINAL DRIVE RATIO spiral bevel

1972

TYPE 4/411 VOLKSWAGEN 1600

GENERAL SPECIFICATIONS

Same as 1971, except:

MODEL AVAILABILITY 2-door Sedan ($2,975)
4-door Sedan ($3,275)
3-door Hatchback Wagon ($3,299)

1973

TYPE 4/412 VOLKSWAGEN 1600

GENERAL SPECIFICATIONS

Same as 1972, except:

MODEL AVAILABILITY 2-door Sedan ($3,299)
4-door Sedan ($3,599)
3-door Hatchback Wagon ($3,699)

SERIAL NUMBERS (412 coupe) 4132000001-up

ENGINE (ALL) Horizontally opposed, overhead-valve four-cylinder (air cooled); displacement: 1,029.5 cubic inches (1,679cc); bore and stroke: 3.54 x 2.60 inches (90 x 66 mm). Compression ratio: 8.2:1; brake horsepower: 76 at 4,000 rpm; torque: 95 lb-ft at 2,700 rpm. Four main bearings, solid valve lifters, Bosch fuel injection.

1974

TYPE 4/412 VOLKSWAGEN 1600

GENERAL SPECIFICATIONS

Same as 1973, except:

MODEL AVAILABILITY 2-door Sedan ($3,299)
4-door Sedan ($3,599)
3-door Hatchback Wagon ($3,699)

SERIAL NUMBERS (412 coupe) 4132000001-up

ENGINE (COUPE) Same as 1973 engine for all models

ENGINE (SEDAN/WAGON) Horizontally opposed, overhead-valve four-cylinder (air cooled); displacement: 109.5 cubic-inch (1,795cc); bore and stroke: 3.66 x 2.60 inches (93 x 66 mm). Compression ratio: 7.3:1; brake horsepower: 72 at 4,800 rpm; torque: 91 lb-ft at 3,000 rpm. Four main bearings, solid valve lifters, Bosch fuel injection.

TYPE 181 VOLKSWAGEN THING

GENERAL SPECIFICATIONS

MODEL AVAILABILITY	2-door Roadster ($2,750)
STARTING SERIAL NUMBER	1973: 183-2000-00 1974: 184-2000-001
WHEELBASE	94.5 inches
LENGTH	148.8 inches
WIDTH	64.5 inches
WEIGHT	1,984 lbs.
TREAD	(front/rear) 53.3/56.9 inches
HEIGHT	63.8 inches
TIRES	155SR14
BRAKES	Hydraulic, front/rear drum
CONSTRUCTION	semiunitized body with platform frame
STEERING	worm and sector
FRONT SUSPENSION	transverse torsion bars with upper/lower trailing arms
REAR SUSPENSION	swing axles with trailing arms and torsion bars
FUEL TANK	11.1 gallons
ENGINE	Horizontally opposed, overhead-valve four-cylinder (air cooled); displacement: 96.7 cubic inches (1,585cc); bore and stroke: 3.36 x 2.72 inches (85 x 69 mm). Compression ratio: 7.3:1; brake horsepower: 46 (SAE net) at 4,000 rpm; torque: 72 ft-lb at 3,000 rpm. Four main bearings, solid valve lifters, single-barrel carburetor, 12-volt electrical system.
TRANSMISSION	four-speed manual
FINAL DRIVE RATIO	spiral bevel

The 1971 Volkswagen Squareback Sedan was really a station wagon, but the company made a different name for it because the passenger bus was marketed as the station wagon. This model was priced at $2,510. *Archives/TEN: The Enthusiast Network Magazines, LLC*

INDEX